THE GREAT MYSTERY OF THE RAPTURE

Virtually all Scripture references are quoted from the King James translation of the Holy Bible.

The Great Mystery of the Rapture
Copyright ©1999
Copyright ©2008 Revised edition by Arno Froese
West Columbia, South Carolina 29170
Published by The Olive Press, a division of Midnight Call Ministries
Columbia, SC 29228 U.S.A.

Copy typist:	Lynn Jeffcoat, Kathy Roland
Copy Editor:	Susanna Cancassi
Proofreaders:	Angie Peters, Susanna Cancassi, Claire Bliesner
Layout/Design:	Michelle Kim
Lithography:	Simon Froese
Cover Design:	Michelle Kim

Library of Congress Cataloging-in-Publication Data

Froese, Arno
   The Great Mystery of the Rapture
   ISBN# 0-937422-43-6

   1. Prophecy

Printed in the United States of America

*This book is dedicated to the
Church of Jesus Christ worldwide.*

*It is intended to contribute toward a better
understanding of God's counsel to men
based on the Scripture.*

*The author does not benefit through
royalties from the proceeds
of the sale of this book. All received funds
are reinvested for the furtherance
of the Gospel.*

CONTENTS

CHAPTER 3 63
THE LORD HIMSELF SHALL DESCEND
FROM HEAVEN

CHAPTER 4 91
WITH THE VOICE OF THE ARCHANGEL

Believed • Believing Prophecy Is Required • The Suffering Servant •
Faith In The Word • Rapture Is Not The Last Resurrection • Who
Are The Two Witnesses? • Prophets Must Be Killed In Jerusalem •
Non Believers-Non Repentance • Michael The Archangel • The
Meeting Place • Two Rapture Categories • The Glorified Body •
Knowledge Of Death Brings Wisdom • Glory Without The Body •
The Best Is Yet To Come • A Warning • No Endtime Signs For The
Rapture • Waiting For Him Alone

CHAPTER 13 283
ISRAEL AND PEACE

Gentile Against Israel • Israel Or Palestine? • Jerusalem: The Stumbling
Stone • The European Union To The Rescue • Land Without Borders
• The Day Of Christ • The Great Deception • Animal Sacrifice •
Israel's Tribulation • Experience Placed Above Faith • Church Differs
From Israel • The Church Has Not Replaced Israel • Israel; The Root
Of The Church • Gentiles Accepted Into The Church

CHAPTER 14 297
PROPHETIC SHADOWS OF THE RAPTURE

Solomon's Temple Made By Gentiles • The Spiritual Temple Will Be
Finished • Church And World Look Alike • Prophetic Necessities Of
The Rapture • Another Gospel=Another Church • When Will The
Church Be Complete? • Replacement Theology • The Significance Of
The Distinction • Before The Foundation Of The World • Victory
Over Death

INTRODUCTION

The book you are about to read, *The Great Mystery of the Rapture*, has been my on-going project for many years. It was not my initial intention to write this book when I first started to study this important subject. But during the years, I had prepared many messages and so ultimately decided to arrange the material into a book form.

Virtually all Bible scholars and theologians agree that the coming of Jesus was prophesied in the Old Testament. Jewish scholars in particular have searched the Old Testament for many thousands of years. They discovered that the long-awaited Messiah would lead Israel to its ultimate glory as prophesied by Moses, *"For thou art an holy people unto the LORD thy God, and the LORD hath chosen thee to be a peculiar people unto himself, above all the nations that are upon the earth"* (Deuteronomy 14:2). The Jews of the Old Covenant and the Church of the New Covenant agree that such a prophecy has not yet been fulfilled.

Moses, likewise, wrote down the words God gave to him regarding the coming Messiah, *"The LORD thy God will raise up unto thee a Prophet from the midst of thee, of thy brethren, like unto me; unto him ye shall hearken"* (Deuteronomy 18:15). These words were simple to understand; a prophet would come to Israel proclaiming the words of God, and would establish Israel into the undisputed leader of all the nations of the world.

However, further study revealed a great controversy, particularly in Isaiah 53. In this section of Scripture, the Messiah is not pictured as the King but rather as a person rejected by the people and shamefully executed as an innocent man.

It became increasingly difficult for many Jewish scholars to avoid recognizing the Messiah as the sacrificial Lamb. The details of His life, crucifixion, and death are clearly given. Thus the question arose, "How can the Messiah lead Israel to glory yet simultaneously become a despised and rejected person to be led as a lamb to the slaughter?" With these facts in mind, we clearly recognize that Jesus must come in two stages. First to die for the sins of mankind as the innocent sacrificial Lamb, establishing the New Covenant, as prophesied in Jeremiah 31:31, *"Behold, the days come, saith the LORD, that I will make a new covenant with the house of Israel, and with the house of Judah."* Then to return in great power and glory to fulfill the original promise which will result in the Lord ruling the nations with a rod of iron, elevating Israel as the supreme nation on planet Earth.

A closer look at the Second Coming in the New Testament also reveals two comings. After His ascension into Heaven, we read of two men in white apparel telling the disciples, *"...Ye men of Galilee, why stand ye gazing up into heaven? this same Jesus, which is taken up from you into heaven, shall so come in like manner as ye have seen him go into heaven"* (Acts 1:11). This was a heavenly message with the assurance that Jesus would come back to earth, more specifically to the Mount of Olives, the exact spot from which He left, to fulfill this prophecy. Zechariah 14:4 confirms this, *"...his feet shall stand in that day upon the mount of Olives, which is before Jerusalem on the east....*" This is the Second Coming of Christ.

It was quite natural for the Jewish disciples to assume that Jesus would literally and physically return to the Mount of Olives at any time to establish the kingdom of God in the land of Israel. Just before He ascended, they asked Him, *"Lord, wilt thou at this time restore again the kingdom of Israel?'* (Acts 1:6). Jesus answered, *"...It is not for you to know the times or the seasons, which the Father hath put in his own power"* (Verse 7). He tells them to wait for the empowering of the Holy Spirit, to proclaim the Gospel in Jerusalem, Judaea, Samaria, and to the outermost parts of the earth.

When we study the verses relating to the Second Coming, we should notice that it is impossible for Jesus to come unless the light of the world is first removed from the earth. That is the first phase of the Second Coming, generally known as the Rapture.

Jesus revealed part of this mystery to His disciples, *"...It is expedient for you that I go away: for if I go not away, the Comforter will not come unto you..."* (John 16:7). This exchange had to take place. Jesus ascended into Heaven so that the Comforter, the Holy Spirit, would come and *"...abide with you* [the disciples] *for ever"* (John 14:16).

This opens our understanding to a further revealed mystery; namely, that Jesus had to depart in order for the Comforter to come. It stands to reason that Jesus cannot come back to earth unless the abiding Comforter is taken out of the way.

In 2nd Thessalonians 2 the apostle Paul, inspired by the Holy Spirit, speaks of two events, *"the coming of our Lord Jesus Christ,"* describing the Second Coming, and *"our gathering together unto him"* describing the Rapture. It is vital to note the very distinct differences between the two. In the first case, Jesus will literally and physically return to the Mount of Olives. In the second case, we will be gathered unto Him, meaning we will come to Him.

The first four verses of 2nd Thessalonians 2 have created much confusion among believers because of their failure to distinguish between these two events. Disappointedly, Paul asked, *"Remember ye not, that, when I was yet with you, I told you these things?'* (verse 5). Then he made a very distinct remark clearly revealing the hindering element, the abiding Comforter in the Church. The Holy Spirit must be taken out of the way in order for the wicked one to be exposed, *"And now ye know what withholdeth that he might be revealed in his time. For the mystery of iniquity doth already work: only he who now letteth will let, until he be taken out of the way"* (verses 6-7).

Scholars and students alike understand that the days of the Great Tribulation will be the most horrendous period of time the world has ever experienced. This is confirmed several times in the Old and New Testaments. Jesus Himself made this statement regarding those days, *"...then shall be great tribulation, such as was not since the beginning of the world to this time, no, nor ever shall be"* (Matthew 24:21). Quite logically, the question should arise, "If it is the work of darkness, how can this horrendous tribulation take place while the light is still present?" Light and darkness are mutually exclusive. Light is stronger than darkness. No matter how weak the light may be, darkness will always be exposed and the light will prevail.

Jesus said to the Church, *"Ye are the light of the world."* Of course, that statement applies only to born again believers. Therefore, it is absolutely impossible for the Great Tribulation

18

to begin unless the light has been taken out of the way.

I repeatedly state throughout this book that the Rapture of the Church is the real reason for the coming Great Tribulation. Once the light has been taken out of the world, darkness can work without hindrance and deception will globally run rampant.

Furthermore, at the first phase of the Second Coming, Jesus doesn't come to us; we come to Him. The meeting place is clearly described in 1st Thessalonians 4:17, *"Then we which are alive and remain shall be caught up together with them in the clouds, to meet the Lord in the air: and so shall we ever be with the Lord."* We approach the Lord; we come to Him. We meet Him in the air; He is not going to meet us on the Mount of Olives.

The teaching of the Pre-Tribulational Rapture becomes unmistakably clear in the Bible when viewed from this angle. The next verse says, *"Wherefore comfort one another with these words"* (verse 18). To what type of comfort is Paul referring? The comfort of the coming Great Tribulation? The comfort of the coming of Antichrist? The comfort of the wrath of God on earth? I believe that each question is categorically answered with a resounding "No." For almost 2,000 years, the comfort of the Church is the promise that Jesus could come today.

In summary, we find that throughout the Bible we are admonished to wait and be ready for His coming at any time. This is reinforced by the Lord Himself when He said, *"Therefore be ye also ready: for in such an hour as ye think not the Son of man cometh"* (Matthew 24:44). The Pre-Wrath, Mid-Tribulation, and Post-Tribulation Rapture theories are fundamentally flawed because in all three cases we do not have to wait for Jesus to come today. We are forced to first wait for the middle of the Great Tribulation, or the indefinite time of the Pre-Wrath. And, in the case of the Post-Tribulational theory, we must first wait for the Great Tribulation to end. In each case, we do not have to wait for Jesus to come today. I believe that every Christian would agree that this is a violation contrary to the clear teaching of the Word of God...

"For our conversation is in heaven; from whence also we look for the Saviour, the Lord Jesus Christ" (Philippians 3:20).

"...waiting for the coming of our Lord Jesus Christ" (1st Corinthians 1:7).

"...to wait for His Son from heaven..." (1st Thessalonians 1:10).

"Looking for that blessed hope, and the glorious appearing of the great God and our Saviour Jesus Christ" (Titus 2:13).

"So Christ was once offered to bear the sins of many; and unto them that look for him shall he appear the second time without sin unto salvation" (Hebrews 9:28).

"And ye yourselves like unto men that wait for their lord, when he will return from the wedding; that when he cometh and knocketh, they may open unto him immediately" (Luke 12:36).

The bottom line is: Who are you waiting for today? If you are waiting for Jesus, you are in the biblical camp, you believe in the imminency of Jesus' coming. Any other waiting, as we have just seen, is contrary to Scripture.

CHAPTER 1

THE REALITY OF THE RAPTURE

"Behold, I shew you a mystery; We shall not all sleep, but we shall all be changed, In a moment, in the twinkling of an eye, at the last trump; for the trumpet shall sound, and the dead shall be raised incorruptible, and we shall be changed. For this corruptible must put on incorruption, and this mortal must put on immortality. So when this corruptible shall have put on incorruption, and this mortal shall have put on immortality, then shall be brought to pass the saying that is written, Death is swallowed up in victory" (1st Corinthians 15:51-54).

The above passage is a description of the Rapture. However, the word "rapture" is not found in the KJV English Bible. Subsequently, some have made claims that the Rapture is an invention of man and therefore, is not biblical. In this chapter, we will show that the Rapture is a reality clearly taught in the Bible and that we can expect this climactic event for the Church to take place at any time.

The fact that the word "rapture" does not appear in our Bible does not mean that it is not taught. For example, the word "trinity," is not found in our Bible either, but the trinity is unmistakably evident in Scripture. In fact, the first three verses of our Bible prove the existence of a Triune God:

Genesis 1:1 - God the Father: *"In the beginning God created the heaven and the earth."*

Genesis 1:2 - God the Holy Spirit: *"And the earth was without form, and void; and darkness was upon the face of the deep. And the spirit of God moved upon the face of the waters."*

Genesis 1:3 - God the Word [Son]: *"And God said, Let there be light: and there was light."* The Word is the Son of God who became flesh. In the New Testament, we read, *"For there are three that bear record in heaven, the Father, the Word, and the Holy Ghost: and these three are one"* (1st John 5:7).

Our Transfiguration

In 1st Corinthians 15, Paul wrote about people who will not all *"sleep;"* in other words, they will not die. Those people will be changed and brought into the presence of God in the twinkling of an eye. This changing process, or translation of the believer, is necessary; otherwise, the Rapture is a non-event for those who are alive at that point. This change must take place because the Bible says that flesh and blood cannot inherit the kingdom of God.

We can determine with certainty that such an event has never taken place in the history of the Church. Verse 54 highlights this fact when it says, *"...then shall be brought to pass the saying that is written, Death is swallowed up in victory."* Is this true for us today? The answer is obviously "No." For the last 2,000 years members of the Church have died. Millions of saints have already gone through the valley of the shadow of death. If the Lord delays His coming this year, even more of us will experience physical death. The Bible says *"it is appointed unto man once to die...."* However, 1st Corinthians 15:54 clearly states that death will be swallowed up in victory. That, we have to admit, has not occurred yet, but will take place at the moment of the Rapture.

Furthermore, the Rapture is the fulfillment of Christ's victory for His Church over death. Paul wrote to the Corinthian church regarding the Rapture in 1st Corinthians 15:54, *"So when this corruptible shall have put on incorruption, and this mortal shall have put on immortality, then shall be brought to pass the saying that is written, Death is swallowed up in victory."* Only at that point—when we have taken on incorruption and immortality— has the prophetic Word been fulfilled, *"Death is swallowed up in victory."*

Traditional Doctrine

In recent years, the doctrine of the Rapture, as set forth in the Bible, has caused many controversies within the Church. In no way should that discourage us from studying the subject and trying to answer the important question, "Will one be taken and the other left behind?"

The answer is not found in our intellect or our knowledge of Hebrew and Greek; we must search for the answer in Scripture.

Of course, this is easier said than done. Thousands, if not

millions of believers in the Lord Jesus Christ search the Scriptures daily, yet not all come to the same conclusion. Each one of us is affected to a certain degree by teachers, preachers, colleges, radio and television programs, books, churches and denominations.

Often we arrive at certain conclusions because of our backgrounds. In the United States alone, hundreds of thousands of pastors preach every week, most of them using the Bible as their foundation. However, every new message should reveal something that was not previously comprehended by those listening.

I think you will agree that each of us who have read our Bible over and over have come to a verse at one time or another that we never really noticed before. Often we are astonished at the depth of it. I experienced this very thing on the Sea of Galilee in Israel. Considered to be the center of Christ's ministry, this place is very important for Christians. From listening to all of the tour guides we have had over the years, I know the significant physical places, including where Jesus preached, healed the sick, cast out the demons, and told Peter to let down the net on the other side of his boat.

Another special place in Israel is where Jesus preached the Sermon on the Mount. I have seen a number of places that look like amphitheaters which could accommodate a great number of people. Jesus could, in fact, have been speaking from the shores of the Galilee so that everyone could hear. One tour guide demonstrated this to us. He stood close to the lake, speaking in a normal voice, and we easily could hear him from 100-150 meters (300-450 feet) away.

One year, an elderly brother took me aside and said, "Arno, Jesus wasn't preaching to the multitudes; He was preaching to the disciples." When I asked him to show me where it said that in the Bible, he read Matthew 5:1-2, *"…seeing the multitudes, he went up into a mountain: and when he was set, his disciples came unto him. And he opened his mouth, and taught them…."* This simple statement shocked me. After all these years, I realized that I had been following tradition instead of the plain Word of God.

Jesus left the multitude and went up into the mountain with His disciples. This revelation was surprising yet refreshing. I had read that passage so many times but only now understood to whom the Lord was speaking. He was not addressing the multitudes; He was teaching His close inner circle, His apostles.

Once again this lesson had shown me how important it is not only to read the Scripture, but to listen to others who read the precious Word of God. We are to permit the Holy Spirit to captivate our minds and hearts so we can understand the depth of the message in the words.

On another occasion, a lawyer asked Jesus, *"Master, what shall I do to inherit eternal life?"* (Luke 10:25). Jesus responded by asking another question, *"… What is written in the law? how readest thou?"* (verse 26). Notice that Jesus not only asked what was written in the Law, but, *"how readest thou?"* It's how we read the Scripture that brings us under the conviction of certain teachings.

Since the beginning of my service in the ministry in 1968, I have met people from all walks of life, including people from different denominations, backgrounds, and education. Most of these Bible-believers– who have no relationship to one another–recognize the truth in the teaching of the Rapture. With that in mind, we will now discuss the reality of the Rapture, highlighting six important points:

1) What is the Rapture?
2) How will the Rapture take place?
3) Why is the Rapture necessary?
4) Who will be raptured?
5) When will the Rapture take place?
6) How can we be ready for the Rapture?

1) What Is The Rapture?

The Rapture is the fulfillment of the Lord's prayer in John 17:24, *"Father, I will that they also, whom thou hast given me, be with me where I am; that they may behold my glory, which thou hast given me: for thou lovedst me before the foundation of the world."* This verse clearly expresses the Lord's desire to be united with His Church. We know from Scripture that when a believer dies, he is immediately in the presence of the Lord. The apostle Paul clearly testified, *"Absent from the body, present with the Lord"* (2nd Corinthians 5:8).

But if all Christians had to die in order to enter into the presence of the Lord, then the Church would certainly not reflect the Lord Jesus Christ who arose from the dead and victoriously ascended into Heaven. Therefore, a bodily resurrection of the Church must take place. The Church is Jesus

Christ's body, and He is the head. It is impossible to separate the head from the body.

It is the Lord's clear, expressed will that His own, whom He has bought with His precious blood, be in His presence so that they may finally behold His glory.

The Rapture is our transformation into the image of Him who was transformed before us: *"Beloved, now are we the sons of God, and it doth not yet appear what we shall be: but we know that, when he shall appear, we shall be like him; for we shall see him as he is"* (1st John 3:2). Thus, we are able to confidently proclaim that the Rapture fulfills Bible prophecy.

We are the *"sons of God"* but we are not like Him. We have not been translated into His image; at this moment we are NOT *"...as He is."* That is yet to come.

In addition to fulfilling Bible prophecy, the Rapture also requires the casting of Satan from Heaven, *"And there was war in heaven: Michael and his angels fought against the dragon; and the dragon fought and his angels, And prevailed not; neither was their place found any more in heaven. And the great dragon was cast out, that old serpent, called the Devil, and Satan, which deceiveth the whole world: he was cast out into the earth, and his angels were cast out with him"* (Revelation 12:7-9).

After the Rapture of the Church, Satan is cast upon the earth to have a field day with mankind because the light has been *"taken out of the way."* Revelation 12:12 summarizes the contrast between these two groups, *"Therefore rejoice, ye heavens, and ye that dwell in them. Woe to the inhabiters of the earth and of the sea! for the devil is come down unto you, having great wrath, because he knoweth that he hath but a short time."*

2) How Will The Rapture Take Place?

The Rapture will take place in "the twinkling of an eye." In other words, it will happen instantaneously and unannounced. No advertising campaign, news coverage, or special announcements will precede the Rapture.

For that reason, it is of utmost importance that we learn to differentiate between our Rapture and the Rapture of the Jews. We will be raptured vertically, from earth to Heaven. The Jews will be raptured horizontally, from the four corners of the earth to Israel. Our meeting place is clearly described in 1st Thessalonians 4:17 as, *"...in the air...."* The destination of the Jewish Rapture will be the land of Israel. God has given them an unconditional promise that He will return them to their land, *"...I have gathered them unto their own land, and have left none of them any more there"* (Ezekiel 39:28).

The Vertical Rapture

So that we don't confuse the two raptures, we must discuss their differences in light of the verses supporting their existence. The Rapture of the Church is described in 1st Corinthians 15:51-53, *"Behold, I shew you a mystery; We shall not all sleep, but we shall all be changed, In a moment, in the twinkling of an eye, at the last trump; for the trumpet shall sound, and the dead shall be raised incorruptible, and we shall be changed. For this corruptible must put on incorruption, and this mortal must put on immortality."* In 1st Thessalonians 4:16-17 we read, *"For the Lord himself shall descend from heaven with a shout, with the voice of the archangel, and with the trump of God: and the dead in Christ shall rise first: Then we which are alive and remain shall be caught up together with them in the clouds, to meet the Lord in the air: and so shall we ever be with the Lord."* In actuality, this is not a very detailed description for such an important event. I believe that this is why Paul writes that he is going to show us *"...a mystery."*

The Horizontal Rapture

Matthew 24:31 describes the horizontal Rapture of the Jews. *"And he shall send his angels with a great sound of a trumpet, and they shall gather together his elect from the four winds, from one end of heaven to the other."* In this context, Jesus is speaking to His people, the Jews, not to the Church. In Matthew 24, we find a geographical reference that does not apply to the Church: *"Then let them which be in Judaea flee into the mountains"* (verse 16). This can't apply to the Church because the majority of Christians live outside of Israel, making it impossible for them to flee to the Judean mountains. Furthermore, verse 20 mentions the *"Sabbath day,"* which was given exclusively to the Jewish people, as confirmed in Exodus 31:17: *"It is a sign between me and the children of Israel for ever...."* When comparing the two, we find distinct contrasting characteristics which enable us to differentiate between the two.

At the Rapture of the Church, *"the Lord himself shall descend from heaven."* However, Matthew 24:31 says, *"...he shall send his angels."* When Jesus comes for the Church, He comes with the *"voice of the archangel"* and with *"the trump of God."* When he comes for Israel, He comes with *"a trumpet."* These vivid descriptions reveal the difference between the two raptures: one exclusively for the Church and the other exclusively for the Jews. One will lead to the clouds in the heavens; the other will lead to Jerusalem.

Why is it necessary that the Jews go to Jerusalem? Scripture would not be fulfilled any other way. The Bible makes it clear that the Jews will look on Him whom they have pierced. The return of the Jews to the land of Israel is something we are witnessing today and is part of the process of Bible prophecy fulfillment. Its climax will come when the entire remnant is back in the land of their fathers. They will all be brought to the land of Israel; no one will be left behind.

A Trumpet Or The Trump Of God?

We noted that Israel will be gathered together with *"a trump"* and the Church with the *"trump of God."* Let us investigate the specific differences between the two. First Corinthians 15:52 states that the Rapture of the Church will take place *"at the last trump of God."* First Thessalonians 4:16 identifies this as the *"trump of God."*

This trump must not be confused with any of the other trumps mentioned in Scripture, such as the trumps of angels, trumps of priests, trumps of war and trumps of peace, or the trumpets in the book of Revelation which announce terrible judgments upon the world. We are dealing here with the "last trump of God." If we are awaiting the *"last trump"* of God, when did the *"first trump"* of God occur?

The First Trump Of God

Exodus 19:16 offers us evidence of the first trump of God,

"And it came to pass on the third day in the morning, that there were thunders and lightnings, and a thick cloud upon the mount, and the voice of the trumpet exceeding loud; so that all the people that was in the camp trembled." Notice the words, *"voice"* and *"trumpet."* We can search the Scriptures from Genesis to Revelation and will not find the presence of the Lord identified by the *"voice of a trumpet"* in any context other than the gathering of Israel to receive the Law, and the gathering of the Church to be united with the Law-giver.

To further establish the identity of the voice, the trumpet, and God, note the following, *"And when the voice of the trumpet sounded long, and waxed louder and louder, Moses spake, and God answered him by a voice"* (Exodus 19:19).

The purpose of this event was to gather His people to hear God's Word. There is no evidence in Scripture that anyone else heard the sound of the first trump of God. I believe we can assume that only those in the camp of Israel heard it. In fact, Hebrews 12:19 substantiates this claim, *"And the sound of a trumpet, and the voice of words; which voice they that heard entreated that the word should not be spoken to them any more."*

In the same way, the last trump of God will go unnoticed by the world and will be heard only by those who have an inner spiritual ear: born again believers. The last trump of God will gather His heavenly people to receive the Word which became flesh!

We observe a prophetic pointer to the resurrection of our Lord Jesus in Exodus 19:11, *"...be ready against the third day: for the third day the Lord will come down in the sight of all the people upon mount Sinai"* (Exodus 19:11). The third day is of tremendous importance in that our Lord arose on that day. Some mistakenly believe that He arose after the third day; however, two disciples testify on the evening of the third day, *"But we trusted that it had been he which should have redeemed Israel: and beside all this, today is the third day since these things were done"* (Luke 24:21).

Do you realize that we are approaching the third day? To the Lord, a thousand years is as one day, and one day is as a thousand years. Our Lord has been gone for almost "two days" and the "third day" is approaching!

3) Why Is The Rapture Necessary?

We will highlight five important points to answer this question:

a) The Rapture is necessary in order to permit sin to reach its culmination. The Church is the light of the world, thus, with the Church (light) gone, sin can fully develop its potential of evil.

When God made His covenant with Abraham regarding the Promised Land, He said, *"But in the fourth generation they shall come hither again: for the iniquity of the Amorites is not yet full"* (Genesis 15:16). God is righteous; He could not punish the Amorites because their measure of sin had not yet been fulfilled. After they had reached that limit, God used Israel as a tool of judgment to destroy that nation.

God cannot send destructive judgment upon the world because the measure of sin has not yet been fulfilled. The fulfillment of sin reaching its climax is now hindered because the light of the world remains in the world. The Church is the obstacle; when that obstacle is removed, sin will reach its prophesied peak.

Some may object and say, "The world is in such a terrible mess; people are so sinful, corrupt, and immoral. God cannot possibly permit this to go on." There is no doubt that evil has increased as prophesied in 2nd Timothy 3:13, *"But evil men and seducers shall wax worse and worse, deceiving, and being deceived."* But in order to see the climax of evil, we must look at the Scripture describing the time when the Church is gone.

After the sixth seal is opened, we read, *"And the kings of the earth, and the great men, and the rich men, and the chief captains, and the mighty men, and every bondman, and every free man, hid themselves in the dens and in the rocks of the mountains; And said to the mountains and rocks, Fall on us, and hide us from the face of him that sitteth on the throne, and from the wrath of the Lamb"* (Revelation 6:15-16). Even when faced with such terrible threats and the promise of coming destruction, they find no room for repentance. Instead, they make a vain attempt to hide themselves from the wrath of the Lamb.

Revelation 9:20-21 reads, *"And the rest of the men which were not killed by these plagues yet repented not of the works of their hands, that they should not worship devils, and idols of gold, and silver, and brass, and stone, and of wood: which neither can see, nor hear, nor walk: Neither repented they of their murders, nor of their sorceries, nor of their fornication, nor of their thefts."* Even after a third of the world's population is killed, these people still find no room in their hearts for repentance.

The worst though, is yet to come. Revelation 9:9-11

describes the most horrendous judgment upon mankind, *"And they had breastplates, as it were breastplates of iron; and the sound of their wings was as the sound of chariots of many horses running to battle. And they had tails like unto scorpions, and there were stings in their tails: and their power was to hurt men five months. And they had a king over them, which is the angel of the bottomless pit, whose name in the Hebrew tongue is Abaddon, but in the Greek tongue hath his name Apollyon."* In addition to the fact that they refused to repent, they also blasphemed the name of God.

b) The Rapture of the Church is necessary in order to allow the Antichrist, who is the highest product of darkness, to be revealed. He cannot take his rightful place until the Church has been removed from this world. The prince of darkness cannot fully develop his diabolical plan while the *"light of the world"* is present. Jesus said, *"Ye are the light of the world."* So darkness can only operate when hidden from the light.

When speaking to the church in Thessalonica about the coming of the Lord Jesus Christ to earth and our *"gathering unto Him,"* the apostle Paul clearly identifies the hindering element. What can hinder darkness? It is the Holy Spirit within the Church who is withholding the revelation of the Antichrist, *"And now ye know what withholdeth that he might be revealed in his time. For the mystery of iniquity doth already work: only he who now letteth will let, until he be taken out of the way"* (2nd Thessalonians 2:7).

The Holy Spirit convicts the world of sin, gives light in

darkness, and dwells in the believer. Jesus testifies, *"...I will pray the Father, and he shall give you another Comforter, that he may abide with you for ever"* (John 14:16).

Few Christians fully realize the incredible significance of being born again: We are the dwelling place of the Holy Spirit! The mystery of iniquity can never fully develop its work of darkness as long as there is but one spark of light present on earth.

Surely, no one can argue that the mystery of iniquity is already at work. It is very evident, especially in our day as we see the entire world turning away from the Living God and turning toward their own selves. From this point of view, we realize that it is an absolute necessity that we are taken out of the way first.

c) The Rapture of the Church is necessary in order to initiate the casting of Satan from Heaven. Some may ask, "How do you know that Satan is in Heaven?" To answer that, we turn to Revelation 12:10, which says, *"...for the accuser of our brethren is cast down, which accused them before our God day and night."* Who is Satan accusing? He is not accusing Israel, or the world, but the *"brethren"* who are redeemed by the saving blood of the Lamb. They live on earth in their tabernacle of flesh and blood. Although these *"brethren"* are born again believers, they are nevertheless subject to sin.

We are redeemed from the power and guilt of sin, but not from the presence of sin. The moment you and I commit a sin, we come under the judgment of the Scripture, *"He who sins is of the devil."* As a result, Satan has a right to stand before God and accuse us. However, when we recognize our sin and confess it to the Lord, our High Priest stands before God defending us against the claims of Satan saying in effect, "I have bought this person with my blood, he has confessed his sin; therefore, it is forgiven, paid in full!" Our advocate in Heaven, our High Priest, intercedes for us.

d) The Rapture is necessary because the Word of God must be fulfilled. When the apostle Paul wrote to the Corinthians, he revealed the mystery of the Rapture, *"So when this corruptible shall have put on incorruption, and this mortal shall have put on immortality, then shall be brought to pass the saying that is written, Death is swallowed up in victory"* (1st Corinthians 15:54). Although Jesus defeated the powers of Satan and of death on Calvary's cross, His victory over death has not been transferred to His body, the Church. We, just like anyone else, must die.

For two millennia, the saints have died and been buried, without having been translated. They are waiting for the fullness of the body so that the whole Church can be raised in *"the twinkling of an eye"* and meet her Lord in the air. The prophecy, *"...then shall be brought to pass the saying that is written, Death is swallowed up in victory,"* can only be fulfilled when the body is united with the head, the Lord Jesus Himself.

e) The Rapture is necessary so that we can come back to judge the world. In his letter to the Corinthians, Paul wrote, *"Do ye not know that the saints shall judge the world?"* (1st Corinthians 6:2). At this point, it is impossible for us to judge the world because we are forbidden to judge, *"Therefore judge nothing before the time, until the Lord come, who both will bring to light the hidden things of darkness, and will make manifest the counsels of the hearts: and then shall every man have praise of God"* (1st Corinthians 4:5). Also, because we are still in our sinful flesh and blood, our judgment is deemed imperfect and would fail to implement the righteousness of God. Even a sinner saved by grace cannot judge righteously. Incidentally, this is an additional confirmation that exposes the vain attempt of some believers to install a righteous government in our nation. Such a promise has not been given to us and any attempt, no matter how well-intended, is destined to fail.

4) Who Will Be Raptured?

The Bible makes it unquestionably clear that only those belonging to the Church of Jesus Christ will be raptured. The apostle Paul did not mince words when he wrote to the Thessalonians, *"Then we which are alive..."* (1st Thessalonians 4:17). He did not specify a certain group within the Church, or a selected number from among the Church; he simply said, *"we."*

Further clarification is found when we read the entire verse, *"Then we which are alive and remain shall be caught up together with them in the clouds, to meet the Lord in the air: and so shall we ever be with the Lord."*

In chapter 2 we will see the distinction between the world (those who are left behind) and us, (the Church of Jesus Christ) is explicitly stated in the following verses, *"For when they shall say, Peace and safety; then sudden destruction cometh upon them, as travail upon a woman with child; and they shall not escape"* (1st Thessalonians 5:3). Note that the words *"they"* and *"them"* are used. Take specific notice of how he addresses the Church with the words *"ye"*; *"we"*; and *"us:"* *"But ye, brethren, are not in darkness, that that day should overtake you as a thief. Ye are all the children of light, and the children of the day: we are not of the night, nor of darkness. Therefore let us not sleep, as do others; but let us watch and be sober"* (1st Thessalonians 5:4-6).

The Rapture of the Church is not based on our level of holiness or service to the Lord; rather, it is based solely on the Lord's will. He wants us to be in His presence. The power of His resurrection will bring us into His presence. All who are born again of the Spirit of God will be raptured.

However, at this point, it is important to mention that not all who claim to be born again are true Christians. Here is where Satan, the great imitator and father of lies, works so desperately–especially in these endtimes. *"Deceiving and being deceived..."* is being fulfilled all over the world. Men refuse to recognize the victorious power of our Lord Jesus Christ. Sadly, we have to admit that the devil is rather successful in causing great confusion even within the Church. However, those who have their hearts set on and grounded in Jesus, and who are awaiting His return, will be raptured because they truly are born again.

Ye Must Be Born Again

The Rapture is the exclusive work of our Lord Jesus Christ demonstrating the power of His resurrection in His body.

Therefore, all born again believers are to be raptured since we constitute the body of Christ. Scripture does not state that the Rapture is our reward or inheritance.

Surely if there were any other prerequisites besides being born again, Paul would have written "they who are ready" or "those who have achieved the spiritual standard." But that is not the case. Paul speaks specifically in 1st Corinthians 15 about "the mystery" when he says, "...*we shall not all sleep but we shall all be changed.*"

It is of great importance that you prove yourself before the countenance of the Lord to see if you really are a child of God. Do not rely on experiences you may have had. Answers to prayer, miraculous healings, supernatural spiritual gifts or even moral turnarounds in your life do not necessarily constitute regeneration. In reality, you may have had an emotional experience rather than the genuine repentance which leads to salvation through faith in Jesus Christ.

5) When Will The Rapture Take Place?

We must strongly emphasize that all speculation regarding the timing of the Rapture are fundamentally wrong. They have been blatantly wrong in the past and will continue to be wrong in the future, for the Bible plainly states, *"Be ye therefore ready also: for the Son of man cometh at an hour when ye think not"* (Luke 12:40).

Date Setting

Much damage has been done by those who have attempted to pinpoint the date of the Lord's return. All of these "datesetters" have been false prophets. Undoubtedly those "prophets" have done great harm to the proclamation of the prophetic Word.

In 1988, Edgar Whisenant wrote a book entitled, *"88 Reasons Why The Rapture Could Take Place In 1988."* The book was well written and expertly researched, but it was also dead wrong. During that time, our office at Midnight Call Ministry was flooded with telephone calls from inquiring believers asking for our position on such a prediction. My answer remained the same, "Jesus will come at an hour when we think not!" In 1989, Whisenant wrote a follow-up book, *"89 Reasons Why the Rapture Could Take Place in 1989."* I consider such speculation an insult to our Lord.

The biggest problem with any prediction is that pinpointing a date takes away the element of surprise. Throughout the Bible, we read of the necessity of being ready at any time. Therefore, if someone predicts that the Lord will come in five days, that means that I don't have to expect Him today or tomorrow because He is going to come on the fifth day. Such teaching violates the principles of the Holy Scripture and therefore must be rejected in totality.

I am reminded of the story of an elderly rabbi in Jerusalem who was interrupted by a young student one day who excitedly exclaimed that he had figured out from Scripture the day of the arrival of the Messiah. This young man said, "The Messiah will come on the Sabbath." The old rabbi replied, "Son, I don't believe you because I am waiting for Him to come today."

Although we emphasize the biblical teaching of the Rapture taking place at any time, it is necessary to state our position regarding the element of time and the different views surrounding the Rapture. Although valid arguments distinguish the Mid-Tribulation and the Pre-Wrath Rapture, I consider these to be fundamentally one and the same. The bottom line is that all theories violate Scripture by taking away the element of surprise and therefore, I reject them completely.

Mid-Tribulation Rapture?

If someone asked me whether the Rapture could take place in the middle of the Tribulation, my answer would be "no." The Tribulation is prompted by the absence of the Church. The Church is the light of the world and the deceptive work of Satan cannot reach its highest point with the Church present. The Mid-Tribulation theory violates Scripture in regard to the element of surprise. It is written in the Word of God, therefore we cannot eliminate it. To believe in the Mid-Tribulation Rapture we must ignore the many Scriptures which support a Pre-Tribulation Rapture, including Titus 2:13, *"Looking for that blessed hope, and the glorious appearing of the great God and our Saviour Jesus Christ."* Belief in a Mid-Trib Rapture prohibits our waiting for Jesus to come today. In actuality, we would be waiting for the beginning of the Tribulation and the appearance of the Antichrist. Such teaching is contrary to the Word of God. We will not find any admonition in the Bible suggesting that we should be looking for the coming Tribulation and the Antichrist!

Post-Tribulation Rapture?

What about the possibility of the Rapture taking place after the Great Tribulation? To such a question, I give a resounding "No!" Not only is this scenario contrary to Scripture, but it would be physically impossible because no one would be left to rapture.

Scripture passages such as Revelation 13:15 illustrate that the existence of believers would be an impossibility. The "other beast," or the false prophet, "*...had power to give life unto the image of the beast, that the image of the beast should both speak, and cause that as many as would not worship the image of the beast should be killed.*" When faced with an alternative, a born again believer will never deny his Lord by bowing down to the image of the beast and worshipping it.

While it is natural to ask, "Wouldn't there be many afraid to lose their lives causing them to deny the Lord, and worship the image of the beast?" I am convinced that such is not the case. In times of great need and severe persecution, the Lord gives the grace needed for His saints to lay down their lives for Him. There is ample evidence of this in Scripture, as well as countless examples of the martyrs throughout the history of Christianity which support this fact.

Therefore this is a pointless debate because we have already seen that the Great Tribulation cannot take place unless the Church is taken out of the way. Only the absence of the Church can initiate the beginning of the Great Tribulation.

Also, it is important to point out that the Great Tribulation cannot instantaneously begin in one day. The preparation for the Great Tribulation began when the Church was born in Jerusalem on Pentecost. From then on, the rivalry between the powers of darkness and the powers of light has resulted in the great persecution of Christians throughout the centuries. Not only has the Church been persecuted by the Roman government, and recently during the reign of Communism, but the longest consecutive persecution of Christians has taken place under the political and religious authority of the Catholic Church.

The point I want to make, however, regards the preparation for the Great Tribulation. These things can't happen overnight; they need to be prepared for, and as I have already stated, this preparation has gone on for almost 2,000 years. Since the re-establishment of the state of Israel, we have seen innumerable signs that point to the preparation for the Great Tribulation.

Assuming that the Great Tribulation is a time when the Antichrist will rule and brutally oppose Christians in particular and force the people of the world to bow down to his authority is a mistake which is often made. Based on the prophetic Word, this will all be accomplished by deception. When you are deceived, you think that you are right when in fact you are wrong. You will even go as far as to fight for your rights because you voluntarily and willingly subject yourself to the deception. Satan comes *"...with all power and signs and lying wonders, And with all deceivableness of unrighteousness in them that perish; because they received not the love of the truth, that they might be saved"* (2nd Thessalonians 2:9-10). As a result, the Bible continues, *"...for this cause God shall send them strong delusion, that they should believe a lie"* (verse 11).

6) How Can We Be Ready For The Rapture?

In order to be ready for the Rapture, you must be born

again. Without regeneration, you will remain in darkness, without hope, and lost for all eternity. John 3:36 testifies to the fact, *"He that believeth on the Son hath everlasting life: and he that believeth not the Son shall not see life; but the wrath of God abideth on him."* It's very simple; the person without Christ is in darkness and shall not see life. To Nicodemus, the religious Pharisee, Jesus says, *"...Verily, verily I say unto thee, except a man be born again, he cannot see the kingdom of God."* Therefore, if you are not born again, you will be left behind.

This may be your last chance to come to Jesus asking for forgiveness of your sins and receive eternal life. Becoming a believer in Jesus is just that simple. Believing that He is the Son of God who has poured out His blood on Calvary's cross for your sin guarantees you eternal life. I urge you to make this decision today, even at this very moment. I cannot help you do this, nor can your pastor or anyone else; you need to come personally to Jesus and ask Him to save you from your sins. The Son of God guarantees, *"He that cometh unto me, I will in no wise cast out."*

Are You Really Born Again?

Unfortunately, the term "rebirth" has been so popularized that often people do not understand its full meaning. How can you be sure you are born again? Take for example, a newborn baby. What does he do first?

1) He cries! Likewise, when you are born again, you will begin to cry out to God. You will begin to pray. Upon the apostle Paul's conversion, we read in Acts 9:11, *"...Saul of*

Tarsus: for, behold, he prayeth."

2) Then the baby eats because he is hungry. You, as a child of God, will hunger for the Word of God, which is essentially spiritual food. You won't do it because you have to, but because you want to.

3) The baby learns to listen. You will begin to heed the Word of God and take His commandments seriously.

4) The baby seeks fellowship. This fellowship is essential for you. It is important that you become active in a local church where you serve the Lord in fellowship with other believers.

5) As the baby grows, he becomes self-conscious. You, too, will become self-conscious of the fact that you are a sinner saved by grace and will continue to seek truth more and more. Paul's prayer was, *"That I may know him, and the power of his resurrection, and the fellowship of his sufferings, being made conformable unto his death"* (Philippians 3:10).

6) As the child grows into adolescence, he begins to look to the future. As a born again person, you will want to study the prophetic Word, which speaks of the future. God invites us to *"ask me of things to come."*

7) When the child grows into an adult, he becomes independent and strives toward goals he sets for himself. As a Christian, our goal is His coming, for He is our beginning and end, the author of our salvation. Desiring Him is only natural.

First Corinthians 1:7 confirms, *"So that ye come behind in no gift; waiting for the coming of our Lord Jesus Christ."* In other words, this gift of waiting for Him must be a reality in your life.

Waiting For Jesus

As we grow older, we begin to realize that our time on earth is limited. As a result, we experience an increased desire for the coming of the Lord. Many passages in Scripture attest to this fact, *"Looking for that blessed hope, and the glorious appearing of the great God and our Saviour Jesus Christ"* (Titus 2:13). As previously stated, this verse supports our looking for the Rapture.

Hebrews 9:28 reinforces this by saying, *"So Christ was once offered to bear the sins of many; and unto them that look for him shall he appear the second time without sin unto salvation."*

Not only are we to look, but we are also *"...to wait for his Son from heaven, whom he raised from the dead, even Jesus, which delivered us from the wrath to come"* (1st Thessalonians 1:10). This verse supports the Pre-Tribulation Rapture; we are delivered from the wrath to come.

While we look and wait, we are also instructed to be patient. James urgently warns that we are to, *"Be patient therefore, brethren, unto the coming of the Lord. Behold, the husbandman waiteth for the precious fruit of the earth, and hath long patience for it, until he receive the early and latter rain. Be ye also patient; stablish your hearts: for the coming of the Lord draweth nigh"* (James 5:7-8). This patience that we are to demonstrate while looking and waiting for Him gives us the additional strength and courage to persevere, ever increasing in His work as the days go by.

Increase In His Work

When the apostle Paul wrote to the Corinthians about the

Rapture, he concluded with an important admonition, *"Therefore, my beloved brethren, be ye stedfast, unmoveable, always abounding in the work of the Lord, forasmuch as ye know that your labour is not in vain in the Lord"* (1st Corinthians 15:58). In writing to the Thessalonians about the Rapture, Paul said, *"Comfort your hearts, and stablish you in every good word and work"* (2nd Thessalonians 2:17). In 1st Thessalonians 4:18, he concludes the description of the Rapture with, *"Wherefore comfort one another with these words."*

It is my sincere prayer that the Lord will comfort you with the hope of His coming and as a result, you will increase in the work of the Lord in these endtimes. How much time we have left, no one knows; however, based on the developments in Israel and the world, we recognize that the end stages of the endtimes are at hand. Therefore, *"...To-day if ye will hear his voice, Harden not your hearts, as in the provocation, in the day of temptation in the wilderness"* (Hebrews 3:7-8). Humble yourself before His countenance and ask Him to give you the grace needed to be ready for Him at any moment.

CHAPTER 2

ISRAEL: THE SURE SIGN OF THE RAPTURE

"Be ye therefore ready also: for the Son of man cometh at an hour when ye think not " (Luke 12:40).

This one short verse puts to rest any attempt to seek a sign for the coming Rapture. Jesus plainly says that He will come *"when ye think not."* If there are to be no signs of this coming event, then why do we title this chapter, "Israel: The Sure Sign of the Rapture"? Simply because we do have an indirect sign which indicates on one hand that God is preparing a replacement for the Church, and on the other, the completion of the Church.

All Bible readers know that Israel is God's chosen people on earth. We also know that Israel rejected the Messiah. As a result, God laid Israel aside and did not use her as His instrument of judgment, light, and salvation. Note that I used the words "laid aside," not "rejected," or "replaced." The Church, primarily from among the Gentiles, is God's organ of salvation on earth today. The Church's message is "come to Jesus and be saved," a message that has been proclaimed for almost 2,000 years.

Based on the clear teaching of the Old Covenant, we know that God promised His people a New Covenant. The prophets explained the details of that covenant and it was established by the Lord Jesus Christ. However–and this is extremely important for us to understand–the New Covenant does not include physical, geographical, political, or material promises. Quite clearly, such promises were given to the people of Israel under the Old Covenant.

A Two-Fold Light Of The World?

God promised that Israel would give light to all the nations of the world. Since that has not been the case in the past, we can be sure that Israel will be restored to its original boundaries in order to fulfill this prophecy. Ultimately, the Jews will have to take a position of leadership here on earth. Deuteronomy 14:2 says, *"For thou art an holy people unto the LORD thy God, and the LORD hath chosen thee to be a peculiar people unto himself, above all the nations that are upon the earth."*

This presents a problem: two groups of people are expected to be light to the world.

Thus, the question we must first answer is, "Is Israel a light to the Gentiles in our days?" Absolutely not. Spiritually speaking, Israel is in darkness. You can't be a light to others if you are in darkness yourself. Actually, the apostle Paul, writing to the Romans, says, *"As concerning the gospel, they (Jews) are enemies for your sakes...."* But in no way does this fact annul

God's eternal promise that Israel will be a light to the Gentiles: *"...It is a light thing that thou shouldest be my servant to raise up the tribes of Jacob, and to restore the preserved of Israel: I will also give thee for a light to the Gentiles, that thou mayest be my salvation unto the end of the earth"* (Isaiah 49:6). Therefore, we have absolute assurance that Israel's becoming a light to the world is yet to come.

Jesus said to the Church, *"Ye are the light of the world."* For almost 2,000 years the Church has been the light-bearer, the torch of God. The Church has provided light to those in darkness. The Holy Spirit has convicted millions of souls of their sin and they have been added to the "kingdom of light."

It is important to emphasize at this point that we are not a light to the world collectively, but individually. Neither Scripture nor church history tells of a whole nation being saved at one time. That has never happened nor will it ever happen in the world of the Gentiles. Having said this, we realize that there are two tasks involved in being a light to the world: the Church to the individual, and Israel to the nations.

We understand that the light of the world is the Lord Jesus Christ. His light, which radiates from believers, reaches the hearts of sinners. This same Jesus has also promised that the Church should be in His presence. Therefore, our task to be light-bearers in this world is only for a limited time. It began on the day of Pentecost and will continue until our departure, the day of our Rapture. The world at that time will indeed experience darkness. There will no longer be any hindering element to the deceptive works of Satan, the father of lies.

When will our task be completed? When the last from among the Gentiles is added to the Church. Then we will be raptured into the presence of the Lord.

When will Israel fulfill her calling to be the light of the world? When the spiritual restoration of Israel has taken place.

Israel Must Be Fully Restored

Historically, it has been impossible for Israel to come into existence as a nation since the Jews were scattered throughout the world. They could not go back to the land of Israel because they would not have been able to survive in a land considered to be a desert. Therefore, God made the necessary preparations that when the Jews did return to the land of Israel, not only would they be able to feed themselves but they would become a dominant factor in that part of the world.

In a similar way, the Lord Jesus assured His Church that He would make preparations for us, *"Let not your heart be troubled: ye believe in God, believe also in me. In my Father's house are many mansions: if it were not so, I would have told you. I go to prepare a place for you. And if I go and prepare a place for you, I will come again, and receive you unto myself; that where I am, there ye may be also"* (John 14:1-3). In Israel's case, the Lord God prepared the land for the people, *"But ye, O mountains of Israel, ye shall shoot forth your branches, and yield your fruit to my people of Israel; for they are at hand to come"* (Ezekiel 36:8). It is quite fascinating to read in verse 4 of Ezekiel 36 the details describing the entire land of Israel, *"Therefore, ye mountains of Israel, hear the word of the Lord GOD; Thus saith the Lord GOD to the mountains, and to the hills, to the rivers, and to the valleys, to the desolate wastes, and to the cities that are forsaken, which became a prey and derision to the residue of the heathen that are round about."* Remember, the land was desolate and forsaken, and actually did become a *"derision to the residue of the heathen that are round about."* This, my friends, is a reality that can be proven unquestionably by recent history.

Since the rebirth of the political state of Israel in May 1948, this country has become a fulfillment of Bible prophecy, a miracle in the eyes of all those who have taken the time to honestly analyze the people and the land. Therefore, the fact that the Jews are coming back to Israel, are building a modern progressive nation, and have become a powerhouse in the Middle East clearly shows that the beginning of Israel signals the end for the Church.

Israel: The Rapture Sign

We continue now to look at this Rapture sign to the Church. *"Moreover, brethren, I would not that ye should be ignorant, how that all our fathers were under the cloud, and all passed through the sea; And were all baptized unto Moses in the cloud and in the sea; And did all eat the same spiritual meat; And did all drink the same spiritual drink: for they drank of that spiritual Rock that followed them: and that Rock was Christ. But with many of them God was not well pleased: for they were overthrown in the wilderness. Now these things were our examples, to the intent we should not lust after evil things, as they also lusted"* (1st Corinthians 10:1-6). Pay specific attention to the admonition, *"these things were our examples."*

If you want to know how to behave, walk, and work as a Christian, read the guidelines; read the message from God to the Church. Take heed of what He is saying: *"Neither be ye idolaters, as were some of them; as it is written, The people sat down to eat and drink, and rose up to play. Neither let us com-*

mit fornication, as some of them committed, and fell in one day three and twenty thousand. Neither let us tempt Christ, as some of them also tempted, and were destroyed of serpents. Neither murmur ye, as some of them also murmured, and were destroyed of the destroyer. Now all these things happened unto them for ensamples: and they are written for our admonition, upon whom the ends of the world are come" (1st Corinthians 10:7-12).

You don't need a Ph.D. in theology to understand these simple instructions, "No idolatry, no fornication, no tempting Christ, no murmuring." Why not? Because you are a chosen person, a member of a special nation, a person who should be a light in a world that is spiritually darkening.

Example For The Christian Life

Another important New Testament passage relates to our pilgrimage toward Heaven, *"Take heed, brethren, lest there be in any of you an evil heart of unbelief, in departing from the living God. But exhort one another daily, while it is called Today; lest any of you be hardened through the deceitfulness of sin. For we are made partakers of Christ, if we hold the beginning of our confidence steadfast unto the end: While it is said, Today if ye will hear his voice, harden not your hearts, as in the provocation. For some, when they had heard, did provoke: howbeit not all that came out of Egypt by Moses. But with whom was he grieved forty years? was it not with them that had sinned, whose carcases fell in the wilderness? And to whom sware he that they should not enter into his rest, but to them that believed not? So we see that they could not enter in because of unbelief"* (Hebrews 3:12-19).

Before we go any further, we must clarify that this passage does not teach that we, as believers, must strive, work, or hope to enter Heaven! The Bible makes it perfectly clear that we are saved by grace, not by works. Jesus paid it all, all to Him we owe!

The verses here should help us recognize the sure sign of the Rapture.

Why Didn't Israel Obtain Salvation?

Israel had the Law, which was used only to identify sin. Therefore, no provision was made for eternal salvation. The opportunity for Israel to "enter in" was offered, but could only be obtained if they believed. However, they could not believe because they did not have a high priest to help with their unbelief. They needed a high priest who was without sin.

They could not "enter in" because they had no perfect sacrifice. At the very most, the blood of all of the animals slaughtered during the time of the Law could cover up their sins, but would never take those sins away! *"For it is not possible that the blood of bulls and of goats should take away sins"* (Hebrews 10:4).

Israel was unable to "enter in" because at that time the New Covenant had not been perfected; the eternal author of salvation had not been made perfect. We read these words in the letter to the Hebrews, *"And being made perfect, he became the author of eternal salvation unto all them that obey him"* (Hebrews 5:9).

I am often amazed as to why some dear brethren desperately try to keep the Law of the Old Covenant, which Israel failed to keep, a covenant which was broken. For that reason, God brought about the New Covenant, which could only be made effective through the sinless sacrifice of Jesus on Calvary's cross. Simple faith in the Lord Jesus Christ makes each believer a full partaker in that eternal covenant.

Another important item answers our question as to why Israel has not yet attained salvation. It concerns the Church of Jesus Christ: *"...blindness in part is happened to Israel, until the fulness of the Gentiles be come in. And so all Israel shall be saved..."* (Romans 11:25-26). Israel cannot be saved unless and until the Church of Jesus Christ is removed.

The Law Cannot Save

As we have previously stated, the Law was used to identify sin. The Bible explains in no uncertain terms that salvation is not obtained through the keeping of the Law:

"I do not frustrate the grace of God: for if righteousness come by the law, then Christ is dead in vain" (Galatians 2:21).

"Are ye so foolish? having begun in the Spirit, are ye now made perfect by the flesh?" (Galatians 3:3).

"Christ is become of no effect unto you, whosoever of you are justified by the law; ye are fallen from grace" (Galatians 5:4).

"Therefore by the deeds of the law there shall no flesh be justified in his sight: for by the law is the knowledge of sin" (Romans 3:20).

The apostle Paul asked the following question in Galatians 3:19, *"Wherefore then serveth the law?"* The answer: *"It was added because of transgressions, til the seed should come...."* This again makes it perfectly clear that the Law cannot save, and was used only to identify sin until the seed came. The SEED is the Lord Jesus Christ, who shed His blood on Calvary's cross to take away the sin of those who believe that His blood is capable of doing just that!

The Law was God's shout to Israel and the world saying in effect, "Listen to me, come to me, obey me, so you will understand that I have prepared salvation for you."

God's Word is still valid; you can still come to Him and obey Him. When you believe in God, the Creator of Heaven and earth, you will be led to the One who created all and perfected salvation.

First Peter 1:19-20 states, *"But with the precious blood of Christ, as of a lamb without blemish and without spot: Who verily was foreordained before the foundation of the world, but was manifest in these last times for you."* God ordained salvation *"before the foundation of the world."*

Long before He made the covenant with Abraham, Isaac, Jacob and the children of Israel, God knew how He would accomplish salvation for lost humanity.

When the time had come, He chose Israel, and gave them the Law so that they might recognize sin and His salvation. While the Law was given directly to Israel, it was given indirectly to all the world. *"That thy way may be known upon earth, thy saving health among all nations. O let the nations be glad and sing for joy: for thou shalt judge the people righteously, and govern the nations upon earth. Selah"* (Psalm 67:2,4). The unique difference between the Old and New Covenants is made visible in Israel and the Church.

I encourage you to read the entire book of Hebrews to gain a better understanding of the indescribable glory of salvation accomplished by our Lord Jesus Christ.

On this side of Heaven, however, the key always was, always is, and always will be the nation of Israel.

Physical And Spiritual Promises

As mentioned in the beginning of this chapter, Israel is the greatest endtime sign for the Church. They are the recipients of God's physical, geographical, political and material promises. On the other hand, the Church only has spiritual promises.

Therefore it is a vain attempt to claim that certain nations have special promises because they are supposed to be Christians. It is a waste of time, energy, and finances to have any involvement in establishing a "Christian" political government on earth. All governments are under the jurisdiction of the devil, who is the god of this world and the prince of darkness. Remember, though, that we are in the world, but not of the world. We have been clearly instructed to be subject to the government which God has established in every country. Jesus was obedient during His short life in the land of Israel, which was occupied by the foreign forces of Rome.

The Gentile Temple

Another sure sign of the Rapture is illustrated in the physical and spiritual temple. We read the following regarding the spiritual temple: *"Ye also, as lively stones, are built up a spiritual house, an holy priesthood, to offer up spiritual sacrifices, acceptable to God by Jesus Christ"* (1st Peter 2:5). With each new member added to the Church through the rebirth, the spiritual temple grows into a perfect habitation of God.

With that in mind, we might ask when that temple will be completed? In order for the spiritual temple to be completed, Acts 15:14 must be fulfilled, *"...God at the first did visit the Gentiles, to take out of them a people for his name."* The moment the last "lively stone" is added to this spiritual temple, the selection will be completed. At that time, the entire temple, which is the Church of Jesus Christ, will be raptured into the presence of the Lord.

It is important to emphasize here that the building of the temple is the Lord's work, which Jesus affirms by saying, *"I will build my church."* Since Jesus is perfect, we can be assured that His Church is also perfect, having no spot or wrinkle.

This may frighten some of you because you are forced to confess that in light of scriptural requirements for holiness, you have failed many times. Even at this moment you must confess that you fall short of the holiness which God wants to see in you. If that is the case, then be of good courage, for the Lord seeks those who are aware of their failures and shortcomings.

One might naturally ask, "If only the perfect 'lively stones' are to be used as building material in the spiritual habitation of God, how can I, a failure, be added to it?" The answer is that you the person, in flesh and blood, will not participate in the glorious building of the spiritual temple; but you the person, born of God, the new, perfect, sinless, holy, and unblemished person will participate. How? Because it is the work of God. First John 3:9 makes this point crystal clear when he says, *"Whosoever is born of God doth not commit sin; for his seed remaineth in him: and he cannot sin, because he is born of God."*

However, your failure while on earth will affect your reward. In fact, 1st Corinthians 3:14-15 says, *"If any man's work abide which he hath built thereupon, he shall receive a reward. If any man's work shall be burned, he shall suffer loss: but he himself shall be saved; yet so as by fire."*

In summary, it is plain to see that the spiritual temple of God, taken primarily from among the Gentiles who have become "lively stones," is perfect and without blemish.

We now turn our attention to the physical temple, the one built of stone in Jerusalem. The architect for that temple is God, the Creator of Heaven and earth. He passed on the heavenly blueprint to Moses, who in turn built the tabernacle. Later, Solomon received clear instructions as to how to go about building this glorious physical temple on Mount Moriah in Jerusalem.

The Temple Of Stone

What is so remarkable, and what I consider to be a technological miracle, is the fact that this temple was prefabricated. Furthermore, this temple was not built by the children of Israel, but by the Gentiles. In 2nd Chronicles 2:17-18 we read, *"And Solomon numbered all the strangers that were in the land of Israel, after the numbering wherewith David his father had numbered them; and they were found an hundred and fifty thousand and three thousand and six hundred. And he set threescore and ten thousand of them to be bearers of burdens, and fourscore thousand to be hewers in the mountain, and three thousand and six hundred overseers to set the people awork."* These *"strangers"* did the actual work in fabricating this glorious temple in Jerusalem.

Since we are citizens of the heavenly Jerusalem, it stands to reason that the fulfillment of being in His presence would require our being raptured into Heaven.

What is most fascinating about this marvelous temple is that when the assembly took place, it was too late to make any alterations, *"And the house, when it was in building, was built of stone made ready before it was brought thither: so that there was neither, hammer nor axe nor any tool of iron heard in the house, while it was in building"* (1st Kings 6:7). This is an amazing achievement unprecedented in history!

At the age of 14, I became a brick-layer apprentice and have accumulated much construction experience throughout the years. I have never seen or heard of prefabricated materials fitting so perfectly that no additional alterations were required. For all practical purposes, it is virtually impossible. But this temple was perfectly built by Gentiles to the glory of Israel and the glory of the God of Israel. When the temple was completed and dedicated, 2nd Chronicles 7:1 reports, *"Now when Solomon had made an end of praying, the fire came down from heaven, and consumed the burnt offering and the sacrifices; and the glory of the LORD filled the house."*

When the spiritual temple is completed, the Rapture will take place. All of the churches, denominations, ministries, publishing houses, TV ministries, radio stations, and mission organizations will be left behind; only the "lively stones" will be snatched away in the twinkling of an eye.

A Voice From 1864

Our forefathers diligently sought for signs of the endtimes. Bible scholars in the 1600's, 1700's, and even the 1800's searched faithfully for signs that would indicate that the Jews were going back to the land of their fathers. Charles Spurgeon, one of the great preachers of this century, knew the Bible well and studied the Old Testament in particular. In 1864, he made the following statements regarding Ezekiel 36 and 37:

The meaning of our text, as opened up by the context, is most evidently, if words mean anything, first, that there shall be a political restoration of the Jews to their own land and to their own nationality; and then, secondly, there is in the text, and in the context, a most plain declaration, that there shall be a spiritual restoration, a conversion in fact, of the tribes of Israel.

They are to have a national prosperity which shall make them famous; nay, so glorious shall they be that Egypt, and Tyre, and Greece, and Rome, shall all forget their glory in the greater splendor of the throne of David. If there be meaning in words this must be the meaning of this chapter.

I wish never to learn the art of tearing God's meaning out of His own words. If there be anything clear and plain, the literal sense and meaning of this passage must be evident that both the two and the ten tribes of Israel are to be restored to their own land, and that a king is to rule over them.

May we learn likewise never to take the Word of God lightly nor interpret it so that it fits into our time. Instead, let the Word of God speak to our hearts so that we will understand the signs of the times.

CHAPTER 3

THE LORD HIMSELF SHALL DESCEND FROM HEAVEN

This chapter is the first in a series of five which primarily deals with the verse: *"For the Lord himself shall descend from heaven with a shout, with the voice of the archangel, and with the trump of God: and the dead in Christ shall rise first"* (1st Thessalonians 4:16).

In this series, we will examine the uniqueness of the only event mentioned in Scripture where millions of people from all over the world will be translated instantaneously and raptured into the presence of the Lord.

It is of great importance that we completely understand what the Rapture is all about, therefore, I make no apology for using certain passages repeatedly or reanalyzing events which support this teaching from different perspectives. I am reminded of the apostle Paul's writings to the Philippians: *"... To write the same things to you, to me indeed is not grievous, but for you it is safe"* (Philippians 3:1). Luther translates this verse as, *"That I always write the same thing to you does not upset me because it does lead you deeper in the assurance."*

The Lord Himself

Because of its immense significance, we will highlight the point that the Lord "Himself" will come. To illustrate this point, consider the following: When the head of state of any nation is invited to a function which may not be important for the nation or for the head of state, he often sends a representative. For example, if the finance minister from Switzerland were to come to Washington D.C., it would serve little or no purpose for the President to personally meet him because the visitor would represent only a small part of Switzerland's government. The President would likely send a representative to meet such a minister. However, if the President of Russia, the Prime Minister of Britain, or the Chancellor of Germany were to come, the President would recognize the importance of such a visit and would make it a top priority to meet the dignitary himself.

The Sick Roman Servant

To further emphasize this point, we will use the event described in Luke 7: *"…a certain centurion's servant, who was dear unto him, was sick, and ready to die. And when he heard of Jesus, he sent unto him the elders of the Jews, beseeching him that he would come and heal his servant. And when they came to Jesus, they besought him instantly, saying, That he was worthy for whom he should do this: For he loveth our nation, and he hath built us a synagogue. Then Jesus went with them. And when he was now not far from the house, the centurion sent friends to him, saying unto him, Lord, trouble not thyself: for I am not worthy that thou*

shouldest enter under my roof: Wherefore neither thought I myself
worthy to come unto thee; but say in a word, and my servant shall
be healed. For I also am a man set under authority, having under
me soldiers, and I say unto one, Go, and he goeth; and to another,
Come, and he cometh; and to my servant, Do this, and he doeth
it" (verses 2-8).

This Roman centurion clearly recognized the position of
the Lord Jesus. It is evident from this passage that the relationship between the Jews and the Romans, particularly this
man, was well established and friendly. The Jews said, *"he*
loveth our nation," and *"he has built us a synagogue."* This centurion was not only a powerful man serving in the army of the
Roman empire, but he also had sufficient financial means to
contribute to the Jews in that he built them a synagogue.

All the centurion was asking was that Jesus simply "say in
a word." In other words, "Command the sickness to leave so
the servant will be healed!" This statement astonished even the
Lord Himself, *"When Jesus heard these things, he marvelled at*
him, and turned him about, and said unto the people that fol-
lowed him, I say unto you, I have not found so great faith, no, not
in Israel" (Luke 7:9).

As we continue to read this passage, we find that Jesus did
not just "say in a word" but He went in person to heal the servant, *"And they that were sent, returning to the house, found the*
servant whole that had been sick" (Luke 7:10).

God Speaks To Men

In expounding on our message, "The Lord Himself Shall
Descend From Heaven" in relation to the Rapture, we will
look at eight different occasions in the Bible that illustrate the

significance of God Himself directly contacting man.

- The Tower of Babel
- Abraham my friend
- Isaac meets his bride
- Moses requests God's presence
- Elijah wants to see God
- Ezekiel meets God's attributes
- God seen in the flesh
- The Lord Himself shall descend

The Tower Of Babel

In Genesis 11, we read the report of many people gathering in one place, speaking one language, and attempting to solidify their union in the building of a city with a tower *"whose top may reach unto heaven."*

This is the beginning of man's vain and unceasing attempt to unify himself outside of God's already established plan.

There are many different opinions among theologians as to whether the people who built the Tower of Babel actually believed that they could reach this indefinable place called "heaven," or whether they reached toward that direction in order to build a spiritual avenue to God. I agree with the latter theory because these people were obviously very intelligent, had great mathematical knowledge, and were well educated in science and architecture–with significant experience in construction. I believe that we must take this literally. Their goal was to "reach heaven," which meant that they wanted to build a religion which would reach their own imagined god.

During the activity of the last Babylon, otherwise known as "Mystery Babylon," again we see the unification of the nations of the world: *"These have one mind, and shall give their power and strength unto the beast"* (Revelation 17:13).

In the case of the Tower of Babel, the presence of God came down to see *"...the city and the tower, which the children of men builded"* (Genesis 11:5). The result was more than the builders had bargained for. Scripture says, *"...the Lord did there confound the language of all the earth: and from thence did the Lord scatter them abroad upon the face of all the earth"* (verse 9).

Why was the Lord against unity? After all, if people come together in a peaceful manner, as they did at the Tower of Babel, to build a city, to create an economic and a political system that is obviously democratic, and to guarantee peace and prosperity for all people, how can that be wrong?

It is wrong because before the foundation of the world, God ordained that He would bring forth His only begotten Son, sacrificing Him on Calvary's cross. He would unify man with God: *"...God was in Christ reconciling the world unto himself..."* (2nd Corinthians 5:19). Calvary was where the Lord Jesus poured out His blood for the forgiveness of sin and thereby created a new people who would have the capacity to understand God's intention. <u>Unity is genuine only if it is established on the Word of God.</u>

Throughout history, and in all religions, man has always attempted to reach God. God, however, did not decree for man to reach God from earth, rather, He sent His Son from Heaven to earth, reaching down toward man.

We reemphasize that the building of the Tower of Babel was so significant that the Lord Himself came down to witness man's manifestation of his imagination, *"...the Lord came down to see the city and the tower..."* (Genesis 11:5).

Abraham; My Friend

Through Abraham God brought forth a nation; from that nation came Jesus, the Messiah of Israel and the Savior of the world.

God spoke to Abraham many times throughout the course of his life. The unique characteristics of Abraham included the fact that he obeyed God instantaneously and without reservation.

Through Abraham, God would demonstrate His intention of saving mankind, as is evident from the following passage, *"...Take now thy son, thine only son Isaac, whom thou lovest, and get thee into the land of Moriah; and offer him there for a burnt offering upon one of the mountains which I will tell thee of"* (Genesis 22:2). Nowhere do we read, or does it imply that Abraham hesitated or talked the matter over with his wife or the leaders of his household. Instead, we read in the next verse, *"And Abraham rose up early in the morning..."* (verse 3).

Scripture does not reveal whether God came down to speak to Abraham or if He appeared in some supernatural way as was the case with Moses.

The audible contact between God and Abraham was apparent; Abraham believed God and it was counted to him as righteousness. The intimate relationship between God and Abraham is clearly expressed in Isaiah 41:8, *"But thou, Israel, art my servant, Jacob whom I have chosen, the seed of Abraham my friend."* This is later reconfirmed in James 2:23, *"And the scripture was fulfilled which saith, Abraham believed God, and it was imputed unto him for righteousness: and he was called the*

Friend of God." The Lord Himself was Abraham's friend.

Isaac Meets His Bride

We will now look at an event in which Scripture does not demonstrate the Lord Himself coming down to meet man, but in a unique way illustrates the meeting of the Lord and His bride.

The event begins in Genesis 24, *"And Abraham was old, and well stricken in age: and the Lord had blessed Abraham in all things"* (verse 1). He called his servant, which we must assume was Eleazer, although the name of the servant is not mentioned during the entire event. This should remind us of the Holy Spirit (also nameless) who was sent by the Father to woo a bride for His Son.

Abraham sent his servant to get a bride for his son Isaac. It is fascinating how this nameless servant totally relied upon the God of Abraham, *"...O LORD God of my master Abraham, I pray thee, send me good speed this day, and shew kindness unto my master Abraham"* (verse 12). Through simple faith and total obedience, the servant went to the right place at the right time, where the right person was busy doing the right things.

The answer to the servant's prayer was seen before he even finished praying, *"And it came to pass, before he had done speaking, that, behold, Rebekah came out..."* (verse 15). She met the qualifications, *"...the damsel was very fair to look upon, a virgin, neither had any man known her..."* (verse 16).

Here we are reminded of the words Paul used to address the Corinthians, *"For I am jealous over you with godly jealousy: for I have espoused you to one husband, that I may present you as a chaste virgin to Christ"* (2nd Corinthians 11:2), and

Ephesians 5:27 confirms, *"That he might present it to himself a glorious church, not having spot, or wrinkle, or any such thing; but that it should be holy and without blemish."*

Willing To Serve

Returning to our text in Genesis 24, we see that this virgin bride demonstrates some rare characteristics. She is not lazy or hesitant, but is eager to serve; she has a servant's heart. We read in verse 18 that, *"she hasted"*; and in verse 20, *"...she hasted, and emptied her pitcher into the trough, and ran again unto the well to draw water..."*

Aren't we advised to be eager and to abound in the work of the Lord until He comes? Romans 12:1 cautions us of the following, *"I beseech you therefore, brethren, by the mercies of God, that ye present your bodies a living sacrifice, holy, acceptable unto God, which is your reasonable service."*

The Gifts

After she was approached by the servant, the bride received gifts from him, *"And it came to pass, as the camels had done drinking, that the man took a golden earring of half a shekel weight, and two bracelets for her hands of ten shekels weight of gold"* (verse 22).

What gift did we receive the moment we trusted the Word which we have heard? *"In whom ye also trusted, after that ye heard the word of truth, the gospel of your salvation: in whom also after that ye believed, ye were sealed with that holy Spirit of promise, Which is the earnest of our inheritance until the redemption of the purchased possession, unto the praise of his glory"* (Ephesians 1:13-14). The moment we are born again, we receive the deposit of our eternal possession. This is the *"earnest of our inheritance."*

The word "earnest" is still used in some business transactions today. For example, a certain amount of money is required as a deposit to purchase a house. In handing over the deposit to the seller, we are expressing that we are earnest to purchase that house. This is a guarantee between the buyer and the seller that no one else can purchase the property.

Rebekah was not in Isaac's possession, but she had already received the *"earnest of the future possession."* How does that apply to the Church? *"Forasmuch as ye know that ye were not redeemed with corruptible things, as silver and gold, from your vain conversation received by tradition from your fathers; But with the precious blood of Christ, as of a lamb without blemish and without spot: Who verily was foreordained before the foundation of the world, but was manifest in these last times for you"* (1st Peter 1:18-20).

Joy Of Salvation

The bride was full of anticipation, eagerly awaiting that which was to come. After the servant explained to Rebekah why he had come, we read the following in Genesis 24: 28-29, *"And the damsel ran, and told them of her mother's house these things. And Rebekah had a brother, and his name was Laban: and Laban ran out unto the man, unto the well."* Isn't it fascinating to see the eagerness of this young virgin lady? The bride didn't walk, send a messenger, or just say, "I'll go when I get around to it." But twice we read that she *"ran."*

What was her message? *"And it came to pass, when he saw the earring and bracelets upon his sister's hands, and when he heard the words of Rebekah his sister, saying, Thus spake the man unto me; that he came unto the man; and, behold, he stood by the camels at the well"* (Genesis 24:30).

This is one of the first signs of a person who is born again of the Spirit of God: he runs and tells everyone about it. He testifies that he has found Jesus, the Bridegroom, the Savior, the Lord.

This remarkable story was then reported to the entire family. As a result, Laban responded, *"...The thing proceedeth from the Lord: we cannot speak unto thee bad or good"* (verse 50). The bride made a decision; she fit all of the requirements of the unknown bridegroom. The entire family became witnesses, *"And the servant brought forth jewels of silver, and jewels of gold, and raiment, and gave them to Rebekah: he gave also to her brother and to her mother precious things"* (verse 53).

The gifts the Holy Spirit gives to the believer at the moment of the rebirth are undeniable, *"But the fruit of the Spirit is love, joy, peace, longsuffering, gentleness, goodness, faith, Meekness, temperance: against such there is no law"* (Galatians 5:22-23). In effect, we become living epistles read by all men, according to Scripture.

Separation From Family

After the initial testimonies and fellowship came the time of separation. The bride's family requested, *"...Let the damsel abide with us a few days, at the least ten; after that she shall go"* (verse 55). The servant, however, was determined to fulfill his task, *"...Hinder me not, seeing the LORD hath prospered my way; send me away that I may go to my master"* (verse 56).

Now, the time had come to pay the price. Family separation is never easy. "*... We will call the damsel, and inquire at her mouth. And they called Rebekah, and said unto her, Wilt thou go with this man?..."* This was obviously a fine, close-knit, trusting and loving family. However, it was now time to let go of their beloved Rebekah. Rebekah had to trust the unnamed servant who would lead her on a long journey to the place where she would meet the bridegroom she had never seen. What was her response? "*...I will go*" (verse 58).

Dr. Wim Malgo, the founder of Midnight Call, wrote on this subject many years ago and illustrated how the bride's relatives can be compared to Israel today. Only the true Church (all born again believers) is Israel's genuine friend. Although Israel is blinded for our sake, we are organically connected to Israel, "*That the Gentiles should be fellow-heirs, and of the same body and partakers of his promise in Christ by the gospel*" (Ephesians 3:6). At this point, Israel may not officially recognize us, but somehow they sense that we are part of Israel. We are drawing life from the roots of the good olive tree: Israel. Therefore, the greatest tragedy will befall Israel the moment the bride is taken away.

New Citizenship

Rebekah's "conversion" was real. She had to make the separation from "flesh and blood" to follow the leading of the unnamed servant (Holy Spirit) to the unknown bridegroom. When tracing Rebekah's route to her bridegroom on a map, you will notice that her travels took her through the desert.

We, as believers, are walking through the "desert of the nations." We may be a citizen of the country we are born in or we may have accepted naturalization, but our real citizenship is in Heaven. Ephesians 2:6 makes this clear, *"And hath raised us up together, and made us sit together in heavenly places in Christ Jesus."* This thought is reinforced in Philippians 3:20, *"For our conversation is in heaven; from whence also we look for the Saviour, the Lord Jesus Christ."*

Rebekah had to say goodbye and leave everything behind, not knowing whether she would ever return to see her family. She simply *"...followed the man: and the servant took Rebekah, and went his way"* (Verse 61).

The Bridegroom

Now Isaac enters the picture, *"...Isaac went out to meditate in the field at the eventide: and he lifted up his eyes, and saw, and, behold, the camels were coming"* (verse 63).

Jesus, the great High Priest and only mediator between God and man, is also our intercessor; He is looking for His Bride *"at the eventide."*

There should be little doubt in our minds that we have reached *"the eventide"* in our day, seeing that the world is developing precisely in accordance with the prophetic Word.

The nations are becoming one, democracy is marching victoriously across the globe, and our economy is so integrated that each nation is dependent upon the other. In addition, the unification of religion is increasing to the point it was when the Tower of Babel was built.

Christians who hold themselves to the true Word of God will experience increasing loneliness in these days. This is an important sign. But the greatest sign that shows that we are in *"the eventide"* is the resurrection of the nation of Israel. Rarely does a day pass without some headline proclaiming news about Israel and Jerusalem.

Approach Of The Bridegroom

The moment Rebekah saw Isaac, she got off of her camel and walked. Rebekah inquired of the servant, "What man is this that walketh in the field to meet us?" The servant responded, *"...It is my master."* Guided by the Holy Spirit, the bride sought to recognize the bridegroom. When she identified him, *"...she took a veil, and covered herself"* (Genesis 24:65). She was the one who then became hidden or isolated.

Likewise, this is our position today; we are being isolated. The Church, in general, is becoming like the world and the world like the Church. Christianity has become "Churchianity."

We haven't seen Jesus; we only know and see Him through His Word, just as in Rebekah's case, the word of the servant was sufficient. The apostle Peter stated, *"Whom having not seen, ye love; in whom, though now ye see him not, yet believing, ye rejoice with joy unspeakable and full of glory"* (1st Peter 1:8). Those who claim to be Christians and do not look and wait for the coming of the Lord should seriously ask themselves whether they are born again of the Spirit of God. The Bible says, *"So Christ was once offered to bear the sins of many; and unto them that look for him shall he appear the second time without sin unto salvation"* (Hebrews 9:28).

Moses Seeks God Himself

One of the most significant figures in the history of Israel undoubtedly is Moses, also known as the Law-giver. Moses was born destined to die in the river of Egypt as an Israelite. By the grace and provision of God, he grew up in the house of Pharaoh, but then was put aside for forty years while he worked an insignificant job as a shepherd, until he met God.

We recall Moses' first encounter with God at the burning bush, *"Moreover he said, I am the God of thy father, the God of Abraham, the God of Isaac, and the God of Jacob. And Moses hid his face; for he was afraid to look upon God"* (Exodus 3:6). Eventually, Moses led the children of Israel out of slavery in Egypt through the desert toward the Promised Land.

Golden Calf

On the way, God prepared the people and gave them His Law. While Moses was in the presence of God on the mountain for forty days and nights, the people of Israel quickly fell away from the commandment of the living God and made themselves an image of gold, a molten calf, and said, *"...These be thy gods, O Israel, which brought thee up out of the land of Egypt"* (Exodus 32:4).

The account continues, *"And the Lord said unto Moses, Go, get thee down; for thy people, which thou broughtest out of the land of Egypt, have corrupted themselves."* We see from this verse that the Lord had separated Himself from His people and His work of redemption, for He says, *"For **thy** (your) people, which **thou** (you) broughtest out of the land of Egypt."* Suddenly, all of the great things that Moses had witnessed–the great miracles, God's leading, the ten plagues upon Egypt and the miraculous parting of the water–seemed irrelevant because of the disobedience of the children of Israel at the base of Mount Sinai.

God recognized Moses' attempt to intercede, but said,

"...let me alone, that my wrath may wax hot against them, and that I may consume them..." (verse 10).

In spite of God's anger, Moses did not give up. He knew that without God he could do nothing.

As a result, he began to seek God's favor, based on His promises. As a matter of fact, he actually contradicted the Lord, *"And Moses besought the Lord his God, and said, Lord, why doth thy wrath wax hot against thy people, which thou hast brought forth out of the land of Egypt with great power, and with a mighty hand?"* (Exodus 32:11).

Moses was saying in effect, "They are not **my** people, they are **your** people; **I** didn't bring them out of Egypt; **you** brought them out of Egypt." Then Moses reminds the Lord, *"Wherefore should the Egyptians speak, and say, For mischief did he bring them out, to slay them in the mountains, and to consume them from the face of the earth? Turn from thy fierce wrath, and repent of this evil against thy people. Remember Abraham, Isaac, and Israel, thy servants, to whom thou swarest by thine own self, and saidst unto them, I will multiply your seed as the stars of heaven, and all this land that I have spoken of will I give unto your seed, and they shall inherit it for ever"* (Exodus 32:12-13).

Not An Angel...But His Presence

After Moses pleaded with the Lord, he received pardon for his people. The Lord said, *"Therefore now go, lead the people unto the place of which I have spoken unto thee; behold, mine Angel shall go before thee..."* (Exodus 32:34). This is a prayer victory for Moses; he was spiritually alert and recognized in the Lord's promise that he would send an angel before them. God told Moses, *"...I will not go up in the midst of thee; For thou art a stiffnecked people: lest I consume thee in the way"* (Exodus 33:3).

Again, Moses did not give up. He knew that the presence of the Lord was absolutely essential; it was the only way Israel could proceed. Moses continued to pray, *"Now therefore, I pray thee, if I have found grace in thy sight, shew me now thy way, that I may know thee, that I may find grace in thy sight: and consider that this nation is thy people"* (Exodus 33:13).

God answered, *"My presence shall go with thee, and I will give thee rest"* (verse 14). We also see a confirmation of the absolute necessity for the Lord's presence with His people, *"...If thy presence go not with me, carry us not up hence"* (verse 15).

After Moses had achieved such great prayer victory, even to the point of offering himself as a sacrifice, *"Yet now, if thou wilt forgive their sin; and if not, blot me, I pray thee, out of thy book which thou hast written"* (Exodus 32:32), the Lord graciously gave Moses an additional assurance, *"...for thou hast found grace in my sight, and I know thee by name"* (Exodus 33:17).

Moses was victorious. He could have relaxed and enjoyed the blessing, but he continued, *"...I beseech thee, shew me thy glory."* We know from verse 11 that *"the Lord spake unto Moses face to face, as a man speaketh unto his friend...."* Moses wasn't satisfied with speaking face to face with God; he wanted to see His face. The Lord God answered, *"...Thou canst not see my face: for there shall no man see me, and live"* (verse 20).

Moses was then placed in the cleft of the rock where he experienced the passing of the glory of God, *"...the Lord said, Behold, there is a place by me, and thou shalt stand upon a rock:*

And it shall come to pass, while my glory passeth by, that I will put thee in a clift of the rock, and will cover thee with my hand while I pass by: And I will take away mine hand, and thou shalt see my back parts: but my face shall not be seen" (verses 21-23).

Elijah Meets The Lord God

During a time of the greatest apostasy, Elijah was the prophet in Israel through whom the Lord would reveal His mighty works. He had just challenged all of Israel, including 450 prophets of Baal, and 400 prophets of the groves, and won victoriously.

In addition, Elijah challenged Israel, *"...How long halt ye between two opinions? if the Lord be God, follow him: but if Baal, then follow him..."* (1st Kings 18:21). The result was that fire came down from Heaven and *"...the people saw it, they fell on their faces: and they said, The LORD, he is the God; the Lord, he is the God"* (verse 39). This was an indisputable victory!

However, in chapter 19, we see a discouraged, defeated and scared man running from Jezebel. When he came to the wilderness, the Bible tells us, *"...he requested for himself that he might die; and said, It is enough; now, O Lord, take away my life; for I am not better than my fathers"* (1st Kings 19:4).

God did not give up on Elijah: *"...he said, Go forth, and stand upon the mount before the LORD. And, behold, the LORD passed by, and a great and strong wind rent the mountains, and brake in pieces the rocks before the LORD; but the LORD was not in the wind: and after the wind an earthquake; but the LORD was not in the earthquake: And after the earthquake a fire; but the LORD was not in the fire: and after the fire a still small voice"* (1st Kings 19:11-12). Elijah had to be led back to the Word of

God! He recognized that the Lord was not in the strong wind that broke the rocks to pieces; nor was He in the earthquake, or the fire. But when Elijah heard the "still small voice," "*...he wrapped his face in his mantle, and went out, and stood in the entering in of the cave. And, behold, there came a voice unto him, and said, What doest thou here, Elijah?*" (verse 13). It strikes me at how casually the Lord spoke to His servant, just as we talk to members of our family or close friends, "What are you doing?" Or, as the younger generation says, "What's up?" Elijah had to become a normal human being, "down to earth," as they say.

The Lord God actually ignored Elijah's plea, his excuses, which he repeats twice in verse 10 and 14, "*...I have been very jealous for the LORD God of hosts: because the children of Israel have forsaken thy covenant, thrown down thine altars, and slain thy prophets with the sword; and I, even I only, am left; and they seek my life, to take it away.*"

The Lord seemed to take no notice of Elijah's problem and said, "*...Go, return on thy way to the wilderness of Damascus...*" (verse 15).

Elijah had a number of important jobs to do: he anointed King Hazael over Syria, he anointed his successor Elisha, and above all, he had to be prepared for the Rapture.

When Elijah went over the Jordan with his successor, Elisha, we read in 2nd Kings 2:11, "*And it came to pass, as they still went on, and talked, that, behold, there appeared a chariot of fire, and horses of fire, and parted them both asunder; and Elijah went up by a whirlwind into heaven.*"

Elisha Alone

Elisha was left alone on the east side of Jordan after Elijah's rapture, *"And Elisha saw it, and he cried, My father, my father, the chariot of Israel, and the horsemen thereof. And he saw him no more: and he took hold of his own clothes, and rent them in two pieces. He took up also the mantle of Elijah that fell from him, and went back, and stood by the bank of Jordan; And he took the mantle of Elijah that fell from him, and smote the waters, and said, Where is the Lord God of Elijah? and when he also had smitten the waters, they parted hither and thither: and Elisha went over"* (verses 12-14).

Note that he does not ask, "Where is the angel of Elijah?" but rather, *"Where is the LORD God of Elijah?"* Elijah had done his job and the Lord took him out of this world into Heaven without him having to taste death. In Elijah's case, God temporarily detoured the Word, *"…It is appointed unto men once to die…"* (Hebrews 9:27). Later in history, we read that it was Elijah and Moses who appeared on the Mount of Transfiguration with our Lord Jesus, talking to Him about His death.

Ezekiel Describes God's Attributes

Almost 600 years before the birth of Christ, Ezekiel gave us this report, *"…the heavens were opened, and I saw visions of God"* (Ezekiel 1:1). In 48 chapters, the prophet gives us an amazingly detailed description regarding the future of Israel, the Middle East and the world. He testified, as we have just read, that he *"saw visions of God."*

Before we go any further, let us emphasize that this prophet was a captive in the land of the Chaldeans. He could not go to the temple, Jerusalem was in ruins, and the land of Israel was far away. He could not cling to anything tangible in relation to the Word or work of God.

It was different in the case of Elijah and Moses. The tabernacle of God, the temple of God existed. Ezekiel, who was in captivity, had nothing; therefore, God opened up the heavens so he could see.

Peculiar Creatures

What did Ezekiel see? A vision that was out of this world. It was something that cannot be analyzed or fully understood with our limited intellect. *"…I looked, and, behold, a whirlwind came out of the north, a great cloud, and a fire infolding itself, and a brightness was about it, and out of the midst thereof as the colour of amber, out of the midst of the fire. Also out of the midst thereof came the likeness of four living creatures. And this was their appearance; they had the likeness of a man. And every one had four faces, and every one had four wings. And their feet were straight feet; and the sole of their feet was like the sole of a calf's foot: and they sparkled like the colour of burnished brass. And they had the hands of a man under their wings on their four sides; and they four had their faces and their wings. Their wings were joined one to another; they turned not when they went; they went every one straight forward"* (verses 4-9).

I cannot even attempt to explain the strange and peculiar vision of these "creatures."

Continuing in verse 10, we read, *"As for the likeness of their faces, they four had the face of a man, and the face of a lion, on the right side: and they four had the face of an ox on the left side; they four also had the face of an eagle."* This Old Testament vision forms a connection to the New Testament, where we read in Revelation 4:7-8, *"And the first beast was like a lion, and the second beast like a calf, and the third beast had a face as a man, and the fourth beast was like a flying eagle. And the four beasts had each of them six wings about him; and they were full of eyes within: and they rest not day and night, saying, Holy, holy, holy, LORD God Almighty, which was, and is, and is to come."*

After reading Revelation 4 and Ezekiel 1, there is little doubt in my mind that both prophets saw the same thing: the glory and attributes of God.

Ezekiel first saw the face of a man, the promised coming Messiah, who would come forth from the tribe of Judah. Revelation 5:5 says, *"And one of the elders saith unto me, Weep not: behold, the Lion of the tribe of Juda, the Root of David hath prevailed to open the book, and to loose the seven seals thereof."* In the ox, he saw the sacrifice, and in the eagle, the ascension of the Lord.

The succession is different for John. First he saw the Lion of the Tribe of Judah, which illustrates absolute victory. Then he saw a calf instead of an ox, pointing to the purity and innocence of the sacrifice. The third attribute is the Son of man, who is the Son of God, the Lord Jesus Christ. And finally, the eagle symbolizes the ascension and return of the Son of man.

In answer to the disciples' inquiry concerning the end-times, Jesus says among other things, *"For as the lightning cometh out of the east, and shineth even unto the west; so shall also the coming of the Son of man be. For wheresoever the carcase is, there will the eagles be gathered together"* (Matthew 24:27-28). In Luke 17:37, the disciples ask Him, *"Where, Lord?"* Jesus responds, *"... Wheresoever the body is, thither will the eagles be gathered together."* This reference is undoubtedly directed to the Church because at the moment of the Rapture, we shall ascend and be with Him forever!

The Glory Of God

Ezekiel goes into detail describing a rather strange activity, *"And they went every one straight forward: whither the spirit was to go, they went; and they turned not when they went. And the living creatures ran and returned as the appearance of a flash of lightning. Now as I beheld the living creatures, behold one wheel upon the earth by the living creatures, with his four faces. The appearance of the wheels and their work was like unto the colour of a beryl: and they four had one likeness: and their appearance and their work was as it were a wheel in the middle of a wheel. When they went, they went upon their four sides: and they turned not when they went. As for their rings, they were so high that they were dreadful; and their rings were full of eyes round about them four. And when the living creatures went, the wheels went by them: and when the living creatures were lifted up from the earth, the wheels were lifted up"* (Ezekiel 1:12,14-19).

These verses have often been misused; even Hollywood has jumped on the bandwagon proclaiming these strange objects to be flying saucers from outer space.

What do we really know about them? Well, I have to confess, nothing except that which is written. According to my understanding, verse 28b is the conclusion, *"This was the appearance of the likeness of the glory of the LORD."*

Let's take a moment to summarize what we have learned so far:

• The Lord came down to see the Tower of Babel.

- Abraham spoke to God as a friend.
- Isaac demonstrated the beautiful picture of the bride being presented to the bridegroom.
- Moses spoke with God face to face.
- Elijah saw the "Lord pass by."
- Ezekiel saw the likeness of the glory of God.

God Seen In The Flesh

The greatest mystery ordained before the foundation of the world undoubtedly was the Word of God becoming flesh.

The Gospel of John testifies, *"...the Word was made flesh, and dwelt among us, (and we beheld his glory, the glory as of the only begotten of the Father,) full of grace and truth"* (John 1:14).

The apostle Paul reinforces this statement in 1st Timothy 3:16, *"And without controversy great is the mystery of godliness: God was manifest in the flesh, justified in the Spirit, seen of angels, preached unto the Gentiles, believed on in the world, received up into glory."* What a marvelous mystery: God manifested into flesh! This was the great surprise hidden from the foundation of the world: God became man.

He Shall Come Himself

The Lord's personal involvement in His plan of redemption has been illustrated in the previous seven points. We now go back to the beginning of our study on 1st Thessalonians 4:16, *"For the Lord himself shall descend from heaven with a shout, with the voice of the archangel, and with the trump of God: and the dead in Christ shall rise first."*

To avoid conflict and possible confusion, we cross reference this verse with the often-quoted and fascinating prophetic chapter in the book of Matthew. In Matthew 24, the Lord repeats the word *"shall"* approximately 59 times. If we want to know the future, the Lord has already told us what "shall be." Matthew 24:31 clearly describes "a" rapture, but not "the" Rapture of His Church, *"And he shall send his angels with a great sound of a trumpet, and they shall gather together his elect from the four winds, from one end of heaven to the other."* We will refer to this verse again in later chapters, but it is important to point out that in this verse the Lord shall not come "Himself;" rather, He *"shall send his angels."*

Who Are The Elect?

What are these angels supposed to do? They are to gather *"his elect from the four winds."* Who, then, are His elect? Of course, we all would agree that the elect comprise the Church. In fact, the word "elect" means "called out" or "to be chosen."

In relation to Israel, James exclaimed in Acts 15:14, *"...God at the first did visit the Gentiles, to take out of them a people for his name."* Undoubtedly this is an election from among the Gentiles; however, we cannot deny that Israel was elected first.

When the Lord God spoke to Pharaoh through Moses, He said, *"...Israel is my son, even my first born"* (Exodus 4:22). That statement was made unconditionally. This is as true today as it was almost 3,500 years ago. We cannot overlook God's statements regarding His chosen people, *"For thou art an holy people unto the Lord thy God, and the Lord hath chosen thee to be a peculiar people unto himself, above all the nations that are upon the earth"* (Deuteronomy 14:2). Doesn't 1st Chronicles 16:13 tell us the same? *"O ye seed of Israel his servant, ye children of Jacob, his chosen ones."* We support Israel's special position with these additional verses: *"For the Lord hath chosen Jacob unto himself, and Israel for his peculiar treasure"* (Psalms 135:4).

"But thou, Israel, art my servant, Jacob whom I have chosen, the seed of Abraham my friend" (Isaiah 41:8).

"Yet now hear, O Jacob my servant; and Israel, whom I have chosen" (Isaiah 44:1).

Therefore, when we ask, "Who are the elect?", we find the answer in Isaiah 45:4, *"For Jacob my servant's sake, and Israel mine elect, I have even called thee by thy name; I have surnamed thee, though thou hast not known me."*

The Jacob Nature

Several times the Lord, through the mouth of the prophets, includes the name "Jacob." The name "Jacob" actually means "deceiver" or "supplanter." In Genesis 32:27-28 Jacob receives his new name: *"And he (God) said unto him, What is thy name? And he said, Jacob. And he said, Thy name shall be called no more Jacob, but Israel: for as a prince hast thou power with God and with men, and hast prevailed."* How striking that God says, *"Thy name shall be called no more Jacob, but Israel..."* Yet, throughout the Bible, we see the appearance of the old name "Jacob" over and over! Why? Because Jacob is not born again yet! Until this very day, Israel stands in opposition to the Gospel. The apostle Paul writes, *"As concerning the gospel, they are enemies for your sakes: but as touching the election, they are beloved for the fathers' sakes"* (Romans 11:28). The Jews are enemies of the Gospel.

Through Grace Alone

The question that should automatically come to mind is, "How can these people, who are enemies of the Gospel, and who have rejected their Messiah shouting *"His blood be upon us and our children,'* be the elect?" The answer is the same and applies to all who have been saved through the Lord Jesus Christ: Grace!

We must never forget that Christ died for us while we were yet sinners. He commended His love toward us while we were lost, without hope and without God.

Will Israel be saved in a different way? No. Do they have to try to keep the Law and be good people in order to be saved? No. If such requirements applied, they would be earning their salvation and grace would be made invalid. As a result, there would be two standards of salvation—a concept contrary to what the Bible teaches, for Jesus plainly said, *"No man cometh unto the Father but by me."* Therefore, the grace of the Lord Jesus will be poured upon His people Israel just as the prophet proclaimed, *"...I will pour upon the house of David, and upon the inhabitants of Jerusalem, the spirit of grace and of supplications: and they shall look upon me whom they have pierced, and they shall mourn for him, as one mourneth for his only son, and shall be in bitterness for him, as one that is in bitterness for his firstborn"* (Zechariah 12:10).

The Jews Will Return

Again, we ask, "How can the Jews look upon Jesus whom they have pierced if they are still scattered among the four corners of the earth?" It is impossible for me to predict how the Jews will act in the future. But right now, considering the fact that modern Israel has existed since 1948, there are Jews residing in rich countries such as Europe and America with no intentions of returning to the land of Israel.

Yet, God clearly tells us through His prophets that ultimately every single Jew will return to the land of Israel. For example, Ezekiel 39:28 says, *"Then shall they know that I am the Lord their God, which caused them to be led into captivity among the heathen: but I have gathered them unto their own land, and have left none of them any more there."*

Reread the last part of that verse: *"have left none of them any more there."* The message is that there will be no Jews among the Gentiles.

Thus the question, "How will the Jews get to Israel?" *"He shall send his angels with a great sound of a trumpet and shall gather his elect from the four winds; from one end of heaven to the other"* (Matthew 24:31).

The Fig Tree

Immediately following this statement, the Lord spoke regarding the fig tree: *"Now learn a parable of the fig tree; When his branch is yet tender, and putteth forth leaves, ye know that summer is nigh"* (Matthew 24:32). We know that the fig tree symbolizes Israel under the Law. It is important to note that the Lord does not say "when the fig tree puts forth *fruit*," but when it *"puts forth leaves."* In understanding this, we realize that when man first sinned he used the leaves of the fig tree to cover his nakedness and hide his sin; Israel never actually had their sin taken away.

The Bible says that it is impossible for the blood of bulls and goats to take away sin. Through the Law and the sacrificial service, Israel's sin was covered up, not removed.

Since 1948, the fig tree has become a reality, and indeed is sprouting forth leaves. This is vividly exemplified in their government, where the religious party has great authority. Israel's national airline, El Al, had to stop flying on the Sabbath because of the law forbidding work on that day. They are bringing forth "leaves," not "fruit." Yet Scripture explains that by the Law, no flesh will be justified. So how will Israel bring forth "fruit"? Through grace!

It is also significant to note one of the Lord's last miracle before the crucifixion was the cursing of the fig tree: *"...seeing a fig tree afar off having leaves, he came, if haply he might find any thing thereon: and when he came to it, he found nothing but leaves; for the time of figs was not yet. And Jesus answered and said unto it, No man eat fruit of thee hereafter for ever. And his disciples heard it"* (Mark 11:13-14). In verse 21 we read, *"And Peter calling to remembrance saith unto him, Master, behold, the fig tree which thou cursedst is withered away."* The fig tree died and for almost 2,000 years Israel was nowhere on the map. The fig tree will not bring forth fruit but the leaves will sprout again as we have read in Matthew 24:32, *"...When his branch is yet tender, and putteth forth leaves, ye know that summer is nigh."*

I hope these illustrations help us to understand that our Lord Jesus must come, Himself, to meet His Bride. He will not come to earth, but we will meet Him in the clouds of Heaven.

After the Marriage Supper of the Lamb, He will come back to Israel, and His feet will stand on the Mount of Olives. Israel will then experience national salvation and the nations of the world will be judged.

CHAPTER 4

WITH THE VOICE OF THE ARCHANGEL

"For the Lord himself shall descend from heaven with a shout, with the voice of the archangel, and with the trump of God: and the dead in Christ shall rise first" (1st Thessalonians 4:16).

After having carefully looked at the first event, *"the Lord Himself shall descend from Heaven,"* and highlighting eight points confirming that the Lord Himself must come, we now turn our attention to the words *"with a shout, with the voice of the archangel."*

Whether the "shout" belongs to the Lord Himself or to the archangel is not clear in this verse. Luther translates the phrase as "with a field command." Other translations confirm this although the word "shout" is somewhat underemphasized in the King James translation. In any event, the source of the "shout" is not the issue. In this study, we want to reveal the deeper meaning of the *"voice of the archangel."* The next five points will clarify its identity, purpose, and result.

- Who is the Archangel?
- Israel's Relation to the Church
- The Difference Between Michael and Gabriel
- The Great Opposer: Satan and His Angels
- The Voice Signifies Beginning and End

1) Who Is Michael The Archangel?

In the King James translation, Michael is the only being who carries the title "archangel." In the German language, *Biblisches Namen Lexikon,* Dr. Abraham Meister also identifies Gabriel as an archangel based on his office and function. (Dr. Meister, who went home to be with the Lord many years ago, was a great Greek and Hebrew scholar who carefully researched over 3,500 Bible names and their meanings.)

So who is Michael? His name means "Who is as God?" In the book of Daniel, he is called *"Michael, one of the chief princes."* Incidentally, this indicates that he is not the only one but obviously one of others (Daniel 10:13). In Daniel 10:21, he is identified as *"Michael your prince"* which is proven in Daniel 12:1, *"And at that time shall Michael stand up, the great prince which standeth for the children of thy people...."* These verses make it unquestionably clear that Michael the archangel, the great prince, can be considered the guardian of God's earthly people: Israel.

The Archangel And Moses

Only one time throughout the Bible do we find a name attached to the title of archangel. In Jude 9 we read, *"Yet Michael the archangel, when contending with the devil he disputed about the body of Moses, durst not bring against him a rail-*

ing accusation, but said, The Lord rebuke thee." This verse is concerned with the body of Moses, considered the greatest Israeli figure in the Old Testament. Apparently the body is very important. In this case, the devil was confronted with a great problem. He could rightfully claim the body of Moses, because flesh and blood cannot inherit the kingdom of God, yet he was opposed by Michael the archangel.

To understand this, we must first realize that something special occurred here. Moses did not die as a result of sin, which, of course, is natural. All of us have an appointment with death unless the Lord comes first. Rather, Moses' death was by a special decree from God Himself. The Bible reports, *"And Moses was an hundred and twenty years old when he died: his eye was not dim, nor his natural force abated"* (Deuteronomy 34:7). Quite obviously he could have lived many more years, he was still strong and well. For this reason Michael the archangel interfered, telling the devil in effect, "This is a special case; you can't have the body of Moses."

It is noteworthy to realize that Michael disputed the devil over Moses' body but he did not condemn the devil in his own power or right. He said, *"...the Lord rebuked thee."* In light of this, we need to be cautious with the practice quite popular in these last days to "rebuke the devil." Never forget, the devil has a legitimate right to our bodies because we are sinners, despite the fact that we are saved. Unimaginable damage has been inflicted on many precious souls who have taken it upon themselves to *"fight the devil,"* and *"cast out demons."* Michael, the mighty archangel does not dare a direct confrontation with the devil; he leaves it up to the eternal God who judges righteously. I sense that it is necessary to revaluate our position as believers. We have not been called to attack the devil, thinking that we have the power within ourselves to destroy the wicked one, but rather we must realize what James 4:7 says, *"...Resist the devil, and he will flee from you."* Note also Paul's strategy for opposing the devil (Ephesians 5). The word *"stand"* is used four times in verses 11,13,and 14. We *"stand"* on the already accomplished victory of Calvary, and when we *"stand"* in that territory, the enemy comes, but finds nothing.

Moses' body was protected for a special purpose. Later he would appear on the Mount of Transfiguration, accompanied by Elijah, to talk with Jesus about His death, *"And, behold, there talked with him two men, which were Moses and Elias: Who appeared in glory, and spake of his decease which he should accomplish at Jerusalem"* (Luke 9:30-31).

2) Israel's Relationship To The Church

Sometimes we tend to oversimplify the Bible by saying the Old Testament is for the Jews and the New Testament is for Christians. It is true that the Jews still do not consider the New Testament as part of their Scripture. At the most, they refer to it as the "Christian" Bible.

During the 80's we offered several "Glory" books, including *Glory of Jerusalem* and *Glory of the Holy Land.* In 1990, two more books followed: *The Glory of the Old Testament* and *The Glory of the New Testament.* While in Israel I visited Shlomo Gaffni, the publisher of these books. I asked him why the two books, *The Glory of the Old Testament* and *The Glory of the New Testament* were not for sale in Jewish bookstores in Jerusalem. He explained that these books gave equal footing to the Old and New Testaments. Many Orthodox Jewish groups were offended and boycotted the sale of the books.

The First Church Was Jewish

The Church of Jesus Christ was founded in Jerusalem by Jews, for Jews, and consisted exclusively of Jews. The Bible, both Old and New Testaments, is a Jewish book written by Jews for Jews. Yet Scripture clearly tells us that during the time of the Gentiles, the Jew, in particular, would be blind to the reality of the Savior, the Messiah of Israel, the Lord Jesus Christ. This is substantiated in Romans 11:28, *"As concerning the gospel, they are enemies for your sakes: but as touching the election, they are beloved for the fathers' sake."*

As far as the Jews in general are concerned, it is important to understand that they see no differences between "churchianity" and Christianity, or between those who by tradition and birth belong to a Christian religion, and those who belong to the Church of Jesus Christ through regeneration.

Throughout the centuries, the Jews have painfully experienced severe persecution under the auspices of "churchianity." They were killed by the Romans and suffered through the Spanish Inquisition. There is not one country on the face of the earth in which they have not experienced opposition, persecution and even death. The most horrendous genocide of all time took place in Germany under the reign of Adolf Hitler, a professing Catholic who frequently quoted Scripture and spiced his speeches with Bible-based slogans. From the Jewish perspective, even Adolf Hitler was a "Christian."

Christians Recognize Jews

From a historical perspective, the Jews have always diametrically opposed anything that is Christian. There seems to be an unbridgeable gap between the two. On the other end of the spectrum, the relationship to Israel and the Jews is different in Bible-believing Christianity.

In Romans 11, the apostle Paul reminds the Gentile church of her roots. In verse 13 Paul identifies the group that he is addressing, *"I speak to you Gentiles."* He reveals that Israel still exists, and he compares Israel to an olive tree, *"...if some of the branches be broken off, and thou, being a wild olive tree, wert grafted in among them, and with them partakest of the root and fatness of the olive tree; Boast not against the branches. But if thou boast, thou bearest not the root, but the root thee. Thou wilt say then, The branches were broken off, that I might be grafted in. Well; because of unbelief they were broken off, and thou standest by faith. Be not highminded, but fear: For if God spared not the natural branches, take heed lest he also spare not thee"* (Romans 11:17-21). Paul clearly explains in verse 24 that Israel will be resurrected, *"For if thou wert cut out of the olive tree which is wild by nature, and wert grafted contrary to nature into a good olive tree: how much more shall these, which be the natural branches, be grafted into their own olive tree?"* The Church has often overlooked God's unconditional guarantee of Israel's perpetual existence. At that time the Church as a whole was making the same mistake that the world makes today: "I only believe what I see."

Israel's Future

From God's point of view, there is no question about Israel's existence–despite the fact that they were not a nation for 2,000 years.

Listen to the words of the prophet Jeremiah, *"Thus saith the Lord, which giveth the sun for a light by day, and the ordinances of the moon and of the stars for a light by night, which divideth the sea when the waves thereof roar; The Lord of hosts is his name. If those ordinances depart from before me, saith the LORD, then the seed of Israel also shall cease from being a nation before me for ever"* (Jeremiah 31:35-36). One cannot simply do away with Israel. It is God's creation and what God creates is eternal! Therefore, let us not repeat the mistake of assuming that Israel has lost her position as God's elect. She was not replaced by the Church; this type of "replacement theology" has been the mother of many heresies.

Of course, it is true that Israel rejected the Messiah, but God never rejected Israel. Instead, He temporarily put Israel aside in His plan of salvation which He ordained before the foundation of the world.

Time Limit Of The Church

Returning to our text in Romans 11, we find a time limit, or dispensation for the Church, *"For I would not, brethren, that ye should be ignorant of this mystery, lest ye should be wise in your own conceits; that blindness in part is happened to Israel, until the fulness of the Gentiles be come in"* (Romans 11:25). The apostle Paul points out that this is a mystery of which we should not be ignorant, otherwise, we would deceive ourselves. The blindness is for the sake of the Gentiles *"Until the fulness of the Gentiles be come in."*

Gospel To The Gentiles

For this reason, we continuously support the urgency of

preaching the Gospel to all people everywhere so that the fullness of the Gentiles may come in soon. The Church is an intermission in God's eternal plan of salvation with His people Israel. This was hidden from the beginning. The apostles didn't even fully understand this great mystery. Ephesians 5:32 states, *"This is a great mystery: but I speak concerning Christ and the church."* The early Church did not fully comprehend that God would first take out a people from among the Gentiles for His name.

Even after Jesus defeated the powers of darkness on Calvary's cross, crying out *"It is finished;"* was buried; arose the third day; and walked among His disciples, they still didn't understand: *"When they therefore were come together, they asked of him, saying, Lord, wilt thou at this time restore again the kingdom to Israel?"* (Acts 1:6). The disciples had one-track minds; they wanted Israel to be an independent kingdom with all of its former glories. They knew Scripture, and hoped for the immediate resurrection of the kingdom of Israel. The only thing they could understand were the "good ole' days." God, however, doesn't look back to old glories, but tells us that He will make *"all things new."*

The disciples were commanded to wait until the Holy Spirit came, *"...I send the promise of my Father upon you: but tarry ye in the city of Jerusalem, until ye be endued with power from on high "* (Luke 24:49). Then they were to be *"witnesses unto me both in Jerusalem, and in all Judaea, and in Samaria, and unto the uttermost part of the earth"* (Acts 1:8). This is a very clear instruction; the beginning is Jerusalem and the end is the outermost parts of the world. The Gospel has literally gone from Jerusalem to the very ends of the earth. For that reason

I believe that the Church has little success when it tries to follow this command in the opposite direction, that is preaching the Gospel to Israel and expecting a mass conversion of Jews.

The Gentile Conflict In The Church

In the beginning, there was a controversy about the Gentiles belonging to the Church. In Acts 15, we read that *"...Paul and Barnabas had no small dissension and disputation with them..."* (verse 2). Why? Because these Jews did not fully grasp the Gospel of grace but tried to convert the Gentiles to Judaism first. They taught, *"...Except ye* (Gentiles) *be circumcised after the manner of Moses, ye cannot be saved"* (verse 1).

To settle this conflict, an apostolic counsel was held in Jerusalem. *"And when there had been much disputing, Peter rose up, and said unto them, Men and brethren, ye know how that a good while ago God made choice among us, that the Gentiles by my mouth should hear the word of the gospel, and believe. And God, which knoweth the hearts, bare them witness, giving them the Holy Ghost, even as he did unto us; And put no difference between us and them, purifying their hearts by faith. Now therefore why tempt ye God, to put a yoke upon the neck of the disciples, which neither our fathers nor we were able to bear? But we believe that through the grace of the Lord Jesus Christ we shall be saved, even as they"* (Acts 15:7-11).

It is significant that the apostle Peter spoke these words because he was the first to recognize that Jesus was the Son of God. Based on Peter's confession, Jesus said, *"...I say also unto thee, That thou art Peter, and upon this rock I will build my church; and the gates of hell shall not prevail against it"* (Matthew 16:18). We emphasize that the statement of our Lord has absolutely no relation to the man-made establishment of the Roman papal system, or to any national or international church entity.

Salvation always was and always will be *"of the Jew,"* as the Lord Jesus Himself stated. Nowhere in the Bible do we read of the Lord giving preference to a certain city or country outside of Israel.

Therefore, any group who claims to be the exclusive and privileged successors of the apostle Peter, or who asserts that they are the exclusive dispensers of salvation, can rightfully be labeled as an anti-Christian cult.

After Peter had spoken, *"…all the multitudes kept silence."* Barnabas and Paul then gave affirmation regarding the Gentiles.

Prophecy Settles Conflict

James confirmed this testimony when he declared, *"Simeon hath declared how God at the first did visit the Gentiles, to take out of them a people for his name. And to this agree the words of the prophets; as it is written, After this I will return, and will build again the tabernacle of David, which is fallen down; and I will build again the ruins thereof, and I will set it up"* (Acts 15:14-16). Here we see the authority of the apostle Peter, for he was the first to preach the Gospel to the Jews, to the half-Jew Samaritans, and to the Gentiles. He was also the first one through whom the Lord performed miracles—including raising the dead to life—to demonstrate the fulfillment of prophecy. James now endorses that which Simon (Peter) had stated is based on the prophetic Word.

According to my understanding, the raising up of the

fallen tabernacle of David is Israel's national identity. This has no relation to the tent-like tabernacle that David built to house the Ark of the Covenant. To establish this point, we turn to Psalm 78:67-68, *"Moreover he refused the tabernacle of Joseph, and chose not the tribe of Ephraim: But chose the tribe of Judah, the mount Zion which he loved."* In other words, the national identity [tabernacle] will not be found in Joseph or Ephraim, but in Judah. As a result, Israelis are Jews and only Jews can instantly and automatically become Israelis the moment they return to the Promised Land.

Turning in our Bibles to the Old Testament book of Amos, the prophet writes, *"That they may possess the remnant of Edom, and of all the heathen, which are called by my name, saith the Lord that doeth this"* (Amos 9:12). This verse prophetically refers to the inclusion of the Gentiles, *"which are called by my name."*

Mystery Of The Church

God's plan for both His people and the Gentiles was a mystery unknown to Israel, the apostles and the prophets; even the angels did not know. The testimony of Peter says the following, *"Of which salvation the prophets have inquired and searched diligently, who prophesied of the grace that should come unto you: Searching what, or what manner of time the Spirit of Christ which was in them did signify, when it testified beforehand the sufferings of Christ, and the glory that should follow. Unto whom it was revealed, that not unto themselves, but unto us they did minister the things, which are now reported unto you by them that have preached the gospel unto you with the Holy Ghost sent down from heaven; which things the angels desire to look into.*

Wherefore gird up the loins of your mind, be sober, and hope to the end for the grace that is to be brought unto you at the revelation of Jesus Christ" (1st Peter 1:10-13).

Gentile's Hopelessness

I am fully convinced that most of us who are saved by grace from among the Gentiles don't fully comprehend the hopelessness of our situation before we became Christians. The apostle Paul explains to the Ephesians, *"Wherefore remember, that ye being in time past Gentiles in the flesh, who are called Uncircumcision by that which is called the Circumcision in the flesh made by hands; That at that time ye were without Christ, being aliens from the commonwealth of Israel, and strangers from the covenants of promise, having no hope, and without God in the world"* (Ephesians 2:11-12). Think of it: *"no hope"* and *"without God."* Could anything possibly be worse than that? Thank God that is not how it ends. *"But now in Christ Jesus ye who sometimes were far off are made nigh by the blood of Christ"* (Ephesians 2:13). Indeed, *"This is a great mystery: but I speak concerning Christ and the church"* (Ephesians 5:32).

Gentile's Hope

At this point, we must stress that the Gentiles, born again of the Spirit of God, are the ones who are addressed by the apostle Paul, for he says, *"I Paul, the prisoner of Jesus Christ for you Gentiles"* (Ephesians 3:1). He also reveals some wonderful news in verse 6, *"That the Gentiles should be fellow-heirs, and of the same body and partakers of his promise in Christ by the gospel."* To the Romans, this same apostle confirms the fulfillment of Bible prophecy for the Gentiles, *"Now I say that*

Jesus Christ was a minister of the circumcision for the truth of God, to confirm the promises made unto the fathers: And that the Gentiles might glorify God for his mercy; as it is written, For this cause I will confess to thee among the Gentiles, and sing unto thy name. And again he saith, Rejoice, ye Gentiles, with his people. And again, Praise the Lord, all ye Gentiles; and laud him, all ye people. And again, Esaias saith, There shall be a root of Jesse, and he that shall rise to reign over the Gentiles; in him shall the Gentiles trust" (Romans 15:8-12). Therefore, the Gentiles have a duty toward Israel, *"It hath pleased them verily; and their debtors they are. For if the Gentiles have been made partakers of their spiritual things, their duty is also to minister unto them in carnal things"* (Romans 15:27). These few verses should validate the fact that although Israel and the Church remain two distinct entities, they are organically united because they both partake of the olive tree.

The Organic Unity Of Jews And Christians

Another verse is often misused and needs to be clarified: *"There is neither Jew nor Greek, there is neither bond nor free, there is neither male nor female: for ye are all one in Christ Jesus"* (Galatians 3:28). The Church consists of both Jews and Gentiles; the two have become one. On a spiritual level there is no distinction between Jew and Gentile.

However, this does not abolish the physical identity of a Jew being a Jew and a Greek being a Greek, which is evident from the statement, *"there is neither male nor female."* Every one of us can attest that the moment we were born again of the Spirit of God, we continued to be what we were: male or female. This further proves that spiritual unity in Christ Jesus is what is meant here and in no way does it indicate that a Jew is no longer a Jew.

3) The Difference Between Michael And Gabriel

We have already determined that Michael is identified with the title "archangel." Whether Gabriel is an archangel is not clear. Some scholars claim that God has three archangels: Michael, Gabriel, and Lucifer, each responsible for one-third of the heavenly power structure. This interpretation was developed on the basis of Revelation 12:4, *"And his tail drew the third part of the stars of heaven, and did cast them to the earth...."* Therefore, it is assumed that Lucifer, in his fallen state, had the power to draw one-third of Heaven's angels to earth. If that is the case, then Lucifer must have been one of the greatest, presumably an archangel. Although this theory sounds fascinating, I cannot find sufficient scriptural evidence to support it. Since Scripture clearly identifies Michael as an archangel, we will not concern ourselves with speculation.

The book of Daniel presents the contrasts between Michael and Gabriel, *"And it came to pass, when I, even I Daniel, had seen the vision, and sought for the meaning, then, behold, there stood before me as the appearance of a man. And I heard a man's voice between the banks of Ulai, which called, and said, Gabriel, make this man to understand the vision"* (Daniel 8:15-16). Daniel had just seen a vision concerning the end-times. The entire future of the Gentile power structure had been shown to him. He then sought the interpretation eager to understand what he had just seen. We then read, *"there stood before me as the appearance of a man."* No further information is given about this "man" other than what we read in the next verse. A commandment instructed, *"Gabriel, make this man to understand the vision."* Gabriel, identified simply as an angel in the New Testament, explained to Daniel what he had just seen. The interpretation is primarily concerned with the Gentile power structure from beginning to end. It will climax with the power of the Antichrist, who *"shall also stand up against the Prince of princes; but he (Antichrist) shall be broken without hand"* (Daniel 8:25).

Gabriel's task is to convey to Daniel, who was a Jew, what will happen to the Gentile world.

We must emphasize here that general terms are given to differentiate between the various power structures of the Gentile world. According to Daniel 7:1, at the time of the vision Daniel was serving, *"Belshazzar king of Babylon."* Daniel 8:20 identifies the ram with the two horns as the next Gentile world empire, *"...the kings of Media and Persia."* Continuing in verse 21, *"the rough goat"* is identified as *"the king of Grecia."* A detailed description of the final Gentile ruler follows.

The Antichrist

In Daniel 8:23, Daniel receives a deeper insight into the last kingdom which will produce the *"king of fierce countenance,"* the Antichrist. Amazingly, although this person has a *"fierce countenance,"* he's apparently very clever because he holds the power of *"understanding dark sentences."* Following in verses 24 and 25 we read, *"And his power shall be mighty, but not by his own power: and he shall destroy wonderfully, and shall prosper, and practise, and shall destroy the mighty and the holy people. And through his policy also he shall cause craft to prosper in his hand; and he shall magnify himself in his heart, and by peace shall destroy many: he shall also stand up against the Prince of princes; but he shall be broken without hand.*" These verses undoubtedly speak of the Antichrist because his power is not his own. In addition, these verses precisely correspond to the description of the Antichrist in Revelation 13, where we read that he receives power from the dragon. Thus, we recognize that he is not a power in his own right, but his success is attributed to the power of Satan himself.

Notice that as a result of his success, *"He shall destroy wonderfully."* His victory will overwhelm even God's people, Israel, for *"he shall destroy the mighty and the holy people."* It seems that nothing will stand in his way; he will be a winner, *"And through his policy also he shall cause craft to prosper in his hand...."* His victory will come not by an act of war, but *"by peace."* This could never happen unless a people-powered democracy ruled.

We must not forget that the Lord Jesus was not crucified through the means of a dictatorship but through the workings of a democracy. The religious authority–along with the people–demanded Jesus' crucifixion; He was executed by the hands of the lawful government of Rome.

In the Gospel of Mark we see democracy in action, *"...Pilate, willing to content the people, released Barabbas unto them, and delivered Jesus, when he had scourged him, to be crucified"* (Mark 15:15). Jesus was killed without opposition!

Jesus did not have to fight against the wicked one nor will He need to fight against him in the end. *"But he* (Antichrist) *shall be broken without hand."* We clearly see the work of the dark force will imitate Jesus to the end.

I find it amazing that the powers of the Gentiles culminating in the Antichrist will not need to be destroyed by war. Jesus, the Prince of Light, will not need to fight in order to win the war; He accomplished that when He cried out on Calvary's cross, *"It is finished."* *"The Lord shall consume* (the Antichrist) *with the spirit of his mouth, and shall destroy with the brightness of his coming"* (2nd Thessalonians 2:8).

Gabriel had to convey this message to Daniel so that he could write it down and we would have record of it until this day.

Medo-Persian Empire

"In the first year of Darius the son of Ahasuerus, of the seed of the Medes, which was made king over the realm of the Chaldeans" (Daniel 9:1).

After receiving such a wonderful revelation, Daniel was still not satisfied. Something was missing. He understood the sequence of the Gentile world empires, culminating with the rulership of the Antichrist, but he failed to see anything concerning his own people, the Jews, particularly regarding Jerusalem. In verse 2 we read, *"In the first year of his reign, I Daniel understood by books the number of the years, whereof the word of the Lord came to Jeremiah the prophet, that he would accomplish seventy years in the desolations of Jerusalem."* More than anything else on Daniel's mind was his beloved homeland, Israel, and the glorious city of Jerusalem.

Sin Confession

Daniel did the right thing; he began to fast and pray. In addition, he confessed the sins of his people, Israel, and his own. It's rather striking that Daniel did not complain about the situation in which he had found himself. After all, it wasn't his fault. He was just a youth when Jerusalem was destroyed and he was led into captivity by King Nebuchadnezzar. Surely he could have prayed, "Our fathers have sinned and they have done wrong; they committed so much evil." This would have been quite normal, but we read just the opposite; Daniel identified himself with the sins of his people by saying, *"We have sinned;" "We have rebelled against him;" "Neither have we obeyed the voice of the Lord our God;"* and *"We have sinned against him."*

He concluded his prayer by confessing his own sins, *"And whiles I was speaking, and praying, and confessing my sin and the sin of my people Israel, and presenting my supplication before the LORD my God for the holy mountain of my God; Yea, whiles I was speaking in prayer, even the man Gabriel, whom I had seen in the vision at the beginning, being caused to fly swiftly, touched me about the time of the evening oblation. And he informed me, and talked with me, and said, O Daniel, I am now come forth to give thee skill and understanding. At the beginning of thy supplications the commandment came forth, and I am come to shew thee; for thou art greatly beloved: therefore understand the matter, and consider the vision"* (Daniel 9:20-23). Notice that Gabriel is not called an angel or archangel in this verse but *"the man Gabriel."*

The Coming Messiah

Daniel received an additional vision explaining the future of Jerusalem, the coming of the Messiah, the death of the Messiah, the establishment of a false covenant and the breaking of the covenant, which would result in *"the overspreading of abominations"* (verse 27). When reading these few chapters, particularly chapters 8-11, we sense that although Daniel's heart was with his people, country and city, the visions he received were primarily concerning the Gentile nations.

Gentile World Empire

"In the third year of Cyrus king of Persia" (Daniel 10:1), Daniel explained that he *"was mourning three full weeks"* (verse 2). Daniel's dedication to his God is unquestionable. He didn't just routinely pray, say "Amen" and get on with his business; he desired to know God's ways. Hadn't what he already experienced been enough? After all, he was the only one in the great Babylonian kingdom who could interpret Nebuchadnezzar's dream. He had been exalted to the chief governor of the entire province of Babylon.

Daniel had also interpreted the handwriting on the wall for Belshazzar–and his interpretation came to pass.

Darius, the next king, had promoted him as one of the three presidents over his entire world empire.

He was thrown into the lion's den because of his faith and was shown the entire history of the Gentile world empires by God.

Still not satisfied, Daniel wanted more: He was concerned about Jerusalem, the land of Israel and his people. Nevertheless, God gave him only a limited view of the restoration of the people of Israel.

We may wonder why Daniel asked for more. I believe that Daniel wanted to know more about the coming Messiah. Instead, he received additional detailed revelation about the final Gentile empire and the Antichrist.

In answer to his extended prayer, we read, *"Then I lifted up mine eyes, and looked, and behold a certain man clothed in linen, whose loins were girded with fine gold of Uphaz: His body also was like the beryl, and his face as the appearance of lightning, and his eyes as lamps of fire, and his arms and his feet like in colour to polished brass, and the voice of his words like the voice of a multitude"* (Daniel 10:5-6). When we compare this description with Revelation 2, where the Lord Jesus revealed Himself to John, we notice that this is the appearance of the *"Alpha and Omega, the first and the last." "His eyes as lamps of fire and his arms and feet like polished brass and the voice of his words like a voice of a multitude."* Revelation 1:17 described John's reaction, *"And when I saw him, I fell at his feet as dead. And he laid his right hand upon me, saying unto me, Fear not; I am the first and the last."* Daniel's reaction to his vision is similar to John's: when he *"saw this great vision...there remained no strength in me: for my comeliness was turned in me into corruption, and I retained no strength...then was I in a deep sleep on my face, and my face toward the ground...And, behold an hand touched me...and he said...Fear not, Daniel"* (Daniel 10:8-12).

Invisible Conflict

The invisible conflict between the powers of darkness and the powers of light were revealed to Daniel, *"And he said unto me, O Daniel, a man greatly beloved, understand the words that I speak unto thee, and stand upright: for unto thee am I now sent. And when he had spoken this word unto me, I stood trembling. Then said he unto me, Fear not, Daniel: for from the first day that thou didst set thine heart to understand, and to chasten thyself before thy God, thy words were heard, and I am come for thy words. But the prince of the kingdom of Persia withstood me one and twenty days: but, lo, Michael, one of the chief princes, came to help me; and I remained there with the kings of Persia"* (Daniel 10:11-13). Who is the *"prince of the kingdom of Persia?"* From the text, it was obviously not a man of flesh and blood, but part of the power structure of darkness.

We must always keep in mind that our planet is ruled by the god of this world, the prince of darkness. He has claim to every human soul on this earth: *"For all have sinned and come short of the glory of God."* The prince of darkness could rightly withstand the messenger of God who brought the message to Daniel concerning the end of the Gentile world empires.

In chapter 10 Gabriel is not identified as the messenger, but we assume he is because chapters 8 and 9 indicate that Gabriel actually spoke the message to Daniel in Daniel 10:11, *"...O Daniel, a man greatly beloved"* and verse 19, *"...O man greatly beloved."* In any event, we do know that Gabriel explained the vision to Daniel regarding the Gentiles. On the other hand, Michael undoubtedly is an archangel who stands for the children of Israel. The angel says, *"But I will shew thee that which is noted in the scripture of truth: and there is none that holdeth with me in these things, but Michael your prince"* (Daniel 10:21).

Gentile Opposition

Clearly, the Gentiles, ruled by the powers of darkness oppose the revelation of the prophetic Word. This mighty heavenly messenger who was sent to Daniel after he had prayed for three weeks was hindered in delivering the message by the prince of the kingdom of Persia. That, however, was not the end, because the messenger also revealed the immediate future, *"...when I am gone forth, lo, the prince of Grecia shall come"* (Daniel 10:20).

We should now better understand why the Lord Himself will come with the voice of the archangel. The moment that the Church is taken out of the way, utter darkness will cover the earth, and Israel, in its unconverted condition will stand helpless, and in great danger. Therefore, Michael will have to intervene on behalf of the children of Israel, *"And at that time shall Michael stand up, the great prince which standeth for the children of thy people: and there shall be a time of trouble, such as never was since there was a nation even to that same time: and at that time thy people shall be delivered, every one that shall be found written in the book"* (Daniel 12:1).

4) The Great Opposer; Satan And His Angels

As children of God, we do well to confirm that we no longer belong to the kingdom of darkness. Paul wrote, *"Ye are all the children of light, and the children of the day: we are not of the night, nor of darkness"* (1st Thessalonians 5:5).

This brings us to a very important point: our earthly association with our nation. During my many years of ministry, I have often met sincere Christians who have been fanatical nationalists. Unfortunately, they are found all over the globe. Somehow these dear Christians are desperately trying to be identified nationally, and they ignore the fact that no matter which nation they belong to, all are under the jurisdiction of Satan, the prince of the power of the air, the god of this world.

The Bible does not distinguish between capitalist or communist, nationalist or Nazi, socialist or dictatorship. From a biblical perspective, they are all Gentiles; therefore they are all the same. Only one kingdom was established and ordained by God: Israel, through which He has brought forth the Church of Jesus Christ. All other nations, no matter how good or evil, fall in the other category: the Gentile world. We must learn to understand that our battle is not against flesh and blood, nationalities, political systems, or moral laws, we are at war against the invisible world.

Our Real Battle

In Paul's letter to the Ephesians, he wrote, *"For we wrestle not against flesh and blood, but against principalities, against powers, against the rulers of the darkness of this world, against spiritual wickedness in high places"* (Ephesians 6:12). Luther translated the last sentence as, *"With the evil spirits under the heaven."* Yes, we are at war, but praise God, the victory is already ours.

In actuality, we no longer have to fight against Satan to gain victory. If that were the case, we would lose the war. Our Lord Jesus Christ already achieved victory. Dr. Wim Malgo once said, "Our greatest fight in life is not to fight." What then must we do? Note very carefully that under the inspiration of the Holy Spirit, the apostle Paul repeatedly used the word "stand." For example, *"that ye may be able to stand against the wiles of the devil"* (verse 11). *"...that ye may be able to withstand in the evil day, and having done all, to stand"* (verse 13). *"Stand therefore, having your loins girt about with truth, and having on the breastplate of righteousness"* (verse 14).

When the devil comes and accuses you of being a miserable creature, a habitual sinner and a failure, don't disagree or defend yourself. Just stand. When your co-workers mock you, don't try to get even. Just stand. When you are falsely accused, don't defend yourself. Just stand. Remember, the battle is over, the war is won; Jesus paid it all, all to Him we owe!

Michael Against The Dragon

Revelation 12 presents the history of the past, present and future of Israel in a nutshell. *"And there appeared a great wonder in heaven; a woman clothed with the sun, and the moon under her feet, and upon her head a crown of twelve stars: And she being with child cried, travailing in birth, and pained to be delivered. And there appeared another wonder in heaven; and behold a great red dragon, having seven heads and ten horns, and seven crowns upon his heads. And his tail drew the third part of the stars of heaven, and did cast them to the earth: and the dragon stood before the woman which was ready to be delivered, for to devour her child as soon as it was born"* (verses 1-4). The "woman" mentioned in this verse is Israel. Salvation is of the Jews. The twelve stars on her crown are the twelve tribes of the children of Israel and the twelve apostles of the Lamb. The dragon, the old serpent called the devil and Satan, had all intentions to *"devour her child as soon as it was born."*

While the children of Israel were still in Egypt, the dragon incited Pharaoh to "devour" the children of Israel as soon as they were born. When Jesus was born, King Herod wanted to rid himself of the newborn King so he sent his henchmen to Bethlehem to kill all male children under the age of two. For thousands of years, many nations, kingdoms, and powers have attempted to destroy the Jews; however, all have failed and will continue to fail.

Petra: The Hiding Place?

This "man-child" will ultimately rule all nations with a rod of iron. Where is this "man-child" now? "...*Her child was caught unto God and to his throne*"(Revelation 12:5). Since that time, Israel was dispersed into the *"wilderness"* of the nations of the world. Continuing in verse 6, we read, "...*the woman fled into the wilderness, where she hath a place prepared of God, that they should feed her there a thousand two hundred and three-score days.*" Here we are given a precise number of days, "*a thousand two hundred and threescore days*"(verse 6). Notice that is just 17 days short of 3 1/2 years.

The general interpretation is that Israel will escape into the wilderness of Petra in Jordan for 3 1/2 years, the second half of the seven-year tribulation.

I have seen the place some scholars believe will be the hiding place for Israel: Petra, in the land of Jordan. If that is the case, then the Jews will have to learn how to live like cave dwellers. In Petra, there is virtually no water, electricity, sewage system, housing, hospitals, police stations, airports, roads, filling stations, or other such essentials that modern man is accustomed to. In addition, Petra is an incredibly dangerous place. When man used horses, arrows and swords as their primary source of weaponry, Petra would have served as a natural defense against attack. However in our day, it's a death trap because even with relatively simple weapons, enemies could bombard it from the outside without the people on the inside even having a chance to defend themselves.

In considering where Israel will escape to, we look to the Bible, which tells us that "*she* [Israel] *has a place prepared of God.*" After much study on this subject, I have concluded that the "place prepared of God" is none other than the land of Israel, which was a "wilderness" for almost 2,000 years.

May I suggest that somewhere in the desert of Israel, God will miraculously establish a place of refuge for His persecuted people in such a way that we cannot describe? Remember, the Bible says that even the angels desire to look into the things which God has prepared for them that love Him. "How could that be, when Israel does not love God?" It is true that a large part of the Israeli population is godless, and the New Testament says that they are enemies for the gospel's sake. Therefore to answer that question, ask yourself, "Did I love God before He loved me?" Of course not. Christ died for us while we were yet sinners. In other words, we were brutal, stubborn, enemies and haters of God, yet despite our condition, God loved us. Is it too much to expect that God would love His chosen people whom He calls "My first love" in the same way He loves the Gentiles?

We know that the Lord's physical appearance on the Mount of Olives will mark the beginning of the end of the Great Tribulation. The Bible tells us that they will see Him whom they have pierced. As previously discussed, that means that the Jews would have to be in the land of Israel, particularly Jerusalem, when Jesus returns. If they all escaped to the land of Jordan and are hiding in Petra, they obviously couldn't be present when the Lord returned to the Mount of Olives. Therefore, I see no resolution other than the Jews fleeing to a wilderness such as the Judean desert or the Negev, where God has miraculously prepared a place for them.

War In Heaven

In the divinely inspired book of Revelation, John writes

about a great conflict, a war in heaven, *"And there was war in heaven: Michael and his angels fought against the dragon; and the dragon fought and his angels"* (Revelation 12:7). Again we see Michael in action. Why is he fighting the dragon? Because he no longer has a claim to any place in Heaven. The Bride is now raptured into Heaven.

When the Church is raptured into Heaven, Satan loses his job as the accuser of the brethren because there is no one left to accuse. There is no reason for him to accuse the world because he owns it; its occupants are the children of darkness who follow in the footsteps of the prince of this world.

It may be important to note here that "Heaven" is much more than our limited intellect can comprehend. For example, the apostle Paul testified that he was *"...caught up to the third heaven"* (2nd Corinthians 12:2). In this particular context, "Heaven" does not mean "in the presence of the glory of God." We saw in Ephesians 6:12 that the powers of darkness have their "spiritual wickedness" in high places, which Luther translates as *"the evil spirit under the heaven."*

I do believe we can say with certainty that the earth, including all who dwell upon it, is ruled by Satan. He has authority which will be broken when Jesus comes in the clouds for the Rapture of His saints. At that moment, Satan is cast out of Heaven onto the earth.

The Universal Church

It is impossible to estimate the number of people who will be raptured. For 2,000 years, the Gospel has been proclaimed in all the world and millions of people have put their trust in the Lord Jesus Christ and have become believers. To the church in Rome, the apostle Paul wrote, *"...your faith is spoken of throughout the whole world"* (Romans 1:8). To the Thessalonians, he wrote, *"For from you sounded out the word of the Lord not only in Macedonia and Achaia, but also in every place your faith to Godward is spread abroad..."* (1st Thessalonians 1:8). Even at the beginning of the Church, faith in Jesus was spread throughout the known world.

Satan does have a claim on us prior to the Rapture because we are subject to the law of sin and death. But now, Jesus' Church is in Heaven, where a great celebration is going on, *"And I heard a loud voice saying in heaven, Now is salvation and strength and the kingdom of our God and the power of his Christ..."* (Revelation 12:10). We can't even imagine the joy, the glory and the happiness that will be experienced in the heavens when Satan and his angels are cast out.

Continuing in verse 10, we read, *"...for the accuser of our brethren is cast down, which accused them before our God day and night."* Satan has lost his job! Each one of us whom he had the right to accuse has now been translated into the image of the beloved Son; our old bodies are left behind. At that time, the prophecy, *"Behold, I make all things new"* will become a reality.

The Bible shows a distinct difference between those in Heaven and those left behind on earth. *"Therefore rejoice, ye heavens, and ye that dwell in them. Woe to the inhabiters of the earth and of the sea! for the devil is come down unto you, having great wrath, because he knoweth that he hath but a short time"* (Revelation 12:12). The devil knows he only has a short time, seven years to be precise. However, the world has been preparing for him since the birth of the Church and is continuing to do so this very day!

The development of the Gentile nations, particularly since the birth of the Church, has, at times, aimed to bring about peace on earth and good will toward men through its own initiative. If we were to compare our time with that of 100, 500, 1,000, or even 2,000 years ago, we would have to confess that the conditions in which we live are better now than ever.

Antichrist Against Israel

We have just read that the one who deceives the whole world was cast down, and arrived to find everything prepared for him. There is, however, an obstacle-the Jew. Israel will be a "thorn in the flesh" of the Antichrist. Although the first 3 1/2 years of the tribulation will seem to be a time of unprecedented prosperity, peace and security, the remaining 3 1/2 years will be evidence that the Jews are different. They are the only people in history who are diverse from all people on earth. Satan will try to change that. In the beginning it will seem as though he succeeds, but when all hope is lost for the Jews, Jesus will appear on the Mount of Olives.

5) The Voice Signifies The Beginning And End

The *"voice of the archangel"* will signify the end of the Church on earth. In that very moment, the Church will be taken into Heaven. The *"voice of the archangel"* will proclaim that the fullness of the Gentiles has come in, and that the Church age has ended.

The *"voice of the archangel"* also marks the beginning of Israel's salvation. Undoubtedly, this amazing event, the coming of our Lord in the clouds of Heaven with a shout with the voice of the archangel, will be hidden from the world.

There are several theories by which the world could explain the disappearance of so many people. A number of articles, books and videos are available on the subject of the Rapture; some accounts are fascinating. However, all of our interpretation is based primarily on speculation. Because this will be a one-time historical event, it is impossible for us to imagine how those left behind will react.

My theory is that the world will be happy because the success of the global world society will have reached such a high point that the preaching of the Gospel, particularly the imminency of the Rapture, will be largely discarded as a theory applicable only to some "fanatics." The world will experience a new beginning that will overwhelm the spirit and soul of man to such an extent that he will gladly believe the deceptive work of the power of darkness.

God Allows The Antichrist

Second Thessalonians 2:9-10 says, *"Even him, whose coming is after the working of Satan with all power and signs and lying wonders. And with all deceivableness of unrighteousness in them that perish; because they received not the love of the truth, that they might be saved."* We believe in either the truth or we believe in a lie. Subsequently, we are either saved or lost.

For 2,000 years, God in His mercy has withheld judgment and has allowed the message that "Jesus saves and He is coming again" to be proclaimed all over the world. However, man has refused to believe this simple truth, and has chosen to believe in lying signs and wonders. Therefore, God confirms the work of the Antichrist, *"And for this cause God shall send them strong delusion, that they should believe a lie"* (2nd Thessalonians 2:11).

How will those who are left behind react? First Thessalonians 5:3 reports, *"For when they shall say, Peace and safety; then sudden destruction cometh upon them, as travail upon a woman with child; and they shall not escape."* The new global system will enjoy a success that has never been experienced. You can't tell people that there is peace when there is none. Remember, at that time, the entire world will be united. Information regarding any area of the world is instantly accessible today. The Antichrist system will establish a tremendous society which says, *"Peace and safety."*

The great truth, however, is that there is no peace or safety outside of the Lord Jesus Christ. That is why as believers we can comfort ourselves with the living reality that this peace and safety has already been eternally established by the Lord Jesus Christ. *"For God hath not appointed us to wrath, but to obtain salvation by our Lord Jesus Christ"* (1st Thessalonians 5:9). In view of this wonderful hope, we read this admonition: *"And the very God of peace sanctify you wholly; and I pray God your whole spirit and soul and body be preserved blameless unto the coming of our Lord Jesus Christ"* (verse 23).

CHAPTER 5

WITH THE TRUMP OF GOD

"For the Lord himself shall descend from heaven with a shout, with the voice of the archangel, and with the trump of God: and the dead in Christ shall rise first" (1st Thessalonians 4:16).

In this chapter, we continue our study on the above verse by concerning ourselves primarily with *"the trump of God."* In the King James version, the "last trump" is found in 1st Corinthians 15:51-52 where the apostle Paul, inspired by the Holy Spirit, speaks about the events of the Rapture, *"Behold, I shew you a mystery; We shall not all sleep, but we shall all be changed, In a moment, in the twinkling of an eye, at the last trump: for the trumpet shall sound, and the dead shall be raised incorruptible, and we shall be changed."* This trump is referred to as the "trump of God."

This trump of God is identified as "the last trump." Keeping this in mind will help us to better understand the uniqueness of the last trump of God in comparison with all of the other trumpets mentioned in the Bible.

What Is A Trump?

A trump is an instrument manufactured from a variety of metals designed to amplify sound. During early history, the trump was an effective means of communication.

Today, our news media are the trumpets. Modern trumpeters can instantaneously proclaim messages around the world.

Unfortunately, the trumpeters in our day often send confusing messages. If we constantly heeded the news media, we would have to change our habits frequently. For example, we were once warned of the danger of eating butter and eggs; recent reports tell us that these foods are now good for our health.

Airbags installed in new cars were initially heralded as the ultimate safety precaution; now auto manufacturers give consumers the option of switching off the airbag device because of the danger that young children could be killed by the bag.

For every claim presented in the media, there are dozens of counter claims. The debate and confusion continues, particularly in regards to politics.

Different Trumpets

The first mention of a trumpet in the Bible was when the children of Israel gathered at Mt. Sinai and God gave Moses the Ten Commandments. This trumpet is significant because it does not relate to the other trumpets mentioned later.

Exodus 19 speaks of God's people gathering to hear His command. Apparently, the trumpet that the people heard was not a trump made by man, but as we will see, was the trump of God.

Trumpet Of Jubilee

"And thou shalt number seven sabbaths of years unto thee, seven times seven years; and the space of the seven sabbaths of years shall be unto thee forty and nine years. Then shalt thou cause the trumpet of the jubile to sound on the tenth day of the seventh month, in the day of atonement shall ye make the trumpet sound throughout all your land. And ye shall hallow the fiftieth year, and proclaim liberty throughout all the land unto all the inhabitants thereof: it shall be a jubile unto you; and ye shall return every man unto his possession, and ye shall return every man unto his family" (Leviticus 25:8-10).

These trumpets were blown to initiate liberty to people in bondage.

This system was ordained by God so that all Israelites would have an equal chance to succeed in their society and would have a second chance if they failed the first time. Furthermore, it would significantly diminish the system of monopoly.

It is fascinating to read how God is concerned about each of His people, providing the opportunity for His children to get back on their feet.

Let's read the instruction that the children of Israel received, *"The land shall not be sold for ever: for the land is mine; for ye are strangers and sojourners with me. And in all the land of your possession ye shall grant a redemption for the land. If thy brother be waxen poor, and hath sold away some of his possession, and if any of his kin come to redeem it, then shall he redeem that which his brother sold. And if the man have none to redeem it, and himself be able to redeem it; Then let him count the years of the sale thereof, and restore the overplus unto the man to whom he sold it; that he may return unto his possession"* (Leviticus 25:23-27).

This passage demonstrates God's intention of forgiveness. It is His desire to forgive; He teaches His chosen people, Israel to forgive one another.

Forty-Nine Times Forgiveness

Later in history, when the Word of God became flesh and dwelt among us, Jesus preached forgiveness: *"Take heed to yourselves: If thy brother trespass against thee, rebuke him; and if he repent, forgive him. And if he trespass against thee seven times in a day, and seven times in a day turn again to thee, saying, I repent; thou shalt forgive him"* (Luke 17:3-4).

When Peter asked the Lord, *"…how oft shall my brother sin against me, and I forgive him? til seven times?"* (Matthew 18:21), the Lord responded, *"I say not unto thee, Until seven times: but, Until seventy times seven"* (verse 22).

Forgiveness was no longer mandated after the 49th year; instead, the Lord proclaimed instant forgiveness throughout the 49 years of bondage!

On a personal note, have your sins been forgiven? If not, then come to Jesus! He is in the business of forgiving sin. John testified, *"Behold the Lamb of God, which taketh away the sins of the world."* Without forgiveness resulting in salvation, there is no foundation for a sustainable society.

Forgiveness is the basis of the message of the Bible. When man fell into sin, God pronounced judgment but simultaneously included a promise of forgiveness, *"And I will put enmity between thee and the woman, and between thy seed and her seed; it shall bruise thy head, and thou shalt bruise his heel"* (Genesis

3:15).

These trumpets of jubilee, blown every 50th year, opened the door to the forgiveness of debts and the restoration of family lands. However, these trumpets must not be confused with the "trump of God."

Trumpets Of Silver

We are introduced to two special trumpets made of silver in Numbers chapter 10. The blowing of these trumpets sent a clear message to the Israelites. When they heard these trumps, they knew that they were either to gather to hear God's Word or to prepare for departure. *"And the Lord spake unto Moses, saying, Make thee two trumpets of silver; of a whole piece shalt thou make them: that thou mayest use them for the calling of the assembly, and for the journeying of the camps. And when they shall blow with them, all the assembly shall assemble themselves to thee at the door of the tabernacle of the congregation. And if they blow but with one trumpet, then the princes which are heads of the thousands of Israel, shall gather themselves unto thee. When ye blow an alarm, then the camps that lie on the east parts shall go forward. When ye blow an alarm the second time, then the camps that lie on the south side shall take their journey: they shall blow an alarm for their journeys. But when the congregation is to be gathered together, ye shall blow, but ye shall not sound an alarm. And the sons of Aaron, the priests, shall blow with the trumpets; and they shall be to you for an ordinance for ever throughout your generations. And if ye go to war in your land against the enemy that oppresseth you, then ye shall blow an alarm with the trumpets; and ye shall be remembered before the LORD your God, and ye shall be saved from your enemies. Also in the day of your gladness, and in your solemn days, and in the beginnings of your months, ye shall blow with the trumpets over your burnt offerings, and over the sacrifices of your peace offerings; that they may be to you for a memorial before your God: I am the LORD your God."* (Numbers 10:1-10).

These trumpets served as a communication system for the people of Israel, but did not constitute the trump of God.

The Feast Of Trumpets

We read the following in Numbers 29:1, *"And in the seventh month, on the first day of the month, ye shall have an holy convocation; ye shall do no servile work: it is a day of blowing the trumpets unto you."*

We notice in this verse that a special occasion was announced by the blowing of the trumpets, but again, they were not the trump of God.

Unger's Bible Dictionary describes the feast of the trumpets: "The Feast of the New Moon, which fell on the seventh month, of Tishri. This differed from the ordinary festivals of the new moon on account of the symbolical meaning of the seventh or sabbatical month, and partly, perhaps, because it marked the beginning of the civil year. This month was distinguished above all the other months of the year for the multitude of ordinances connected with it, the first day being consecrated to sacred rest and spiritual employment, the tenth being the day of Atonement, while the fifteenth began the Feast of Tabernacles."

This was a special trumpet used for a special occasions, but was not the trump of God.

Trumpets Of Ram's Horn

It is important for us to point out that a number of the

trumpets used in the judgment of Jericho, including the trump of priests and the trump of war, were trumpets made of ram's horn, not metal. *"And the Lord said unto Joshua, See, I have given into thine hand Jericho, and the king thereof, and the mighty men of valour. And ye shall compass the city, all ye men of war, and go round about the city once. Thus shalt thou do six days. And seven priests shall bear before the ark seven trumpets of rams' horns: and the seventh day ye shall compass the city seven times, and the priests shall blow with the trumpets. And it shall come to pass, that when they make a long blast with the ram's horn, and when ye hear the sound of the trumpet, all the people shall shout with a great shout; and the wall of the city shall fall down flat, and the people shall ascend up every man straight before him"* (Joshua 6:2-5). This ram's horn trumpet was identical to those used by Ehud, Gideon and Joab as signals for the people in their wars.

Given the previous examples, it is clear to see that trumpets were blown on different occasions and for many purposes: war, assembly, warnings, and announcements for holy days. Each of these, as well as other trumpets that have not been mentioned, all had a distinct purpose. The people who heard them knew what they meant.

An Uncertain Trumpet

The apostle Paul referred to the sound of a trumpet in relation to the preaching of the Gospel. In 1st Corinthians 14, he targeted the practice, or actually, the misuse of speaking in tongues in the church in relation to prophecy.

Inspired by the Holy Spirit, he declared that the prophetic Word should have preeminence because, *"…he that prophesies speaketh to man to edification and exhortation and comfort."* The simplicity of intelligible spoken words results in people hearing the Gospel, responding to it and becoming born again through the Spirit of God.

The primary task of the Church, and the only way to fulfill His command is to, *"Go ye into all the world, and preach the gospel to every creature"* (Mark 16:15).

The confusion created in the Corinthian church had muffled the clear call in response to God's command. Thus Paul writes in 1st Corinthians 14:8, *"For if the trumpet give an uncertain sound, who shall prepare himself to the battle?"*

Interpreting The Trumpet

Not only were trumpets used in Israel, but Gentiles were also familiar with the use of trumpets in relation to wars.

When the two silver trumpets were blown, the sound targeted a specific group (as we saw in Numbers 10) and meant that the congregation should assemble at the tabernacle.

When one trumpet was blown, only the princes and leaders of Israel were to gather. When the trumpet alarm sounded, the east part of the camp had to go forward first.

Can you imagine what would have happened if the people had not carefully listened to the sound of the trumpets, or if the trumpeters did not sound the proper notes? Utter chaos and catastrophe might have befallen the people of Israel.

Let us consider what those practices mean in the Christian realm. A distinct sound of the trumpet in relation to the preaching of the Gospel is absolutely essential! Whatever we do, or to whatever office the Lord has called us, if the sound of the "trumpet,"-which is the Gospel of salvation-is not our ultimate goal, then we are guilty of giving forth *"an uncertain sound."*

Heavenly Trumpets

Now that we know what a trump is, as well as its purpose and use, let us take a closer look at the heavenly trumpets.

In the last book of the Bible, the first three chapters of Revelation address seven churches in Asia Minor. These churches represent what I believe to be all churches throughout the dispensation of the Church age.

I believe this because after addressing each local church, John states, *"He that hath an ear, let him hear what the Spirit saith unto the churches"* (Revelation 3:22). That means that the warnings, and/or praises uttered to each of the seven churches apply to all churches at all times.

Chapter 4 begins, *"After this I looked, and, behold, a door was opened in heaven: and the first voice which I heard was as it were of a trumpet talking with me; which said, Come up hither, and I will shew thee things which must be hereafter"* (verse 1). In this context the trumpet is not an instrument of communication, but the trump itself speaks, *"...a trumpet talking with me..."* What did the trumpet say? *"...Come up hither, and I will shew thee things which must be hereafter."*

This "talking trumpet" differs from the other trumpets we've read about in the Old Testament because it was not built by man; it is in Heaven!

In the fourth and fifth chapters of Revelation, John was confronted with the indescribable attributes of God. The next two chapters show the judgments which will come upon the earth as each of the seven seals of the book are broken. As a result, devastating catastrophes will take place.

Seven Angels And Seven Trumpets

The opening of the seven seals initiates the appearance of seven angels, *"And I saw the seven angels which stood before God; and to them were given seven trumpets"* (Revelation 8:2). These seven angels blow their trumpets one at a time from first to last.

Revelation 8 and 9 illustrate the result of the first six trumpets being blown. These destructive judgments do not result in repentance, in fact, quite the opposite takes place, *"Neither repented they of their murders, nor of their sorceries, nor of their fornication, nor of their thefts"* (Revelation 9:21).

Still missing is the seventh angel with the seventh trumpet. Before this final destructive judgment comes upon the earth, *"...another mighty angel came down from heaven, clothed with a cloud: and a rainbow was upon his head, and his face was as it were the sun, and his feet as pillars of fire"* (Revelation 10:1).

You can almost sense the coming climax revealed in Revelation 10:7, *"But in the days of the voice of the seventh angel, when he shall begin to sound, the mystery of God should be finished, as he hath declared to his servants the prophets."*

The Two Olive Trees

Before the Bible tells us the event that follows the sounding of the seventh trumpet by the seventh angel, we are informed of the future of Jerusalem and its temple. Following that is the description concerning the two witnesses, who are also called the "two olive trees." This is the last testimony of God on earth specifically for Jerusalem. These two men will prophesy in the city of Jerusalem and will be equipped with the unique power to shut off the heavens so that no rain will fall, and they will turn water into blood. Only when they have finished their testimony will the beast make war on them and kill them.

Upon their death, an international "Christmas party" will take place, *"And they that dwell upon the earth shall rejoice over them, and make merry, and shall send gifts one to another; because these two prophets tormented them that dwelt on the earth"* (Revelation 11:10).

How were these two men able to "torment" the entire world? The two conditions have already been mentioned: 1) no rain, which means the end of most of the life on earth, and 2) the transformation of water into blood, which would have the same result. I believe that this "torment" includes something else: the truth. The truth hurts. People will be deceived to such an extent that they will deliberately and gladly believe the lie of the Antichrist. They will be wrong! These two prophets will proclaim that no true peace can come about on earth until the Prince of Peace comes, the Lord Jesus Christ. That message, however, will come in blatant opposition to the New World Order. We must keep in mind that at that time, this new global system will be so successful that opposition will not be tolerated. As a matter of fact, it will be unthinkable!

The Resurrection Of The Two Witnesses

At the conclusion of these three and a half days, the Spirit of God will enter the dead bodies of the two witnesses and they will stand on their feet in view of the world's news media. As a result, *"...great fear fell upon them which saw them."* Then, we hear a great voice, *"Come up hither!"* (Revelation 11:12).

Undoubtedly, this is the same voice heard by John in chapter 4, where he testified, *"...a trumpet talking with me; which said, Come up hither...."* The resurrection power is the same; it is the power that has defeated death and Hell.

The Seventh Trumpet

After all these events, we read in Revelation 11:15-17, *"And the seventh angel sounded; and there were great voices in heaven, saying, The kingdoms of this world are become the kingdoms of our Lord, and of his Christ; and he shall reign for ever and ever. And the four and twenty elders, which sat before God on their seats, fell upon their faces, and worshipped God, Saying, We give thee thanks, O Lord God Almighty, which art, and wast, and art to come; because thou hast taken to thee thy great power, and hast reigned."*

This verse reinforces the absolute power of the Lord and His ultimate visible victory over all opposition.

The Unique Last Trump

At this point, we must clarify some misunderstandings that are prevalent in the Church today. We are concerned with the event of the Rapture, so let us again read 1st Corinthians 15:51-52, *"Behold, I shew you a mystery; We shall not all sleep, but we shall all be changed, In a moment, in the twinkling of an eye, at the last trump: for the trumpet shall sound, and the dead shall be raised incorruptible, and we shall be changed."*

The conclusion that some have come to has been that the Rapture will take place *"at the last trump."* Therefore, all we would have to do is look for the last trumpet in the book of

Revelation to determine the time of the Rapture. However, the careful reader has already noticed that the trumpets mentioned in Revelation are not the same as the "last trump of God" we have already read so much about.

Furthermore, we must reiterate that this "last trump of God" is not the trumpet described in Matthew 24:31, *"And he shall send his angels with a great sound of a trumpet, and they shall gather together his elect from the four winds, from one end of heaven to the other."* This is simply *"a great sound of a trumpet,"* not related to the trumpets in the Old Testament we have discussed, or the trumpets we just read about in the book of Revelation. Neither is it identical to the last trump of God.

The Trumpet For Israel

The trumpet mentioned in Matthew 24 serves to gather His elect from the four corners of the earth and relates to the prophecy of Isaiah. Over 700 years before the birth of Christ, Isaiah, inspired by the Holy Spirit wrote, *"And it shall come to pass in that day, that the great trumpet shall be blown, and they shall come which were ready to perish in the land of Assyria, and the outcasts in the land of Egypt, and shall worship the LORD in the holy mount at Jerusalem"* (Isaiah 27:13). This trumpet clearly signals the ingathering of the children of Israel to the Promised Land.

We must add that the fulfillment of the ingathering of the exiles is vehemently opposed by the spirit of the Antichrist. His policy states, in effect, "Under no circumstances must the prophetic Word be fulfilled!" Thus, the spirit of Satan, who guides the political leaders of the world in a united fashion, opposes the fulfillment of Bible prophecy!

God gave the Jews the Promised Land from the Euphrates River to the river of Egypt and has ordained Jerusalem as the capital city of the Jewish nation.

Not one nation on earth agrees with the Scripture. We see, once again, the absolute reliability of the prophetic Word, which so plainly states that all nations of the world will oppose Jerusalem!

Another reference to the ingathering of the exiles and the defense of Zion is found in Zechariah 9:14, *"And the LORD shall be seen over them, and his arrow shall go forth as the lightning: and the Lord GOD shall blow the trumpet, and shall go with whirlwinds of the south."*

In this case, we read that *"the Lord God shall blow the trumpet."* According to my understanding of the Bible, this has never occurred before. In the end stages of the Great Tribulation, when it looks hopeless for Israel to continue her existence and the Jews have come to the end of their intellectual capacity and ingenuity, the Lord will supernaturally intervene, resulting in the conversion of all Israel!

Israel And The Rapture

In Psalm 47 we find an amazing description of the restoration of Israel, the establishment of the thousand-year kingdom of peace, and the Rapture of the Church: *"O clap your hands, all ye people; shout unto God with the voice of triumph. For the LORD most high is terrible; he is a great King over all the earth. He shall subdue the people under us, and the nations under our feet. He shall choose our inheritance for us, the excellency of Jacob whom he loved. Selah. God is gone up with a shout, the Lord with the sound of a trumpet. Sing praises to God, sing praises: sing praises unto our King, sing praises. For God is the King of all the earth: sing ye praises with understanding. God reigneth over the heathen: God sitteth upon the throne of his holiness. The princes of the people are gathered together, even the people of the God of Abraham: for the shields of the earth belong unto God: he is greatly exalted"* (Psalm 47:1-9). This Psalm, addressed "To the chief musician, a psalm for the sons of Korah," is primarily concerned with the victory of God over the nations and the salvation of the children of His people, *"Jacob, whom he loved."*

In verse 2, we read that the Lord *"is a great King over all the earth"* because *"He shall subdue...the nations."* He must use force to end the great rebellion of all the nations of the world.

The Lamb's Wife

In verse 8 we clearly see that He reigns over the heathen because of His holiness. However, in the middle of this Psalm we read *"God is gone up with a shout, the LORD with the sound of a trumpet."* When I read that He has *"gone up,"* I asked myself, "Shouldn't He be coming down?"

Victory for Israel will be when the Lord comes back to the land and His feet stand upon the Mount of Olives. Why then does it say that God has *"gone up"*? I believe that this refers to the Rapture.

The Lord cannot come back to earth to save Israel unless His body, the Church, also known as the "bride of the Lamb," is taken up. You can't have the bridegroom in Heaven without the bride. He went to prepare a place for us and He promised that He will return so that we are where He is, just as we read in John 17:23, *"I in them, and thou in me, that they [the*

Church] may be made perfect in one...."

We must keep in mind that God does not dwell in temples built by hands. Since Christ fulfilled His sacrificial work on Calvary's cross, He now dwells in the hearts of millions who have accepted Him as their Savior. The apostle Peter wrote about this in 1st Peter 2:5, *"Ye also, as lively stones, are built up a spiritual house, an holy priesthood, to offer up spiritual sacrifices, acceptable to God by Jesus Christ."* Since there is no visible temple on earth any longer, the spiritual temple consisting of *"lively stones"* is currently being built. When the last "lively stone" from among the Gentiles is added to this temple, it will be completed and must be removed from the earth.

The Rapture Psalm

This Psalm for the sons of Korah identifies the Lord, the shout, and the sound of the trumpet. Allow me to summarize this 47th Psalm: In the first three verses, the Lord King is the ruler of an opposing world. He brings about salvation to Israel in verse 4. The nations become obedient to His rulership in verses 6-8. The seed of Abraham is identified as the center of God's action on earth in verse 9. However, in the midst of this Psalm, it says, *"God is gone up with a shout...with the sound of a trumpet."*

The Glory On The Mount Of Olives

Ezekiel the prophet also described the departure and return of the glory of God. *"And the glory of the LORD went up from the midst of the city, and stood upon the mountain which is on the east side of the city"* (Ezekiel 11:23).

Jesus went out of the city of Jerusalem onto the Mount of

Olives located on the east side of the city. From there He ascended into Heaven, thus, *"the glory of the Lord went up."*

This corresponds precisely with the testimony of Acts 1:9-11, *"And when he had spoken these things, while they beheld, he was taken up; and a cloud received him out of their sight. And while they looked stedfastly toward heaven as he went up, behold, two men stood by them in white apparel; Which also said, Ye men of Galilee, why stand ye gazing up into heaven? this same Jesus, which is taken up from you into heaven, shall so come in like manner as ye have seen him go into heaven."*

Where were the disciples when this occurred? We find our answer in verse 12, *"Then returned they unto Jerusalem from the mount called Olivet, which is from Jerusalem a sabbath day's journey."* From the Mount of Olives the Glory of Israel departed and to the Mount of Olives the Glory of Israel will return!

Ezekiel makes the following comment regarding His return, *"Afterward he brought me to the gate, even the gate that looketh toward the east: And, behold, the glory of the God of Israel came from the way of the east: and his voice was like a noise of many waters: and the earth shined with his glory"* (Ezekiel 43:1-2). This describes the glorious return of the Lord to earth for the redemption of His people Israel, and to place judgment upon the nations.

Additionally, this will fulfill Zechariah's prophecy of hundreds of years ago, *"Thus saith the LORD of hosts; I was jealous for Zion with great jealousy, and I was jealous for her with great fury. Thus saith the Lord; I am returned unto Zion, and will dwell in the midst of Jerusalem: and Jerusalem shall be called a city of truth; and the mountain of the LORD of hosts the holy mountain"* (Zechariah 8:2-3).

Today, the nations of the world are trying to burden them-selves with Jerusalem; however, the Bible says, *"...in that day will I make Jerusalem a burdensome stone for all people: all that burden themselves with it shall be cut in pieces, though all the peo-ple of the earth be gathered together against it"* (Zechariah 12:3).

The First And Last Trump

At this point in our study, we have established that the Rapture will take place at the *"last trump of God."* This trump of God is not isolated from the Lord because He will descend from Heaven Himself with a shout and with the voice of the archangel. They cannot be separated. The moment that the Church is gathered to her heavenly home, Israel will have lost her only true friend. Born again Christians all over the world are praying for Israel and for the peace of Jerusalem. They comfort Israel on the basis of Isaiah 40, but when the Rapture takes place, that comfort will be gone and Israel will stand alone.

Israel, for the most part, does not recognize or acknowl-edge the Church. They can't, because the Church is not an organization or denomination. Rather, it consists exclusively of born again believers all over the world. Thus, for all practical purposes, the Church has no geographical identity.

For that reason, Israel desperately tries to cling to an orga-nized, literal and physical church. The Vatican, ruled by the pope, embodies the largest and most powerful religious orga-nization in the world.

Christians and Israel published an article entitled "The Vatican" in their winter 1997 issue.

On April 10, 1997, Israel's second envoy to the Holy See,

Ambassador Aharon Lopez, presented his credentials to Pope John Paul II at the Vatican. The first ambassador, who recently completed his tour of duty, was Mr. Shmuel Hadass.

In his speech accepting the new ambassador's credentials, the pope described the fundamental agreement between the Holy See and Israel, signed in December 1993, as 'an important step in the continuing process of normalization that we have undertaken.'

He referred to the legal agreement, subsequently to be ratified by the Government of Israel as 'a most significant juridical instrument for the life of the Catholic Church in Israel and for the Catholic faithful who are Israeli citizens.'

Ambassador Lopez said that part of his task was 'to build a basis for coexistence and meeting points along the way to a fruitful dialogue between the Catholic Church and the Jewish people.'

In a highly unusual gesture, Pope John Paul II on July 7 performed the rite of baptism on Zaki Farhud, a baby born to an Arab Catholic family in Israel.

The Farhud family had requested the help of the Israeli Embassy to the Holy See in arranging the event - following two earlier tragedies that had struck the family: the death of Zaki's older brother, of a rare skin disease, and the loss of an embryo during pregnancy.

The rite was performed in the Pope's private chapel and was attended by two high-ranking papal officials, two Franciscan monks from Hong Kong, several nuns and members of the Farhud family. Also present was a delegation from the Embassy of Israel to the Holy See, headed by Ambassador Aharon Lopez (at whose special request the ceremony was moved from Saturday, the Jewish Sabbath, to Monday).

Israel attaches great significance to any and all friendly words from the pope and his organization.

We must remember that Israel is an enemy of the Gospel, according to Romans 11:28, *"As concerning the gospel, they are enemies for your sakes: but as touching the election, they are beloved for the fathers' sakes."* Therefore, they cling hopelessly to any religious support with diplomatic credentials. The Vatican is supported by a very impressive organizational infrastructure, strengthened and supported by beautiful buildings and priceless objects in her many museums. The Vatican is a very tangible source of reality.

The real Church, as I already mentioned, is not officially recognized by Israel, although during the many times I've been to Israel, I have noticed that a certain bonding is taking place between Israelis and true born again Christians. However, their primary aim is to be on good terms with the Vatican, which has great influence throughout the world.

Therefore, when the Rapture takes place, Israel will enter a period of the greatest danger they have encountered in their entire history.

Where Was The First Trump?

We have dealt with the fact that 1st Corinthians 15:51-52 speaks of the "last trump of God", and have seen that this trump cannot be compared with the other trumpets mentioned in the Old and New Testaments.

Therefore, the next logical question is, "Where was the first trump of God?" To answer this, we must first ask the question, "Why does the Lord come with a shout, with the voice of the archangel and with the trump of God?" I believe we all know the answer: the Word became flesh, dwelt on earth, fulfilled His task, died on Calvary's cross, arose on the third day, was seen by many witnesses, ascended into Heaven, and will come back to gather His own unto Himself. Jesus will now receive the fruit of the Word. Subsequently, we must search for an event in Israel's history where God gathers His people to receive His Word.

In Exodus 19, we read of Israel having arrived in the wilderness of Sinai, after their victorious exodus from Egypt in the third month of their departure.

Notice that Moses, a man of God, needed direction. He went up to meet the Lord, who gave him clear instructions, *"...Thus shalt thou say to the house of Jacob, and tell the children of Israel; Ye have seen what I did unto the Egyptians, and how I bare you on eagles' wings, and brought you unto myself. Now therefore, if ye will obey my voice indeed, and keep my covenant, then ye shall be a peculiar treasure unto me above all people: for all the earth is mine: And ye shall be unto me a kingdom of priests, and an holy nation. These are the words which thou shalt speak unto the children of Israel"* (Exodus 19:3-6).

This is a simple matter of God telling Israel, in effect, "Look, this is what I did for you. Are you now willing to believe and follow my commandments?"

Moses, the faithful servant, presented this to the people, *"And Moses came and called for the elders of the people, and laid before their faces all these words which the LORD commanded him"* (verse 7).

How did they react? *"...all the people answered together, and said, All that the LORD hath spoken we will do. And Moses returned the words of the people unto the LORD"* (verse 8). Israel had collectively promised that they would do everything that the Lord had said to Moses.

The Lord God took this promise seriously and said to Moses, *"Lo, I come unto thee in a thick cloud, that the people may hear when I speak with thee, and believe thee for ever..."* (Verse 9). This was a historic first; the audible voice of the

Eternal Creator, the God of Heaven and earth, the God of Abraham, Isaac and Jacob, was heard.

Three Day Sanctification

Moses received the following instructions, *"...Go unto the people, and sanctify them today and tomorrow, and let them wash their clothes, And be ready against the third day: for the third day the LORD will come down in the sight of all the people upon mount Sinai"* (Verses 10-11). The people had to be ready on *"the third day."* Preparations would have to be made in two days, and on the third day, the Lord would speak to them.

This extended prophecy points to the Church. As previously mentioned, one day with the Lord is as a thousand years and a thousand years is as one day. Our Lord has been gone for two days (almost 2000 years) and we are quickly approaching the third day. What will happen on this "third day?" Will we hear the Lord Himself coming with a shout saying, *"Come up hither?"*

Let us return to Mount Sinai: *"And it came to pass on the third day in the morning, that there were thunders and lightnings, and a thick cloud upon the mount, and the voice of the trumpet exceeding loud; so that all the people that was in the camp trembled"* (verse 16).

Interesting! On the morning of the third day, the people heard *"the voice of the trumpet."* This mysterious talking trumpet is the "first trump of God." How do we know that? Because it is the only "talking trumpet" and it is identical to the "last trump of God" found in the New Testament. Hebrews 12:19 confirms the fact that this was a talking trumpet, *"And the sound of a trumpet, and the voice of words; which voice they that heard entreated that the word should not be spo-ken to them any more.*"

What was the result of the sound of this trumpet? *"The people...trembled...."* They had every reason in the world to tremble because they were still in their sin. Imagine, a holy God meeting with a group of sin-laden people! As mentioned in an earlier chapter, during the Old Testament times, sins were not forgiven, they were only covered up. The blood of a lamb that saved them from the angel of death in Egypt covered their sins, but it did not take away their sins. The complete remission of sin occurred approximately 1,500 years later when Jesus came and John said *"Behold, the Lamb of God which taketh away the sins of the world."*

Therefore, it is quite natural that the people were afraid and trembled in their bones.

This should help us understand that it is necessary for us to be changed, and only in our translated bodies will we be raptured into the presence of the Lord.

Israel was not translated; they were still in their sinful nature. Nevertheless, they were specially chosen by God based on His mercy. The blood of sacrificed animals was sufficient to temporarily cover their sins so that they could meet the Living God. Those sacrifices, however, were a foreshadow of the final, all-sufficient sacrifice of the Lamb at Calvary.

Meeting God

This must have been an overwhelming experience for them: *"And Moses brought forth the people out of the camp to meet with God; and they stood at the nether part of the mount. And mount Sinai was altogether on a smoke, because the LORD descended upon it in fire: and the smoke thereof ascended as the smoke of a furnace, and the whole mount quaked greatly.* " (verses 17-18).

The people not only trembled, but they also experienced a "mountain quake." There was no question in anybody's mind that this was the work of the Living God; the voice of the talking trumpet was clear and audible. They knew that they were in the presence of a holy and righteous God!

The First Sinners

This unmistakable voice of God was also heard by two sinners: our original parents, Adam and Eve. *"...Adam and his wife hid themselves from the presence of the LORD God amongst the trees of the garden"* (Genesis 3:8). They had a reason to hide from the presence of God because sin had entered into their lives.

Sinful man and a holy God cannot have fellowship. They are separate entities and mutually exclusive. God is perfect, therefore sin cannot stand before a holy God and God cannot tolerate sinful man. In Adam and Eve's case, we know that God gave them a promise of the coming Redeemer who would save them from their sins.

The Uniqueness Of Israel

To hear the voice of God and live was extraordinary. In his summary, Moses amplified the significance of Israel thereby revealing the uniqueness of God's chosen people, *"Did ever people hear the voice of God speaking out of the midst of the fire, as thou hast heard, and live?"* (Deuteronomy 4:33).

"...Behold, the LORD our God hath shewed us his glory and

his greatness, and we have heard his voice out of the midst of the fire: we have seen this day that God doth talk with man, and he liveth" (Deuteronomy 5:24).

"For who is there of all flesh, that hath heard the voice of the living God speaking out of the midst of the fire, as we have, and lived?" (Deuteronomy 5:26).

This three-fold emphasis of the significance of hearing God's word audibly should clearly establish Israel's unique position as a chosen people.

Back at Sinai we read, *"And when the voice of the trumpet sounded long, and waxed louder and louder, Moses spake, and God answered him by a voice"* (Exodus 19). In this verse we see the "voice of the trumpet" identified again. This is the first trump of God. Its purpose was to gather His people to receive the Word.

In the New Testament, which speaks of the people of the New Covenant, we read in 1st Thessalonians 4:16 about the Word which became flesh, gathering His heavenly people to their heavenly home!

It is important to point out that when the Church is raptured into her heavenly home by her heavenly Bridegroom, she will no longer belong to the earth. At that very moment, a translation will take place; our mortal bodies will be changed into immortality.

Moses The Friend Of God

Another significant point which we will discuss at the close of this chapter is the fact that Moses did not experience this change, yet he appeared at the Transfiguration, directly in the presence of the Lord with Elijah.

The Bible tells us that He spoke to Moses in person, as we read in Exodus 33:11, *"...the Lord spake unto Moses face to face, as a man speaketh unto his friend...."* From among God's chosen people, God called Moses as a representative.

This special position was emphasized by God during a family quarrel when Moses' sister Miriam and brother Aaron spoke against him. We read of their complaint: *"...Hath the Lord indeed spoken only by Moses? hath he not spoken also by us? And the Lord heard it"* (Numbers 12:2).

How did the Lord respond? *"And the LORD came down in the pillar of the cloud, and stood in the door of the tabernacle, and called Aaron and Miriam: and they both came forth. And he said, Hear now my words: If there be a prophet among you, I the Lord will make myself known unto him in a vision, and will speak unto him in a dream. My servant Moses is not so, who is faithful in all mine house. With him will I speak mouth to mouth, even apparently, and not in dark speeches; and the similitude of the Lord shall he behold: wherefore then were ye not afraid to speak against my servant Moses?* (verses 5-8).

Moses believed God and acted according to His will. May the Lord grant that many of us become like Moses, and seek the counsel and the countenance of the Lord–wherein lies the secret to a blessed and victorious life.

CHAPTER 6

THE DEAD IN CHRIST SHALL RISE FIRST

"For the Lord himself shall descend from heaven with a shout, with the voice of the archangel, and with the trump of God: and the dead in Christ shall rise first" (1st Thessalonians 4:16).

The question, "Why should the dead in Christ rise first?" is answered by a simple statement, "They have been waiting longer." Of course, that's not all there is to it, as we will discuss in this chapter.

First of all, the dead in Christ have been led one step closer to the Lord by drinking the cup of physical death. If the dead in Christ shall rise first, that makes *"we which are alive"* last.

However, this succession belongs to the same great event, the Rapture of the Church.

In previous chapters, we looked at the details surrounding the Lord's coming by Himself, with the *"voice of the archangel"* and with the *"trump of God;"* however, all of these characteristics are incorporated into one event.

The Bible makes the time-frame very clear when it says in 1st Corinthians 15:52, *"In a moment, in the twinkling of an eye...."* A number of different translations give us a little more insight into what this *"twinkling of an eye"* means.

Luther translated it, *"Suddenly, in the twinkling of an eye."*

Another translation emphasizes the word, *"instantaneously."*

One Dutch language translation says, *"In an individeable moment of time."*

And one book I've read describes the Rapture with the words, "In an atom of time." After years of study, I cannot believe the Rapture will take place in stages, as some suggest.

Some scholars have used Matthew 27:52-53 as a comparison to the Rapture event. *"And the graves were opened; and many bodies of the saints which slept arose, And came out of the graves after his resurrection, and went into the holy city, and appeared unto many."* Therefore, some theorize that the dead in Christ will rise first in order to appear on earth to prepare for the coming Rapture. I do not share that view because of the distinct emphasis placed on the time frame, *"In a moment, in the twinkling of an eye."*

While the Matthew 27 event shows the power of the resurrection of our Lord affecting the Old Testament saints who were already dead, we clearly read, *"many bodies,"* which means not "all bodies." I understand that only those Old Testament saints were resurrected who were ready to be resurrected. Undoubtedly, they were a special group. So then we ask, "What happens to the rest of the saints?" We must first clarify the phrase, *"which slept."* This does not mean that they were in a state of unconsciousness because this verse specifically refers to "the bodies," not to the spirit or soul, which is immortal. I believe from the text that they received their glorified bodies that very moment.

Our Lord's Resurrection Power

The initiating power of this translation was, of course, the resurrection power of our Lord. We all know that He appeared in the same body He had before His death. The disciples recognized Him, as did many other people.

The apostle Paul later writes about the resurrected Lord and confirms in 1st Corinthians 15:5-8, *"...that he was seen of Cephas, then of the twelve: After that, he was seen of above five hundred brethren at once; of whom the greater part remain unto this present, but some are fallen asleep. After that, he was seen of James; then of all the apostles. And last of all he was seen of me also, as of one born out of due time."*

The resurrection of the Lord is a major event in God's history of salvation. When Jesus victoriously arose on the third day, we read, *"...behold, there was a great earthquake: for the angel of the Lord descended from heaven, and came and rolled back the stone from the door..."* (Matthew 28:2). That was an earth-shaking event! The power of that resurrection caused the awakening and subsequent translation of the bodies of some of the saints.

Paul's Desire For Resurrection

Most of our New Testament instruction was written by the apostle Paul. When writing to the Philippians, he emphasized his position in the flesh, *"Circumcised the eighth day, of the stock of Israel, of the tribe of Benjamin, an Hebrew of the Hebrews; as touching the law, a Pharisee"* (Philippians 3:5). Regarding the law, he says in verse 6, *"blameless."*

Paul indeed had something to brag about! He came from the stock of Israel, of the tribe of Benjamin, the first tribe to be integrated into the royal tribe of Judah.

He was a genuine Hebrew; and as far as the law was concerned, he was a Pharisee—one who really took the Word of God seriously, studied it, meditated upon it, and defended it fiercely.

However, in comparing his position, heritage, nationality, family, and religion to his position in Christ, he says, *"Yea doubtless, and I count all things but loss for the excellency of the knowledge of Christ Jesus my Lord: for whom I have suffered the loss of all things, and do count them but dung, that I may win Christ"* (Philippians 3:8). Paul had only one goal: to please Christ, to follow Him, and to suffer for Him.

In general, we pray that the Lord will bless us, keep us, protect us, and give us good health to live comfortably. Not the apostle Paul. Listen to his prayer in verse 10, *"That I may know him, and the power of his resurrection, and the fellowship of his sufferings, being made conformable unto his death."* He was praying to be integrated into the fellowship of "His suffering," even unto "death."

Why was Paul so keen to suffer with Christ and experience death? He gives us the reason in Philippians 3:11, *"If by any means I might attain unto the resurrection of the dead."* Many have speculated that Paul expressed this strange goal to *"attain the resurrection of the dead."* Doesn't everyone experience the resurrection? Of course, all who are saved through Jesus participate in the first resurrection. The last resurrection will result in every lost soul who ever lived to stand before the Great White Throne of judgment. At that throne, there is no Jesus, no Lamb, and no blood, and it results in the second death, which is eternal. What is this resurrection Paul desired to attain? During the 1999 Christian Booksellers Convention in Orlando, Florida, I asked my friend, Dr. Moody Adams about this matter. He graciously supplied me with his answer:

Union With Christ

Philippians 3:10-15, *"That I may know him, and the power of his resurrection, and the fellowship of his sufferings, being made conformable unto his death; If by any means I might attain unto the resurrection of the dead. Not as though I had already attained, either were already perfect: but I follow after, if that I may apprehend that for which also I am apprehended of Christ Jesus. Brethren, I count not myself to have apprehended: but this one thing I do, forgetting those things which are behind, and reaching forth unto those things which are before, I press toward the mark for the prize of the high calling of God in Christ Jesus. Let us therefore, as many as be perfect, be thus minded: and if in any thing ye be otherwise minded, God shall reveal even this unto you."*

The Goal Of Paul's Life

Paul's great ambition was *"That I may know Him."* Lorne Sanny, the founder of the Navigators, called these the five greatest words in the Bible. William Barclay says, "It is important to note the verb which he uses for to know...It is the personal experience of another person. We may see the depth of this word from a fact of Old Testament usage. The Old Testament uses "to know" of sexual intercourse...(Genesis 4:1). In Hebrew the verb is "**yada**" and in Greek it is translated by "**ginoskein**." This verb indicates the most intimate knowledge of another person. It is not Paul's aim to know about Christ, but to personally to know Him." (William Barclay, *The Daily Study Bible Series*, Philippians, p.63).

Then Paul says, in vs. 14, *"I press toward the mark,"* repeating that this is the goal of his life. The central theme of Paul's letters was "union with Christ," or becoming one with Him. He discusses four aspects of this repeatedly:

Romans 6:1-7, *"What shall we say then? Shall we continue in sin, that grace may abound? God forbid. How shall we, that are dead to sin, live any longer therein? Know ye not, that so many of us as were baptized into Jesus Christ were baptized into his death? Knowing this, that our old man is crucified with him, that the body of sin might be destroyed, that henceforth we should not serve sin. For he that is dead is freed from sin."*

Paul urges us to "know" that we were crucified with Him!

Romans 6:11, *"Likewise reckon ye also yourselves to be dead indeed unto sin, but alive unto God through Jesus Christ our Lord."*

Paul also urges us to *"reckon"* this to be true. That we died at the cross. Sin doesn't bother a dead man.

2. Union with Christ in burial

"Therefore we are buried with him by baptism into death: that like as Christ was raised up from the dead by the glory of the Father, even so we also should walk in newness of life. For if we have been planted together in the likeness of his death, we shall be also in the likeness of his resurrection" (verses 4-5).

Baptism is a symbol of what we are believing. We died in Christ and we were buried with Him. Nothing is more loathsome than a corpse. Spiritually, nothing is more loathsome than a person displaying his death to sin - his righteousness. It is not enough to die to sin; we must also be buried and out of public view, not boasting our righteousness.

3. Raised with Christ

Ephesians 2:5-6, *"Even when we were dead in sins, hath quickened us together with Christ, (by grace ye are saved;) And hath raised us up together."*

Here, in a letter containing the deepest spiritual truths Paul speaks of union with Christ in resurrection. He states it as an historic fact: we were raised with Him. In Philippians 3:10 he is wanting to know the power of the resurrection to which he is entitled; to grow in faith through suffering until he is experiencing the power to which all believers are entitled - the power of the resurrection. Again we must know this is an historic fact and through recognizing or believing it to be true we come to experience that power.

4. Seated with Christ in Heaven

Ephesians 2:6, *"...and made us sit together in heavenly places in Christ Jesus."*

It is reasonable to believe that Paul was not talking about achieving the bodily resurrection that comes at the Rapture in Philippians 3:13. It was quite obvious that he had not died, and therefore he could not have been bodily raised. It is also reasonable to believe he was talking about the spiritual resurrection that takes place when we discover "union," that we died and were raised with Christ and by faith claim the power of the resurrection. The argument here is that he states Christ had (past tense) made us to sit in heavenly places. This is obviously not talking about a physical presence at the throne. But when we know the truth of "union" and recognize it to be true, you can say as Luther said, that when we discover union with Christ we can look to Jesus upon the throne and say, "I am that Christ" and He can look to us and say "I am that sinner."

Again Paul alludes to union in Colossians 3:1-4, *"If ye then be risen with Christ, seek those things which are above, where Christ sitteth on the right hand of God. Set your affection on things above, not on things on the earth. For ye are dead, and your life is hid with Christ in God. When Christ, who is our life, shall appear, then shall ye also appear with him in glory."* He says we are hid with Christ in God.

Union is a thing that cannot be understood. It is something that must be embraced by faith.

I write of these things but have not "apprehended" them in my experience. Oh God, that I might take my position each morning as one who had already died, been buried, raised in power and was sitting at the right hand of the Father "in my Savior Jesus." I press on to this goal.
-Moody Adams Evangelistic Association, 7/99

Five Important Points

To better understand our message "And the Dead in Christ Shall Rise First," we should consider five important points:

- What does the word "resurrection" mean?
- The eight-fold resurrection in our Bible.
- The resurrection as a fulfillment of prophecy.
- The first and second resurrection.
- The restoration resurrection.

1) What Does "Resurrection" Mean?

In simple terms, the word "resurrection" means to go from death to life. Obviously, this must be preceded by the change from life to death. Resurrection reverses that process.

Resurrection from the dead is essential to Christian doctrine, and concerns itself primarily with the resurrection of our Lord. Later, we will see different types of resurrections; however, none of them compare to the resurrection of the Lord Jesus Christ because His is the firstfruit of the resurrection to eternal life.

We must highlight the reversal from death to eternal life. When the apostle Paul wrote to the Corinthians about the Rapture in 1st Corinthians 15:12-14, he specifically emphasized the absolute necessity of the resurrection of the Lord Jesus Christ. *"Now if Christ be preached that he rose from the dead, how say some among you that there is no resurrection of the dead? But if there be no resurrection of the dead, then is Christ not risen; And if Christ be not risen, then is our preaching vain, and your faith is also vain."* Paul's point is very clear. Without Christ's resurrection, the preaching of the Gospel is invalid; furthermore, our faith is in vain.

We are saved through faith, not based solely on the death of Christ itself but because of the scriptural fact that He victoriously arose from the dead on the third day, ascended into Heaven and by His promise, He is coming again! We can't divide this event and believe only parts of it. The event belongs together in totality. The components which make up the resurrection can be identified in this order: life, death, resurrection, ascension, and return.

Paul continues, *"...we are found false witnesses of God; because we have testified of God that he raised up Christ: whom he raised not up, if so be that the dead rise not. For if the dead rise not, then is not Christ raised: And if Christ be not raised, your faith is vain; ye are yet in your sins"* (Verses 15-17).

Without the resurrection of Christ, there would be no salvation: *"Ye are yet in your sins."*

Equally, we would have no hope of resurrection if Christ had not been raised from the dead. Subsequently, with no resurrection of the dead in Christ, we which are alive could not be caught up in the Rapture, and *"...they also which are fallen asleep in Christ are perished"* (verse 18).

Faith in the Rapture is a requirement for the Rapture. First Thessalonians 4:14 says, *"For if we believe that Jesus died and rose again, even so them also which sleep in Jesus will God bring with him."* Notice the word "if." This is a clear revelation that those who do not believe in the physical resurrection of the Lord Jesus are in reality not believers. As a result, they will not be raptured.

Christ: The Firstfruits

Paul dismisses the theory prevalent in the Corinthian church regarding the non-resurrection and confirms the absolute reality of the resurrection of Christ, *"But now is Christ risen from the dead, and become the firstfruits of them that slept. For since by man came death, by man came also the resurrection of the dead. For as in Adam all die, even so in Christ shall all be made alive. But every man in his own order: Christ the firstfruits; afterward they that are Christ's at his coming"* (1st Corinthians 15:20-23).

In this passage, Paul identifies Christ as *"the firstfruits"* two times. This is significant because none of the other resurrections documented in the Bible belonged to the "firstfruits." More importantly, the Lord's resurrection is the one that leads to eternal life.

This addresses a crucial point regarding Hebrews 9:27, which reads, *"…it is appointed unto men once to die, but after this the judgment."* Obviously, this does not apply to those who died before God's plan of salvation was established and accomplished through the Lord Jesus Christ.

For example, Moses died in the land of Moab and was buried by God. However, approximately 1,500 years later, he appeared on the Mount of Transfiguration with Elijah and they spoke with the Lord Jesus about His death on Calvary's cross.

Therefore, when Revelation 11 speaks of the two witnesses, also referred to as the "two olive trees" and "two candlesticks" who have the power to *"…shut heaven, that it rain not…and have power over waters to turn them to blood, and to smite the earth with all plagues, as often as they will"* (Revelation 11:6), then I have no problem believing that they will be Elijah and Moses. God gave Elijah the power to shut up the heavens, and Moses the power to turn water into blood.

National Resurrection Of Israel

Ezekiel documents a special resurrection that doesn't belong to the resurrection of the firstfruits. It is the national resurrection of Israel. *"The hand of the LORD was upon me, and carried me out in the spirit of the LORD, and set me down in the midst of the valley which was full of bones, And caused me to pass by them round about: and, behold, there were very many in the open valley; and, lo, they were very dry. And he said unto me, Son of man, can these bones live? And I answered, O Lord God, thou knowest"*(Ezekiel 37:1-3).

It is helpful to understand that in the previous chapter the Lord caused the resurrection of the land. For example, we read, *"Therefore, ye mountains of Israel, hear the word of the Lord GOD; Thus saith the Lord GOD to the mountains, and to the hills, to the rivers, and to the valleys, to the desolate wastes, and to the cities that are forsaken, which became a prey and derision to the residue of the heathen that are round about"*(Ezekiel 36:4).

What is the reason for the resurrection of the land? We find the answer in verse 8, *"But ye, O mountains of Israel, ye shall shoot forth your branches, and yield your fruit to my people of Israel; for they are at hand to come."* If the Jews had come back to the land of Israel, a desert, they could not exist because there was no food. Someone has said that a country can function without politicians, a military, or a police force, but it cannot function without farmers. People must eat and food comes from the ground. For that reason, the Lord speaks to the land of Israel to resurrect it to productivity. Today, it is no secret that Israel is a leading country in the technology of irrigation, particularly drip irrigation. Israel produces enough to feed herself, as well as plenty for export.

National Resurrection

National identity had to be resurrected as well. For all practical purposes, this was virtually impossible because the Jews were scattered over the entire face of the earth.

It seemed as though wherever they settled they were always faced with oppression and persecution. Where they have been permitted to remain, they have become part of the landscape of the nation in which they lived. In Europe they have become European Jews; in Africa they have become African Jews; in Asia they have become Asian Jews; and in America, American Jews. Despite the odds, they have remained Jews; an invisible bond has kept them together. This bond centers on the Bible, their heritage. The Bible has been the only cord of unity binding the Jews throughout the Diaspora.

We must magnify the fact that this is totally unique. For example, approximately 40 million Europeans migrated to America but lost their heritage within one or two generations.

My wife and I are both German-born and our children were born in the United States. Although they speak German, it is unlikely that our grandchildren will. As a result, within two generations, our heritage will be completely erased. That has not been the case with the Jews; 2000 years after the Diaspora, they are still Jews.

That raises the question, "How is it possible for these Jews–who are so diverse with their languages, cultures, mentalities and levels of civilization–to return to the land and become a nation?"

Before the state of Israel was founded, many leading anthropologists predicted that it would take hundreds of years for Israel to become a nation of one people.

During a 1974 prophecy conference in Israel, Professor Pinchas E. Lapide made the following statement:

In 1949, one year after the establishment of the state, we already had had to welcome Jews from 112 countries-I say HAD TO because none wanted to wait and many had no homes. During that year, a group of anthropologists from America and Scandinavia visited us.

For anthropologists and also archaeologists, Israel is truly a paradise! Nowhere do such anthropological and sociological processes take place with such speed and in such a dispersion and amongst such varied nationalities, on such a small area of ground as in Israel.

These anthropologists visited our land for eight months. I was present at their farewell dinner in Jerusalem at the end of 1949. The leader of the group (a very well-known expert whose name I shall not disclose) said, 'Ladies and gentlemen, we are very impressed by your new state but one thing you must realize: you have not yet achieved one people. You are not a nation. You have a mixture of people from more than 112 different countries, they are immigrants, to mold these into a national unity will take at least one or two centuries.'

When he saw the look of disappointment on all our faces, he tried to comfort us by saying, "Look, I come from America. I have a Swedish background but my great great grandmother was already born in America. But we nevertheless celebrate all the Swedish feasts in our home in Mississippi. We give our children Swedish names. We speak Swedish with our parents and grandparents and we look upon ourselves as Swedish-Americans. You have not even such a thing as Israeli nationality, so how can you expect new immigrants to adapt themselves to something that does not even exist? In short: if you can manage to become Israeli by the end of the 21st century you can be happy, but certainly not before."

At the end of 1972, many of these same experts visited Israel again to make a "follow-up examination." They went to the same kibbutz and the same villages and suburbs. After two months they concluded, against all their expectations, that this mixture of nations representing five continents, 112 countries, dozens of cultures, languages and civilizations which had as good as nothing in common to start with, had now, in 25 short years, been molded into one nation not only psychologically but also demographically.

During the discussion with these gentlemen after dinner, we said, 'Perhaps Nasser had something to do with it,' to which the aforementioned man replied, 'That could well be. Nothing unites different people and types more quickly than a common danger from outside.'

It would not surprise me if in the future, Abdul Nasser, who has since died, will no longer be described as Israel's arch enemy, but rather as one of the architects of the Jewish state. Surely he would turn in his grave if he heard such a thing.

But I think it could be said that, biblically-speaking, this Nasser often reminds me of a reincarnation of Balaam, the Gentile prophet who wanted to curse Israel three times - he even received money for cursing Israel - and yet he blessed Israel three times.

I suspect that Mr. Nasser did a similar thing although it is probably yet too early to be able to analyze Nasser's part theologically. But I can no longer think of him as an enemy."

(*Midnight Call*, September 1974, pp.10-11).

The national resurrection of Israel is the subject of the vision of the dry bones. The impossibility is revealed in Ezekiel 37:11, *"Then he said unto me, Son of man, these bones are the whole house of Israel: behold, they say, Our bones are dried, and our hope is lost: we are cut off for our parts."*

Surely, they had no hope when they were herded like sheep to the slaughter in Hitler's Nazi Germany.

Even after the war, their situation was hopeless. As they desperately tried to return to the land of their fathers, the mighty British Navy forced them back.

Yet, in spite of these seemingly impossible odds, Israel survived and has become a nation. It would have been natural to assume that the Jews, who dreamed of unity, would never see it due to their diverse culture. However, that matter was taken care of by the Lord as well, *"Say unto them, Thus saith the Lord*

God; Behold, I will take the stick of Joseph, which is in the hand of Ephraim, and the tribes of Israel his fellows, and will put them with him, even with the stick of Judah, and make them one stick, and they shall be one in mine hand" (Ezekiel 37:19). They came from virtually all the nations of the world, yet they became *"...one nation in the land upon the mountains of Israel..."* (verse 22).

Thus, we see the miracle of the resurrection of the nation of Israel. However, more is yet to come, *"...and one king shall be king to them all: and they shall be no more two nations, neither shall they be divided into two kingdoms any more at all"* (verse 22b). That is Israel's future.

Resurrection reverses the process from death to life.

2) The Eight-Fold Resurrections In The Bible

In the Old Testament, three resurrections prophetically symbolize Israel's three-fold resurrection. In the New Testament, five resurrections testify to the five Gentile world empires.

Resurrection One

In 1st Kings 17, we read about Elijah the prophet being sent to a Gentile widow in the town of Zarephath. Elijah found this lady and her son in extreme poverty and ready to give up on life. In answer to Elijah's request for a little water and some bread, the widow said, *"...I am gathering two sticks, that I may go in and dress it for me and my son, that we may eat it, and die"* (1st Kings 17:12). Here we see a parallel of Israel being in the foreign land of Egypt, enslaved under extreme poverty with no hope for the future and ready to perish.

In this hopeless situation, Elijah appeared. Through him, her poverty was alleviated. But something even worse than poverty happened next! The widow's son died.

We see another parallel of the many mothers who lost their sons in the foreign land of Eygpt because of Pharaoh's decree that all the male children be drowned in the Nile.

In the case of the widow of Zarephath, there was a remedy, a "redeemer," the man of God. He cried unto his Lord and as a result, "...*the soul of the child came into him again, and he revived. And Elijah took the child, and brought him down out of the chamber into the house, and delivered him unto his mother: and Elijah said, See, thy son liveth. And the woman said to Elijah, Now by this I know that thou art a man of God, and that the word of the Lord in thy mouth is truth*" (1st Kings 17:22-24). What a glorious prophetic picture of Israel's future: The great Son, the Messiah, who was dead now lives forevermore and will return to Israel.

Resurrection Two

We find evidence of the second resurrection in 2nd Kings 4:9-10; only this time it wasn't a poor Gentile widow, but a rich Israeli woman. The prophet in this case is Elisha, the successor of Elijah.

This well-to-do religious woman asked her husband, "...*Behold now, I perceive that this is an holy man of God, which passeth by us continually. Let us make a little chamber, I pray thee, on the wall; and let us set for him there a bed, and a table, and a stool, and a candlestick: and it shall be, when he cometh to us, that he shall turn in thither*" (verses 9-10).

Such a guest room could only be built by those who were

financially well off. In this passage, Elisha received all of the Shunammite couple's favors.

This should remind us of Israel's second dispersion and subsequent return from the land of Babylon. When they came back to Jerusalem they were not poor, but loaded with the riches from the kingdom of Persia. They came back under the authority of the government which instructed everyone to assist the Jews in their return.

But then tragedy struck the Shunammite household, *"And when the child was grown, it fell on a day, that he went out to his father to the reapers. And he said unto his father, My head, my head. And he said to a lad, Carry him to his mother. And when he had taken him, and brought him to his mother, he sat on her knees till noon, and then died"* (2nd Kings 4:18-20). Lo and behold, Elisha, the man of God was there, who, by the power of God, reversed the cycle from death to life, *"...So he called her. And when she was come in unto him, he said, Take up thy son. Then she went in, and fell at his feet, and bowed herself to the ground, and took up her son, and went out"* (2nd Kings 4:36-37). This second resurrection parallels Israel's return to Jerusalem and the resurrection of the destroyed temple.

Resurrection Three

"And Elisha died, and they buried him. And the bands of the Moabites invaded the land at the coming in of the year. And it came to pass, as they were burying a man, that, behold, they spied a band of men; and they cast the man into the sepulchre of Elisha: and when the man was let down, and touched the bones of Elisha, he revived, and stood up on his feet" (2nd Kings 13:20-21).

This amazing resurrection occurred after Elisha had died.

It was marked by extreme hopelessness for Israel. They didn't have the time to prepare a proper funeral for this unnamed man. In fact, they hadn't even closed the grave where the great prophet Elisha was buried.

At that very moment, danger approached. A band of Moabites came to plunder and destroy. This added to their hopelessness, tragedy, suffering and loss of life. But the moment they dropped this man into the open pit with Elisha's corpse, the man stood up. He arose from the dead!

This third resurrection in the Old Testament symbolizes Israel's desperate situation before and during their third and final return to the Promised Land, which resulted in the establishment of the state of Israel in 1948.

We must recall that the Jews were being murdered by the millions and their enemies were oppressing them mercilessly. In addition, the Arab settlers within the land of Israel also intended to cast every Jew into the Mediterranean. The Arab nations were united against the newly founded state and proclaimed that they would end the attempt to establish the state of Israel. Despite all odds, Israel arose from the grave. Today, Israel is a mighty, vibrant and prosperous nation in the Middle East—to the envy of its surrounding Arab nations.

Elisha's death illustrates the gravity of the time because Elisha was a prophet, and with his death the prophetic Word was silenced. That is exactly what happened to the Jews for almost 2,000 years. They heard no word of prophecy, and had no hope of being returned to the land of Israel. But then suddenly, at the epitome of their suffering after approximately six million Jews were murdered in cold blood, the resurrection of their nation began.

The resurrection of these people reflect the three times the Jews returned to their land: 1) from Egypt to the land of milk and honey; 2) from Babylon; and 3) from the entire world.

Resurrection Four

The first resurrection in the New Testament is described in Matthew 9. It concerned a twelve-year-old girl and only daughter. *"But when the people were put forth, he went in, and took her by the hand, and the maid arose"* (Matthew 9:25).

This resurrection reminds us of the Babylonian Empire, the first and the best Gentile power represented by the head of gold. In this resurrection, we see a young girl dependent on her mother in much the same way Israel was taken care of by the king of Babylon.

Resurrection Five

This resurrection involved a young man, *"Now when he came nigh to the gate of the city, behold, there was a dead man carried out, the only son of his mother, and she was a widow: and much people of the city was with her"* (Luke 7:12).

In this account, we see a mother dependent on her son. Without the support of this young man, the mother, who was a widow, would be condemned to live a meager existence. However, Jesus, who is life eternal, came on the scene. *"And when the Lord saw her, he had compassion on her, and said unto her, Weep not. And he came and touched the bier: and they that bare him stood still. And he said, Young man, I say unto thee, Arise. And he that was dead sat up, and began to speak. And he delivered him to his mother"* (verses 13-15).

Today, we may not realize the magnitude of this widowed mother's situation. The death of her son would leave her alone.

She would not fit properly in society because the head of her household was gone. All she had was the hope that her son would marry, have children, and establish a household in which she could find protection and sustenance for the rest of her life.

This event draws parallels to the Medo-Persian Empire. During the reign of Ahasuerus, Haman came on the scene and threatened the annihilation of the Jewish people. That threat eliminated Israel's hope of returning to the Promised Land one day and re-establishing her former glory. But then came a "savior," Mordecai, who trusted in the God of Israel. The Jews' mourning was turned into joy. During that time, the Jews were established in the Diaspora and were rather prosperous. From the books of Esther and Daniel, we see the Jews reach such a powerful position that even the Gentiles desired to become Jews! Evidence of this is recorded in Esther 8:17, *"And in every province, and in every city, whithersoever the king's commandment and his decree came, the Jews had joy and gladness, a feast and a good day. And many of the people of the land became Jews; for the fear of the Jews fell upon them."*

Resurrection Six

Resurrection six does not concern a girl dependent on her mother, or a young man in whom a mother had placed her hope. It involved Lazarus, an independent adult who was beloved by his immediate family and apparently had many friends.

Mary's sister testified to Jesus, *"...Lord, if thou hadst been here, my brother had not died"* (John 11:21).

Martha even seemed to oppose Jesus' interference, for she, too, believed that it was too late, *"...Lord, by this time he stin-*

keth: for he hath been dead four days" (John 11:39).

Jesus lifted up His eyes, thanked His Father, and then, *"...when he thus had spoken, he cried with a loud voice, Lazarus, come forth. And he that was dead came forth, bound hand and foot with graveclothes: and his face was bound about with a napkin. Jesus saith unto them, Loose him, and let him go"* (John 11:43-44).

This resurrection parallels the Grecian Empire. The Jews were back in their land, the temple was rebuilt, but now there was a threat from Greece. This fierce new empire had conquered the known world in a very short time. Israel had been an "adult" but had died - with no hope of resurrection because it had been "dead four days." Four thousand years had passed since Adam and Eve had fallen into sin. They had been in bondage to death with no hope of spiritual life until the seemingly impossible happened, *"the dead came forth"* to life. The Grecian Empire perished; but Israel remained.

Resurrection Seven

"Now there was at Joppa a certain disciple named Tabitha, which by interpretation is called Dorcas: this woman was full of good works and almsdeeds which she did. And it came to pass in those days, that she was sick, and died; whom when they had washed, they laid her in an upper chamber" (Acts 9:36-37).

At that time, Rome ruled the known world. Dorcas' activity demonstrates the Roman Empire, which brought forth the most glorious kingdom. *"This woman was full of good works."* She had made *"coats and garments."* Surely, this symbolizes the riches and prosperity of the Roman Empire.

It is also significant that this event occurred in Joppa, which is today's Tel Aviv. The Roman stronghold was on the coast of Israel from Joppa to Caesarea. Although Jerusalem was the capital, the political, military and economic power structure developed on the coast in Roman times, Jerusalem was only a religious capital.

Incidentally, this is also the case today. Jerusalem is the capital city of the Jewish state, but the embassies to the nations of the world are located in Tel Aviv, not Jerusalem.

When we read the story of Dorcas and her resurrection, we find a veiled prophecy of the resurrection of the Roman Empire which is in the process of being re-established in our day.

This resurrection took place in the following manner, *"But Peter put them all forth, and kneeled down, and prayed; and turning him to the body said, Tabitha, arise. And she opened her eyes: and when she saw Peter, she sat up. And he gave her his hand, and lifted her up, and when he had called the saints and widows, presented her alive. And it was known throughout all Joppa; and many believed in the Lord"* (Acts 9:40-42).

As a result of Dorcas' resurrection, *"many believed in the Lord."* Likewise, our resurrection/rapture will result in the salvation of 144,000 in Israel who will become the heralds of the Lord.

Resurrection Eight

"And upon the first day of the week, when the disciples came together to break bread, Paul preached unto them, ready to depart on the morrow; and continued his speech until midnight. And there were many lights in the upper chamber, where they were gathered together. And there sat in a window a certain young man named Eutychus, being fallen into a deep sleep: and as Paul was long preaching, he sunk down with sleep, and fell down from the

third loft, and was taken up dead. And Paul went down, and fell on him, and embracing him said, Trouble not yourselves; for his life is in him. When he therefore was come up again, and had broken bread, and eaten, and talked a long while, even till break of day, so he departed. And they brought the young man alive, and were not a little comforted" (Acts 20:7-12).

The apostle Paul preached until midnight. The young man named Eutychus went to sleep and fell out of the window to his death. I find it significant that Paul said, *"Trouble not yourselves; for his life is in him."* Why? Because the Roman Empire never disappeared completely; it has always been present. Virtually all western nations are founded upon Roman law to this day. Today, for the first time, we can clearly see that the Roman Empire is not dead but *"life is in him."*

For centuries, scholars have eagerly sought a suitable explanation for the resurrection of the Roman Empire. This search has never been completed as one key ingredient has been missing: the resurrection of the nation of Israel.

Serious scholars who have read the prophet Daniel have realized that the power structure under which Jesus was crucified must reign again when He returns.

Comparing historical and political developments with the prophetic Word never led to any conclusions because Israel had to first become a nation again. For all practical purposes, that seemed impossible.

Even in the beginning of the 1900's, there was no chance of the Jews going back to the land of Israel to establish a nation.

We must add that the resurrection of Eutychus took place outside of Israel in the Roman Empire, indicating that the reestablishment of the Roman Empire will not take place in Israel, or through Israel. It will develop independently, and only later will Israel be added to it.

Bodily Resurrection

The Lord Jesus Christ is *"the firstfruits of them that slept."* He is the first One who arose from the dead and lives forevermore.

He is followed by *"them that slept."* First Corinthians 15:23 gives us the order, *"But every man in his own order: Christ the firstfruits; afterward they that are Christ's at his coming."* This includes all who are in Christ, who belong to Him, and are saved based on His shed blood.

This additional statement demonstrates that the dead in Christ must rise first because their spirit-souls are already in the presence of the Lord without their glorified bodies. Keep in mind that the glorified body can only be attained through the resurrection of the old body. For that reason we unconditionally believe in the physical resurrection of the Lord.

When Jesus arose from the dead, His own disciples could not comprehend, as the Bible reports they *"believed not"* and *"...neither believed they them"* (Mark 16:11,13).

When Jesus appeared in their midst and said, *"...Peace be unto you"* (Luke 24:36), they could not conceive the reality of the physical resurrection, *"...they were terrified and affrighted, and supposed that they had seen a spirit"* (verse 37). Jesus had to treat His disciples as one treats little children, *"...Why are ye troubled? and why do thoughts arise in your hearts? Behold my hands and my feet, that it is I myself: handle me, and see; for a spirit hath not flesh and bones, as ye see me have. And when he had thus spoken, he shewed them his hands and his feet"* (verses 38-40).

Jesus specifically emphasized that He was not a spirit, *"...for a spirit hath not flesh and bones...."* He arose bodily, physically, and when He arose, He was instantaneously translated into His glorified body.

But even such an overwhelming miracle did not lead the disciples to believe, for the Bible says, *"...while they yet believed not for joy, and wondered..."* (verse 41). Jesus had to do something very natural in order to convince them, so He asked, *"...Have ye here any meat?"* This act demonstrated that He had arisen bodily, *"And they gave him a piece of a broiled fish, and of an honeycomb. And he took it, and did eat before them"* (verses 42-43).

Resurrection Is Fulfillment

Now comes the important part: Jesus led His disciples to the prophetic Word. He knew that miracles which we see and hear do not necessarily lead to a living faith, *"And he said unto them, These are the words which I spake unto you, while I was yet with you, that all things must be fulfilled, which were written in the law of Moses, and in the prophets, and in the psalms, concerning me. Then opened he their understanding, that they might understand the scriptures, And said unto them, Thus it is written, and thus it behoved Christ to suffer, and to rise from the dead the third day"* (Luke 24:44-46).

The resurrection is a fulfillment of Bible prophecy and this fulfillment will continue until He has accomplished all things, *"The last enemy that shall be destroyed is death"* (1st Corinthians 15:26). Death will be destroyed when His Body is completed.

When will that take place? When the last one is added to the Church. Only then can the Rapture take place, *"So when this corruptible shall have put on incorruption, and this mortal shall have put on immortality, then shall be brought to pass the saying that is written, Death is swallowed up in victory. O death, where is thy sting? O grave, where is thy victory?"* (1st Corinthians 15:54-55).

The First And Second Resurrection

We cannot emphasize strongly enough that there is no salvation outside of the Lord Jesus Christ. He clearly stated *"No one cometh unto the Father, but by me."* He is the door, He is the way, He is the truth, He is the light, and He is the life. That means that all people at all times who will be saved before the Church and after the Church are saved only through the shed blood of the Lamb of God.

When John penned the book of Revelation, he said that he was commanded into Heaven, *"Come up hither."* He then described the events of the future. Even though these events are described from a heavenly perspective, they are a present-day reality. In Heaven, there is no past and future; all things are eternally present.

Worthy Is The Lamb

Just before the seven seals are opened, we learn in Revelation 5 that no one is found worthy to open the book except for the Lion of the tribe of Judah.

The reason is related in Revelation 5:9, *"And they sung a new song, saying, Thou art worthy to take the book, and to open the seals thereof: for thou wast slain, and hast redeemed us to God by thy blood out of every kindred, and tongue, and people, and nation."* There is no other salvation; we are saved by the blood of the Lamb!

Furthermore, in Revelation 7:9 we read, *"After this I beheld, and, lo, a great multitude, which no man could number, of all nations, and kindreds, and people, and tongues, stood before the throne, and before the Lamb, clothed with white robes, and palms in their hands."* Who are these people? *"... These are they which came out of great tribulation, and have washed their robes, and made them white in the blood of the Lamb"* (verse 14).

All believers of all times who have trusted the Lord and are saved for all eternity belong to the first resurrection, *"Blessed and holy is he that hath part in the first resurrection..."* (Revelation 20:6). The first resurrection nullifies the power of death, *"...on such the second death hath no power..."* (verse 6).

The Last Resurrection

The last resurrection is described in the latter verses of this chapter, *"And I saw the dead, small and great, stand before God; and the books were opened: and another book was opened, which is the book of life: and the dead were judged out of those things which were written in the books, according to their works. And the sea gave up the dead which were in it; and death and hell delivered up the dead which were in them: and they were judged every man according to their works. And death and hell were cast into the lake of fire. This is the second death"* (verses 12-14). Grace is not included in this last resurrection. Neither the Lamb nor the Son of God are present, only the Great White Throne where all will stand before God.

These souls have rejected God's free offer of salvation in

Jesus Christ, and are now separated from eternal salvation for-ever, *"And whosoever was not found written in the book of life was cast into the lake of fire"* (Revelation 20:15).

Not only are these lost people separated from salvation, but they are also tormented forever because they are cast into the same place as the devil, *"And the devil that deceived them was cast into the lake of fire and brimstone, where the beast and the false prophet are, and shall be tormented day and night for ever and ever"* (Revelation 20:10).

Some have objected to this truth and have said, "God is love and He would not permit a place of torment for all eter-nity." I don't quite understand how they come up with this idea because while it is true that God is love, He is also just. Therefore, if the Bible says *"for ever and ever"* that must mean eternity. Otherwise, *"for ever and ever"* in relation to our own salvation is not eternal. We must reject such theories because they can only lead us astray. At the moment of the Rapture, we will be in His presence *"...and so shall we ever be with the Lord."* That word, *"ever"* means exactly what it says.

The Restoration Resurrection

We have seen in several instances that the resurrection restores life. The resurrection we are speaking of encompasses much more than human life.

Jesus, who is the firstfruits from among the dead, is also the author of all things. The Gospel of John begins with the words, *"In the beginning was the Word, and the Word was with God, and the Word was God. The same was in the beginning with God. All things were made by him; and without him was not any thing made that was made"* (John 1:1-3). Because in Him dwells the Godhead bodily, He has to restore all things.

In relation to the Rapture, 1st Corinthians 15:24-28 says, *"Then cometh the end, when he shall have delivered up the kingdom to God, even the Father; when he shall have put down all rule and all authority and power. For he must reign, till he hath put all enemies under his feet. The last enemy that shall be destroyed is death. For he hath put all things under his feet. But when he saith all things are put under him, it is manifest that he is excepted, which did put all things under him. And when all things shall be subdued unto him, then shall the Son also himself be subject unto him that put all things under him, that God may be all in all."* This is the full and final restoration.

The Son has completed all tasks and now becomes subject to God the Father, *"that God may be all in all."* From this we realize that not only will the dead in Christ rise first, followed by *"we which are alive,"* but the world we leave behind will also be restored.

Restoration Of All Creatures

In his letter to the Romans, the apostle Paul reveals some significant, sometimes overlooked truths, *"For the earnest expectation of the creature waiteth for the manifestation of the sons of God. For the creature was made subject to vanity, not willingly, but by reason of him who hath subjected the same in hope, Because the creature itself also shall be delivered from the bondage of corruption into the glorious liberty of the children of God. For we know that the whole creation groaneth and travaileth in pain together until now. And not only they, but ourselves also, which have the firstfruits of the Spirit, even we ourselves groan within ourselves, waiting for the adoption, to wit, the redemption of our body"* (Romans 8:19-23).

In this passage we see the result of our resurrection, the restoration and liberation of the creatures from the bondage of corruption. They will participate in *"the glorious liberty of the children of God."*

This can only happen after we are taken out of the way; then evil can progress without hindrance, until the climax of evil is reached. At that point, the Lord will return physically and literally to the land of Israel to save His people and confront the powers of darkness, *"...whom the Lord shall consume with the spirit of his mouth, and shall destroy with the brightness of his coming"* (2nd Thessalonians 2:8). Therefore, resurrection restores all things. Not only does it bring man back into the image of the beloved Son, but Israel, the animal world, and finally, a new Heaven and a new earth will come into existence, *"And I saw a new heaven and a new earth: for the first heaven and the first earth were passed away; and there was no more sea. And I John saw the holy city, new Jerusalem, coming down from God out of heaven, prepared as a bride adorned for her husband"* (Revelation 21:1-2).

CHAPTER 7

THEN WE WHICH ARE ALIVE

"For the Lord himself shall descend from heaven with a shout, with the voice of the archangel, and with the trump of God: and the dead in Christ shall rise first: Then we which are alive and remain shall be caught up together with them in the clouds, to meet the Lord in the air: and so shall we ever be with the Lord" (1st Thessalonians 4:16-17).

What a tremendous encouragement! We will meet the Lord and then be with Him forever. This is a fundamental teaching in the Holy Scriptures. Someone once said, "The Bible can be summarized with one word: Come!" This should remind us of the Lord's invitation, *"Come unto me, all ye that labour and are heavy laden, and I will give you rest"* (Matthew 11:28). The next to the last verse in our Bible reads, *"...Surely I come quickly, Amen. Even so, come, Lord Jesus"* (Revelation 22:20). Those who have accepted His invitation now desire His coming, which is expressed throughout the entire Bible.

For almost 2,000 years, believers in Christ have yearned for the experience described in the above verses. This unique, one-time event in the Church of Jesus Christ has not yet happened. Before and during this event, which will take place suddenly, and without announcement, the news media will be silent. However, they will quickly try to conjure up an explanation for this occurrence soon after. Judging by the media and entertainment industry today, we can well imagine that they will concoct some explanation.

A number of novels and movies have attempted to explain this prophesied disappearance of a pre-selected group of people. One book describes outer space aliens invading planet Earth to remove those who do not cooperate with the new universal system and transport them somewhere for reprogramming. Sadly, such ideas are being expressed more and more in our day. When the Rapture does take place, the removal of millions of "fanatic, fundamental Bible-believing Christians" will be easily accepted by those who have been left behind.

It is doubtful that the media will recognize what really happened because so many verses in Scripture indicate that apostasy, or a departure from faith in the Living God, will run rampant. Based on the succession of events in the book of Revelation, recognition of the truth and subsequent repentance will virtually be non-existent.

The following verses indicate that those left behind will remain unrepentant. *"And the kings of the earth, and the great men, and the rich men, and the chief captains, and the mighty men, and every bondman, and every free man, hid themselves in the dens and in the rocks of the mountains; And said to the mountains and rocks, Fall on us, and hide us from the face of him that sitteth on the throne, and from the wrath of the Lamb"* (Revelation 6:15-16); *"And the rest of the men which were not killed by these plagues yet repented not of the works of their hands, that they should not worship devils, and idols of gold, and silver, and brass, and stone, and of wood: which neither can see, nor hear, nor walk: Neither repented they of their murders, nor of their sorceries, nor of their fornication, nor of their thefts"* (Revelation 9:20-21); and Revelation 16:11, *"And blasphemed the God of heaven because of their pains and their sores, and repented not of their deeds."*

The Two-Phase Coming

Another critical verse that accentuates this point is 2nd Thessalonians 2:1, which begins with the statement, *"Now we beseech you, brethren, by the coming of our Lord Jesus Christ, and by our gathering together unto him."* This verse depicts two events: the coming of our Lord Jesus Christ and our gathering unto Him.

The coming of Jesus Christ is clearly identified as "the day of Christ." This is not speaking of the Rapture, but of the literal return of the Lord Jesus Christ to earth. Quite apparently, the believers during Paul's time were confused by some false teachers who were proclaiming that "the day of Christ is at hand." Paul corrects them and writes, *"...for that day shall not come, except there come a falling away first, and that man of sin be revealed..."* (verse 3). Paul is referring to the revelation of the Antichrist, which must take place before the day of Christ, not before the Rapture.

Surprisingly, he asks, *"Remember ye not, that, when I was yet with you, I told you these things?"* (verse 5). Notice that Paul reverses the direction of events, then reveals the answer in verses 6-7, *"And now ye know what withholdeth that he might be revealed in his time. For the mystery of iniquity doth already work: only he who now letteth will let, until he be taken out of the way."* As a result, the revelation of the Antichrist cannot take place while the Church remains on earth. The Holy Spirit, who dwells in the Church and within each believer for eternity, must "be taken out of the way." Only *"...then shall that Wicked be revealed...."*

His Coming At His Appointed Time

When the media and government officials state that the hindering element for a global society has been removed, they will almost be telling the truth; however, they will have reversed the facts. The saved will be gathered to the Lord and the lost will be left behind, ready to be fully deceived by the powers of darkness.

In addition, the Rapture will also put to shame all of the prognosticators who have vainly attempted to calculate a date for the Rapture. Therefore, we reinforce the indisputable fact that the coming of the Lord for His saints is based upon His appointment alone. When the Lord Himself shall descend from Heaven, He will not consult anyone as to when He will arrive. He is not dependent upon our understanding of the fulfillment of the prophetic Word, nor does He depend on the world's attitude toward the Church or Israel. The Lord's coming will be based solely on His own eternal resolution.

Based on my understanding of the Bible, Israel will be just as surprised as the rest of the world. This element of surprise makes the Rapture so exciting. We know with absolute certainty that it will take place; we just don't know when.

A Summary

Before we go any further in our study, it is vital to highlight some key points from the previous chapters.

• *"The Lord Himself shall descend from Heaven"* is a unique, one-time event. On a similar occasion in Scripture, when *"...the Lord came down..." "to see the city and the tower, which the children of men builded"* (Genesis 11:5). Yet, this passage does not specify that "the Lord Himself" came to see the Tower of Babel and the city. The purpose of His coming at that time was to visibly determine that the people had indeed trespassed His intentions with their imagination. As a result, we read, *"...the Lord said...nothing will be restrained from them, which they had imagined to do"* (verse 6). To put an end to their imagination, He determined, *"...let us go down, and there confound their language, that they may not understand one another's speech"* (verse 7).

The Lord's personal coming for the Rapture has a completely different purpose. He will come to receive the Bride whom He purchased with His own blood. There is no doubt in my mind that instead of confusing the languages as He did during the building of the Tower of Babel, He will unite us, so that we will understand each other perfectly as we communicate in a heavenly language.

• The *"Voice of the Archangel"* is also unprecedented. No where else in Scripture do we read about the Lord Himself coming from Heaven with the *"voice of the archangel."* Furthermore, we've determined that the archangel would be Michael, who will defend the children of Israel. The moment the Rapture takes place, Israel will lose her spiritual protection, and she will be exposed to the enemy. Therefore, Michael will have to intervene on her behalf: *"...at that time shall Michael stand up, the great prince which standeth for the children of thy people..."* (Daniel 12:1).

• *"The trump of God"* is another absolutely unique occurrence. We learned that this *"trump of God"* must not be confused with any of the other trumpets mentioned in the Bible. Because it is the *"last trump of God,"* we asked about the first trump of God. We found the answer in Exodus 19:16-19, which revealed that the trump is identical to the voice of God, which was so loud that the people in the camp could not bear the sound. This obviously illustrates that in their sinful state, they were not able to face the Living God as He spoke directly to them.

• *"The dead in Christ shall rise first"* brought us to the conclusion that this is only natural because *"the dead in Christ"* will have waited longer for the coming of the Lord.

It is important to understand that the statement, *"The dead in Christ shall rise first,"* is not addressed to all people who have died; only those who have died *"in Christ"* will rise first.

Two Types Of Dead

1) Those who die without faith

More than 700 years before the birth of Christ, Isaiah spoke of those who died without faith in the substitutionary sacrifice that was to be accomplished in the fullness of time through Jesus, the Son of God (Isaiah 26). Those who rejected faith in God's prophesied salvation were considered this way,

"They are dead, they shall not live; they are deceased, they shall not rise: therefore hast thou visited and destroyed them, and made all their memory to perish" (Isaiah 26:14). Clearly there is no hope for those who refuse to accept God's provided atonement; they are lost for all eternity. The Bible does not make any provisions regarding a second chance in such cases.

The Roman Catholic Church teaches the existence of purgatory, which is supposed to purify sinners and make them ready to enter Heaven. On the contrary, the Word of God makes no such promise.

2) Those who live by faith

The second type of "dead" are those who lived by faith. Verse 19 reads, *"Thy dead men shall live, together with my dead body shall they arise. Awake and sing, ye that dwell in dust: for thy dew is as the dew of herbs, and the earth shall cast out the dead."* Here we see a very clear contrast between *"They are dead, they shall not live"* and *"Thy dead men shall live."* Prophetically speaking, this is a picture of the Rapture, during which the dead in Christ will rise first.

First Thessalonians 4:18 clearly shows that the Rapture has been the hope of the Church from the very beginning: *"Wherefore comfort one another with these words."* Throughout the millennia, believers in the Lord Jesus Christ have been comforted by knowing that Christ could come at any moment. Think of those who have suffered so terribly during times of persecution, particularly under the Roman government and later under the Roman church. Those believers who were condemned to death and prepared to die drew strength from knowing that Jesus could come at any moment, and indeed, they were greatly comforted.

The First Living Rapture

In the listing of biblical genealogy, beginning with Adam, we read in Genesis 5:22-24, *"And Enoch walked with God after he begat Methuselah three hundred years, and begat sons and daughters: And all the days of Enoch were three hundred sixty and five years: And Enoch walked with God: and he was not; for God took him."* What a testimony! Twice we read that *"Enoch walked with God."* We will discuss Enoch later in this chapter.

Prophetically speaking, we are reminded of Ephesians 2:6, *"And hath raised us up together, and made us sit together in heavenly places in Christ Jesus."* Further, we read in Philippians 3:20, *"For our conversation is in heaven; from whence also we look for the Saviour, the Lord Jesus Christ."* Luther translates the first sentence with these words, *"But our walk is in heaven...."* As born again children of God, we have already been spiritually translated, therefore, based on the above verses, we are already in His presence.

We must never underestimate the fundamental fact taught in Scripture that the Spirit of God dwells in us: *"But if the Spirit of him that raised up Jesus from the dead dwell in you, he that raised up Christ from the dead shall also quicken your mortal bodies by his Spirit that dwelleth in you"* (Romans 8:11). This pertains to the living believers. For all practical purposes, we are dead in sins and trespasses. But in Christ we have died with Him, as proclaimed in Romans 6:6, *"Knowing this, that our old man is crucified with him, that the body of sin might be destroyed, that henceforth we should not serve sin."* Our body is only the vehicle in which the newly-born Spirit dwells.

Church Denominations Serve As Scaffolding

To the untrained eye, a construction site may look like utter chaos. In the beginning stages of construction, a fence usually surrounds the site. Later, when the actual building is under way, a scaffolding hides most of the construction work–making the project look even worse. However, when the building is completed, the scaffold is taken down, the trash is removed, and landscaping surrounds the building with shrubs, trees, flowers, and grass. Upon completion, we see the true purpose of all the infrastructures related to finishing the project. Then we may enjoy the beauty of the new building.

This illustrates the purpose of the organizational infrastructures of the Church, whether they are local church buildings, missionary organizations, denominational headquarters, or anything else. Virtually all organizations are temporary and only **contain** the true Church of Jesus Christ. We already know that the Church exclusively consists of born again believers. However, at the moment of the Rapture, all things, including our highly sophisticated infrastructures, buildings, machinery, and electronic gadgetry will be left behind; only believers will be taken.

This illustration should also point out that our flesh and blood, in which the Holy Spirit dwells during the very short span of our lifetime, is not what counts. Our bodies (outward man) will perish; they must be done away with. However, our inner man, created through the new birth, is what is important.

This helps us understand the apostle Paul's admonition in

Romans 8:13, *"For if ye live after the flesh, ye shall die: but if ye through the Spirit do mortify the deeds of the body, ye shall live."*

This may be a very difficult fact to accept, but for all practical purposes, our body is dead. Having said that, I ask you, "Have you died with Christ? Do you accept the cross for yourself personally?" If your answer is "Yes!", then you will be able to walk in a Christ-like manner at all times. When someone offends you it won't hurt; if you are insulted it won't matter; when you experience extreme unrighteousness it won't harm you because you have accepted the cross in exchange for your life. You are "dead in Christ."

Go to a funeral home and try to insult a dead person. There will be no defense, no offense, no reaction because the person is dead. Dead people don't defend themselves.

The devil, who is the father of lies, has reversed this simple, biblical doctrine in the opposite direction. Satan says, "You must recognize your self-worth, build your self-esteem and consider yourself extremely important. When someone insults you, be sure to defend yourself to the utmost to preserve your 'good name.'

Anti-Christianity

This is typical of the spirit of the Antichrist, *"Who opposeth and exalteth himself above all that is called God, or that is worshipped; so that he as God sitteth in the temple of God, shewing himself that he is God"* (2nd Thessalonians 2:4).

Daniel describes the Antichrist in chapter 11:36 with the following words, *"And the king shall do according to his will; and he shall exalt himself, and magnify himself above every god, and shall speak marvellous things against the God of gods...."*

Only when we are spiritually alert can we clearly recognize the ways of the spirit of Antichrist within the Church today.

The gospel of the Antichrist is being preached with great success around the world. A perfect description of end-time Christianity is given to us in 2nd Timothy 3:1-4, *"This know also, that in the last days perilous times shall come. For men shall be lovers of their own selves, covetous, boasters, proud, blasphemers, disobedient to parents, unthankful, unholy, Without natural affection, trucebreakers, false accusers, incontinent, fierce, despisers of those that are good, Traitors, heady, highminded, lovers of pleasures more than lovers of God."* From pulpits all over the world, we are being taught to love ourselves, yet the Bible clearly identifies those who are *"lovers of their own selves"* as anti-Christians. In writing to his spiritual son Timothy, the apostle Paul concludes his description of anti-Christians with these words, *"Having a form of godliness, but denying the power thereof: from such turn away"* (2nd Timothy 3:5).

Fellowship Of Suffering

What is this power that they are denying? It is none other than the power to forgive sins and the power which enables us to live a holy life in the presence of God. What power do they deny? The power of the precious blood of Jesus that cleanses the sins of the worst sinner and presents that person spotless before the throne of the Father. It is the same power which made the apostle Paul pray this prayer, *"That I may know him, and the power of his resurrection, and the fellowship of his sufferings, being made conformable unto his death"* (Philippians 3:10).

This prayer request diametrically opposes the tendencies

of our day. Paul is actually praying to be integrated into *"the fellowship of his suffering."* Who wants to suffer? Surely, no one does. Our church bulletins are filled with prayer requests for the sick. Why? Because we don't want to suffer. It is contrary to our nature, for we want to pamper the flesh and serve our egos.

I must make myself clear so as not to be misunderstood. We need to pray for one another more than ever! It definitely should be the Church's position that the believer can come and request prayer. However, such prayer should not hinder the spiritual building of the Church.

Paul sought the Lord in prayer three times for an unspecified physical ailment. That was and is quite normal; however, the answer to his prayer was contrary to his request. Yet he accepted it, *"My grace is sufficient."*

When Paul prayed about being integrated into the fellowship of his suffering, he was speaking on a much higher level. He no longer cared about his physical body; he wanted to be closer to his Lord.

In today's world, the greatest battles are not being fought against politicians, or against the abominable practices of sodomy, abortion, or crime. The greatest battle is described in Galatians 5:17, *"For the flesh lusteth against the Spirit, and the Spirit against the flesh: and these are contrary the one to the other: so that ye cannot do the things that ye would."* Who is winning the battle in your life?

If we could fully understand that the Bible teaches that flesh and blood cannot inherit the kingdom of God, we would better understand Paul's prayer. Our bodies, in the flesh, are never sanctified and will always remain under the curse of sin.

Therefore, our task is to subject our physical bodies–with all of their desires, habits and passions–to the guidance of the Spirit. The Bible says, *"... Walk in the Spirit, and ye shall not fulfil the lust of the flesh"* (Galatians 5:16).

Fellowship With Death

The apostle Paul goes one step further in his prayer, *"... being made conformable unto his death"* (Philippians 3:10). This fact testifies that he had, in practical terms, accepted the death of Christ for himself. He was finished with his life on earth; he knew that there was no future for him in his mortal body.

We live in our bodies on this earth temporarily, yet within these perishable tabernacles dwells that which is born again of the Spirit of God, and is eternal. Thus, we understand the contradictory relationship between flesh and blood and the Spirit. Paul testified, *"For I am in a strait betwixt two, having a desire to depart, and to be with Christ; which is far better: Nevertheless to abide in the flesh is more needful for you"* (Philippians 1:23-24).

Enoch Walked With God

We have discussed what it means to walk with God, and as mentioned earlier, we know from the Bible that Enoch did just that. As a result, *"he was not, for God took him."*

Not only did Enoch "walk with God," but he believed God to the extent that God was pleased, *"By faith Enoch was translated that he should not see death; and was not found, because God had translated him: for before his translation he had this testimony, that he pleased God"* (Hebrews 11:5). Enoch did not die; the Bible testifies that he did "not see death." Instead, we read three times that he was "translated." This is precisely what we are waiting for! The coming of our Lord for us will result in our translation.

What will happen at the moment of our translation? We will no longer be burdened with the "old tabernacle," our bodies, which are not subject to the Spirit. For that reason, Paul rejoices, *"Looking for that blessed hope, and the glorious appearing of the great God and our Saviour Jesus Christ"* (Titus 2:13).

Rapture Of Enoch

Enoch demonstrated how we are to walk with God. His testimony was very clear: he believed God and as a result, the Lord had pleasure in him. Jude 14 confirms that Enoch prophesied about the coming of the Lord, *"...Enoch also, the seventh from Adam, prophesied of these, saying, Behold, the Lord cometh with ten thousands of his saints."* Clearly, this is not a prophecy of the coming of the Lord in humility, born in a stable in Bethlehem. Rather He comes *"with ten thousands of his saints."* Enoch, therefore, was a prophet for the endtimes. Before Abraham, Isaac, Jacob and Israel, Enoch had already spoken of the return of the Lord. Undoubtedly, he meant the Rapture as well, because the Lord cannot come with the saints unless He first comes for His saints, that is, His Church. Enoch experienced the translation of his body into the glorious image of the Lord. Had he not, he would not have been with God.

When Enoch spoke of the coming of the Lord, as many prophets had throughout the Old Testament, he mentioned all three comings in one breath: His first coming in Bethlehem when the Word became flesh and dwelt among us; His Second

Coming which will take place in the clouds of the air to call His blood-bought Church to Himself; and His third coming when His feet stand on the Mount of Olives.

At that time, He will implement salvation for Israel and pronounce judgment upon the world. Verse 15 of Jude reads, *"To execute judgment upon all, and to convince all that are ungodly among them of all their ungodly deeds which they have ungodly committed, and of all their hard speeches which ungodly sinners have spoken against him."* That verse refers to the final coming of the Lord for the purpose of judgment. The word "all" and "ungodly" are each mentioned four times in this verse. This will be the result of the Great Tribulation when the Lord Himself will descend upon the Mount of Olives and cause unprecedented change in Israel and world history.

When Enoch spoke about the endtimes, he included the coming of the Lord, the Rapture. We must not make the mistake of separating one event from the other. The coming of the Lord is one, yet it occurs in three stages.

They Shall Prophesy

The book of Acts offers a biblical example of the day the Church was born in Jerusalem. Peter preached to the people of Israel, *"But this is that which was spoken by the prophet Joel; And it shall come to pass in the last days, saith God, I will pour out of my Spirit upon all flesh: and your sons and your daughters shall prophesy, and your young men shall see visions, and your old men shall dream dreams: And on my servants and on my handmaidens I will pour out in those days of my Spirit; and they shall prophesy: And I will shew wonders in heaven above, and signs in the earth beneath; blood, and fire, and vapour of smoke: The sun shall be turned into darkness, and the moon into blood, before that great and notable day of the Lord come"* (Acts 2:16-20). Undoubtedly, Peter is highlighting the prophecy of Joel. However, he does not stop with verse 18, *"...and they shall prophesy,"* but continues to show events that will take place in the end stages of the endtimes, known collectively as the Great Tribulation. Peter, on the day of Pentecost, told his listeners what the prophet had said, how parts had been fulfilled and how it all would end. That's a package deal.

The Rapture Of Elijah

The Rapture of Elijah is an event from which we can learn a great deal regarding our walk with the Lord. Elijah worked in Israel when great apostasy prevailed throughout the land. During the early days of his ministry, King Ahab and the wicked Queen Jezebel ruled. Courageously, Elijah faced King Ahab, the prophets of Baal and all of Israel. Atop Mt. Carmel, he boldly challenged them, *"...How long halt ye between two opinions? if the LORD be God, follow him: but if Baal, then follow him. And the people answered him not a word"* (1st Kings 18:21). Clearly God was on Elijah's side because of this man's obedience to His Word. In verse 36, Elijah prayed, *"...LORD God of Abraham, Isaac, and of Israel, let it be known this day that thou art God in Israel, and that I am thy servant, and that I have done all these things at thy word."* As a result of his prayer, fire came down from Heaven. Not only did it consume the burnt sacrifices and the wood, but the stones, the dust and the water in the trench as well. Why did the fire of God consume all of this? Because it was a work of faith, *"...I have done all these things at thy word!"* Due to this visible manifestation of the power of God, the people confessed, *"...The LORD, he is the God; the LORD, he is the God"* (verse 39). Sadly, this undeniable miracle by the power of God did not lead the people to repentance; in fact, quite the opposite occurred: their hearts were hardened. They showed no evidence of revival; all apparently stayed the same!

Next, we see courageous Elijah running for his life from Queen Jezebel. By His grace, however, the Lord restored Elijah both spiritually and physically to continue to do His bidding and proclaim the message of God to the people.

Bethel

Second Kings 2 offers a blow-by-blow description of Elijah's rapture. First we read, *"And Elijah said unto Elisha, Tarry here, I pray thee; for the LORD hath sent me to Bethel. And Elisha said unto him, As the LORD liveth, and as thy soul liveth, I will not leave thee. So they went down to Bethel"* (verse 2). Elisha, the successor of Elijah, stood with the prophet and went with him to Bethel. The word "Bethel" means "the house of God."

Incidentally, that is the foundation of our doctrine and faith, "the house of God" which is found in the form of the 66 books which make up our Bible. If we desire to know more about the past, the present, or the future, we simply need to read the precious Word of God. The Lord actually challenges us to *"ask me of things to come."*

Jericho

After Bethel, *"...Elijah said unto him, Elisha, tarry here, I pray thee; for the LORD hath sent me to Jericho. And he said, As the Lord liveth, and as thy soul liveth, I will not leave thee. So they came to Jericho"* (verse 4). The city of Jericho reminds us of judgment. God instructed Israel to take this city and destroy everything within its boundaries.

Judgment is something that we, as individual believers must go through as well. The Lord, by His Spirit, continues to judge us. The Bible says, *"…we must through much tribulation enter the kingdom of God"* (Acts 14:22). Therefore, we should never be surprised when the Lord sends difficulties our way, whether it is sickness, unspoken burdens, or even tragedies. We must always remember that we are in the hand of the Eternal One, and His promises apply to all children of God: *"…we know that all things work together for good to them that love God, to them who are the called according to his purpose"* (Romans 8:28).

Many of God's dear children are going through deep distress and inner turmoil. They have often asked, "Why Lord, why me?" Yet, the Lord in His love is silent and only when all is over will we understand that His hand of judgment was used against us because of His great love, *"For whom the Lord loveth he chasteneth, and scourgeth every son whom he receiveth"* (Hebrews 12:6).

Jordan

The next step of this journey was the Jordan, *"…Elijah said unto him, Tarry, I pray thee, here; for the LORD hath sent me to Jordan. And he said, As the LORD liveth, and as thy soul liveth, I will not leave thee. And they two went on"* (2nd Kings 2:6). Jordan is also pictured as death. The Jordan River empties itself into the lake of death, the Dead Sea. As Elijah and

Elisha approached the Jordan River we read, *"And fifty men of the sons of the prophets went, and stood to view afar off: and they two stood by Jordan"* (verse 7). It is interesting that the sons of the prophets did not come along, but only watched from *"afar off."* I have often wondered about the meaning of this and have never really come to any conclusion other than the explanation Dr. Wim Malgo used to give. The sons of prophets prophetically present a Christianity which confesses to believe in the Bible, but which does not put the Word of God into practice. They do not walk with the Lord. They say "yes" to Jesus, "yes" to salvation, "yes" to the truth of the Bible, but when it comes time to put their lives on the line, they would rather "view from afar off."

The story of the Rapture unfolds when the Jordan River is divided: *"...they two went over on dry ground"* (verse 8). Elijah and Elisha walked side-by-side to their destination. Then came the point of their parting, *"And it came to pass, when they were gone over, that Elijah said unto Elisha, Ask what I shall do for thee, before I be taken away from thee. And Elisha said, I pray thee, let a double portion of thy spirit be upon me. And he said, Thou hast asked a hard thing: nevertheless, if thou see me when I am taken from thee, it shall be so unto thee; but if not, it shall not be so"* (verses 9-10). Although this is not a direct prophecy, we can conclude that this is an indirect prophecy demonstrating the Church of Jesus Christ pictured by Elijah, and Israel pictured by Elisha. The Church will be taken out of the way, but Israel will be left behind.

The Church was founded when the Holy Spirit was poured out on the waiting disciples. From that day forward, the Spirit continues to flow into the empty vessels of repentant sinners and will continue to do so until the fullness of the Gentiles has come in. It may be significant to note that in spite of almost 2,000 years of church history, we really cannot claim to have reached the entire world with the Gospel. With a population of 1.25 billion, China is predominantly atheist, and India, whose population is over 1 billion, is primarily Hindu. Currently, over 1 billion people remain under the dictate of the pope in Rome, and there are almost a billion followers of Islam. Based on these figures, we have to admit that the Church has barely scratched the surface.

We must remember that it is the Lord who builds His Church. Despite the seemingly impossible odds, we find those He has redeemed in every area of the globe. There isn't a nation on the face of this earth where there are no Christians. Therefore, this double portion of the spirit of Elijah which came upon Elisha is yet to see its greatest fulfillment. The Word of God will go out from Jerusalem and the earth will be filled with the knowledge of the Lord.

Undoubtedly, Israel is yet to experience mighty things unprecedented in history. Through Israel, the Lord will fill the world with His precious Word.

Rapture By A Whirlwind

Finally we come to the Rapture of Elijah, *"And it came to pass, as they still went on, and talked, that, behold, there appeared a chariot of fire, and horses of fire, and parted them both asunder; and Elijah went up by a whirlwind into heaven"* (2nd Kings 2:11).

As far as the Church and Israel are concerned, this will definitely happen. Although organically we belong together, we will be parted. Let's take a closer look at the unity of Israel and the Church.

The Olive Tree

Israel, symbolized by the olive tree, never ceased to exist. Contrary to nature, the Gentiles were grafted in, as Romans 11:24 confirms, *"For if thou wert cut out of the olive tree which is wild by nature, and wert grafted contrary to nature into a good olive tree: how much more shall these, which be the natural branches, be grafted into their own olive tree?"* Israel will stand alone when the Church is raptured. For the first time in history, they will be threatened with the integration of the Gentile nations, as we see in Daniel's prophecy, *"...whereas thou sawest iron mixed with miry clay, they shall mingle themselves with the seed of men: but they shall not cleave one to another, even as iron is not mixed with clay"* (Daniel 2:43). Quite often we hear about the great danger facing Israel geographically. Not only do they have to deal with the hatred of the Arabs, but the Jews have suffered more persecution than any other race throughout the centuries. However, all these terrible things pale in comparison to the greatest danger they are yet to face: the mixing of the "iron with the clay," or the integration of the Gentiles with the Jews.

Church To Be Separated

This calling to be a peculiar people also applies to the Church. Hear the words of the apostle Peter, *"But ye are a chosen generation, a royal priesthood, an holy nation, a peculiar people; that ye should shew forth the praises of him who hath called you out of darkness into his marvellous light"* (1st Peter 2:9). The distinct difference between Israel and the Church lies in the fact that Israel has a national calling, *"above all the nations"* and we have a spiritual calling as a *"royal priesthood"* to let His light shine in the darkness. The danger of mixing with the world is a strong warning to every child of God.

I am afraid that it is becoming more and more difficult to distinguish Christians from non-Christians. Both speak the same language, use the name of Jesus, claim to believe the Bible, build churches, proclaim the message of God over the radio, publish literature, operate successful television ministries, and even send out missionaries. Both do everything that can possibly be done, yet one is real and the other counterfeit.

The False Gospel

The apostle Paul warns us emphatically of the false Jesus that is preached by another spirit, that constitutes another gospel, and that is promoted by false apostles and ministers of unrighteousness. He writes in 2nd Corinthians 11:2, *"For I am jealous over you with godly jealousy: for I have espoused you to one husband, that I may present you as a chaste virgin to Christ."* Then he explains, *"But I fear, lest by any means, as the serpent beguiled Eve through his subtilty, so your minds should be corrupted from the simplicity that is in Christ. For if he that cometh preacheth another Jesus, whom we have not preached, or if ye receive another spirit, which ye have not received, or another gospel, which ye have not accepted, ye might well bear with him. For I suppose I was not a whit behind the very chiefest apostles...For such are false apostles, deceitful workers, transforming themselves into the apostles of Christ. And no marvel; for Satan himself is transformed into an angel of light. Therefore it is no great thing if his ministers also be transformed as the ministers of righteousness; whose end shall be according to their works"* (verses 3-5, 13-15). Only those who are born again of His Spirit heed the clear call to separate from the things of the world. The true Church is in the world but not of the world and the true members hear the voice of the one true Shepherd. Those are mentioned in 1st Thessalonians 4:17, *"Then we which are alive and remain shall be caught up together with them in the clouds, to meet the Lord in the air: and so shall we ever be with the Lord."* May the Lord, by His grace, protect each one of us from the deceitfulness of the works of Satan. As our time on earth is rapidly coming to an end, *"He who hath an ear, let him hear what the spirit saith unto the churches."*

CHAPTER 8

ISRAEL: THE BEGINNING OF THE CHURCH

The Church And Israel

It is not our intention to debate the various interpretations regarding the Rapture because we believe that would only lead to additional confusion. The Rapture is an orthodox doctrine which cannot be denied. The purpose of this chapter is to encourage the Church to believe in the words of Jesus, *"Let not your heart be troubled: ye believe in God, believe also in me. In my Father's house are many mansions: if it were not so, I would have told you. I go to prepare a place for you. And if I go and prepare a place for you, I will come again, and receive you unto myself; that where I am, there ye may be also"* (John 14:1-3) Therefore, we joyfully await the Lord! The apostle Paul warns believers to be *"Looking for that blessed hope, and the glorious appearing of the great God and our Saviour Jesus Christ"* (Titus 2:13). Therefore, based on the Scripture, we believe in the imminency of the Rapture!

The Bible refers to the Rapture as a "mystery!" For that reason we refuse to support the many sensational claims that circulate among believers about amazing new discoveries that allegedly "prove" the Bible is the absolute Word of God. Because the Bible must be believed, truth stands on its own merits. Truth does not need or depend on so-called scientific facts. The truth we proclaim is a person; His name is Jesus. He is in person, the TRUTH.

The Necessity Of Faith

The Bible says, *"...he that cometh to God must believe that he is"* (Hebrews 11:6). God gave us His Word and we believe it unconditionally. Whether we understand all of its content or only a little does not make a difference. We categorically dismiss all allegations of those who criticize the truth of the Bible because of our own limited human ability. In other words, some claim that since you cannot humanly explain something, it does not exist. Such conclusions are faulty because the Bible says, *"While we look not at the things which are seen, but at the things which are not seen: for the things which are seen are temporal; but the things which are not seen are eternal"* (2nd Corinthians 4:18).

Even the apostle Peter had to confess that some of the things Paul wrote were difficult to understand, *"...even as our beloved brother Paul also according to the wisdom given unto him hath written unto you; As also in all his epistles, speaking in them of these things; in which are some things hard to be understood..."* (2nd Peter 3:15b-16a).

It is good to ask questions about the Word of God. It indicates that we are searching and striving for the truth so that we may further comprehend the wonderful mysteries of the depths of God. Paul expressed this hope which comes from the increased understanding of His Word, with these words, *"The eyes of your understanding being enlightened; that ye may know what is the hope of his calling, and what the riches of the glory of his inheritance in the saints"* (Ephesians 1:18).

Scripture is absolute; it is the Word of God.

Faith—Not Science

Scripture cannot be presented to scientists for a study to determine its truth. God has disallowed the intellectual process of recognizing Him: *"For after that in the wisdom of God the world by wisdom knew not God, it pleased God by the foolishness of preaching to save them that believe"* (1st Corinthians 1:21). He has revealed the truth to those who believe, regardless of our social status or educational level. It may be humbling for some of us to realize that we are not so smart after all. As the Bible points out, *"…God hath chosen the foolish things of the world to confound the wise; and God hath chosen the weak things of the world to confound the things which are mighty"* (1st Corinthians 1:27).

The Bible is a book of faith, and only to the extent that we are willing to subject our intellect to the authority of the Holy Scriptures are we able to understand its message. Hebrews 11:1 says, *"Now faith is the substance of things hoped for, the evidence of things not seen."* This verse speaks in scientific and legal terms: Faith is "substance" and "evidence."

For this very reason, it is futile to argue the doctrine of the Rapture with those who deny the absolute authority of the Holy Scriptures. The apostle Paul wrote to the Thessalonians in the simplest of terms and listed only one condition when he described the coming Rapture, *"For if we believe that Jesus died and rose again…"* (1st Thessalonians 4:14). Therefore, if we do not believe in the death and resurrection of Jesus, we cannot be born again. As a result, we will not be raptured.

Israel: The Endtime Sign

When we talk about the Rapture, we must realize that this is not an isolated event concerning only the Church of Jesus Christ, nor is it a doctrine established only in the New Testament. That is far from the truth. We notice from many passages, Romans 11 in particular, that the Church of Jesus Christ mainly consists of Gentiles and is actually part of Israel; we are organically one. The Bible clearly supports the position of the Gentiles with the following words, *"...wert cut out of the olive tree which is wild by nature, and wert grafted contrary to nature into a good olive tree: how much more shall these, which be the natural branches, be grafted into their own olive tree?"* (verse 24). Verse 17 gives further clarification, *"...thou, being a wild olive tree, wert grafted in among them, and with them partakest of the root and fatness of the olive tree."*

Since the olive tree represents Israel, the Gentiles who believe in Jesus have been joined with Israel, making us one. When the Rapture takes place, it will undoubtedly affect Israel, as we will see later on.

This organic unity is also emphasized in Ephesians 2:12, *"That at that time ye were without Christ, being aliens from the commonwealth of Israel, and strangers from the covenants of promise, having no hope, and without God in the world."* And of course, we must not forget to mention Ephesians 3:6, *"That the Gentiles should be fellow heirs, and of the same body and partakers of his promise in Christ by the gospel."* Therefore, if part of the promise was addressed to the Church from among the Gentiles, we can conclude that Israel must be the greatest endtime sign for the Church and that the Rapture is close at hand.

With that in mind, let us take a closer look at Israel.

Israel's Separation From Egypt

The Old Testament deals with the people of Israel whom God specifically chose to establish His kingdom on earth. He gave them the law and the prophets. This law was exclusively intended for the descendants of Abraham, Isaac, Jacob, (later named Israel) and the twelve sons who constituted the twelve tribes of Israel. It is evident that God chose them by separation. They were set apart right from the beginning when they became a nation in Egypt so that they would not be integrated and ultimately become Egyptians.

Just before Israel left Egypt, God said, "*...against any of the children of Israel shall not a dog move his tongue, against man or beast: that ye may know how that the LORD doth put a difference between the Egyptians and Israel*" (Exodus 11:7).

Israel: God's Tool Of Judgment

In many instances, God continuously separated Israel from the nations with which she came in contact. When the Israelites entered the Promised Land, they received God's clear instruction that they should destroy everything and that they should not leave a soul alive. The judgment of God executed by Israel was all-inclusive.

God gave them instructions and the reason why this separation was necessary, "*When the LORD thy God shall bring thee into the land whither thou goest to possess it, and hath cast out many nations before thee, the Hittites, and the Girgashites, and the Amorites, and the Canaanites, and the Perizzites, and the Hivites, and the Jebusites, seven nations greater and mightier than thou; And when the LORD thy God shall deliver them before thee; thou shalt smite them, and utterly destroy them; thou shalt make no covenant with them, nor shew mercy unto them: Neither shalt thou make marriages with them; thy daughter thou shalt not give unto his son, nor his daughter shalt thou take unto thy son. For they will turn away thy son from following me, that they may serve other gods: so will the anger of the Lord be kindled against you, and destroy thee suddenly"* (Deuteronomy 7:1-4).

Joshua later warned the people that if they did not fully execute this commandment of God that those nations which were left alive would become a stumbling stone for the people of Israel.

Israel To Be Separate

Very few seem to realize that the union of the Jews and Gentiles clearly violates God's order. According to Deuteronomy 14:2, Israel cannot be integrated into the nations of the world, *"For thou art an holy people unto the Lord thy God, and the Lord hath chosen thee to be a peculiar people unto himself, above all the nations that are upon the earth."* Prior to Moses' death, he blessed the twelve tribes and addressed Israel, *"Happy art thou, O Israel: who is like unto thee, O people saved by the LORD, the shield of thy help, and who is the sword of thy excellency! and thine enemies shall be found liars unto thee; and thou shalt tread upon their high places"* (Deuteronomy 33:29). God set the Jews apart, *"above all other nations."* They are chosen for God's purpose. If Satan, the prince of this world, who is also called the god of this world, is successful in mixing the Jews with the Gentiles, then he can eradicate the Jews, dissolving them in the ocean of Gentiles, ruining God's promises. We know from the Bible that in the end, Satan will not succeed. The Lord will see to it that Israel will be saved out of this terrible coming day, the Great Tribulation.

Israel Failed To Separate

From reading the Old Testament, we know that Israel failed to completely fulfill this commandment of God. For as long as Joshua lived, the people followed the Lord's instruction to destroy their enemies. However, after Joshua died, we read over and over in the book of Judges that the tribes of Israel did not completely drive out the enemies from within their allotted territory. We arrive at this conclusion based on the following examples:

- Judah and Simeon *"…could not drive out the inhabitants of the valley…"* (Judges 1:19).
- *"And the children of Benjamin did not drive out the Jebusites that inhabited Jerusalem…"* (Judges 1:21)
- *"Neither did Manasseh drive out the inhabitants of Bethshean…"* (Judges 1:27).
- *"…when Israel was strong…they put the Canaanites to tribute, and did not utterly drive them out"* (Judges 1:28).

Israel failed to execute God's commandment. This has carried over to the present problem in the Middle East and is nothing other than the result of Israel's disobedience, even thousands of years ago! Israel deliberately refused to separate herself from the nations and has continuously allowed some degree of integration.

Israel Failed To Receive The Kingdom Of God

In the fullness of time, Jesus, Son of God and Messiah came and proclaimed that the kingdom of God was at hand.

Finally, Israel had the opportunity to be a unique nation above all others as a visible testimony to the heathen.

John the Baptist, the herald of the coming Messiah, proclaimed, *"…Repent ye: for the kingdom of heaven is at hand"* (Matthew 3:2). John did not come out with this statement of his own initiative, but quoted the prophetic Scripture, *"For this is he that was spoken of by the prophet Esaias, saying, The voice of one crying in the wilderness, Prepare ye the way of the Lord, make his paths straight"* (Matthew 3:3). When Jesus was baptized by John, we hear the heavenly Father's confirmation, *"This is my beloved Son, in whom I am well pleased"* (Matthew 3:17).

The Great Temptation

To destroy God's counsel, Satan tempts the Son of God by offering Him a false, substitute kingdom. We read, *"…the devil taketh him up into an exceeding high mountain, and sheweth him all the kingdoms of the world, and the glory of them"* (Matthew 4:8). Jesus was to come and proclaim the kingdom of God, but the devil wanted to bring about his own kingdom through the world. To each of Satan's temptations Jesus quoted the Scriptures, saying, *"It is written."* Jesus came to fulfill the prophetic Word. His works were not produced by Himself out of His own will, but He came to do the will of the Father.

Fulfilled Prophecy

It is fascinating to notice that all of these events took place in accordance with the prophetic Word, *"…that it might be fulfilled which was spoken of the Lord by the prophet…"* (Matthew 1:22). Even the religious people who in reality did not wait for the coming of the Messiah had to confess, *"…for thus it is written by the prophet"* (Matthew 2:5). In verse 15 we read, *"...that it might be fulfilled which was spoken of the Lord by the prophet...."* And in verse 17, *"Then was fulfilled that which was spoken by Jeremy the prophet..."* When His parents had settled in Nazareth, we read, *"...that it might be fulfilled which was spoken by the prophets, He shall be called a Nazarene"* (Verse 23). Jesus came to fulfill the perfect will of God the Father. The New Testament repeatedly testifies of His works as being the fulfillment of prophecy.

The scribes, the Pharisees, and the other religious authorities should have recognized that Jesus was the Messiah, but they did not. Why not? Because prophecy had to be fulfilled. Matthew 13:14-15 bears witness that, *"...in them is fulfilled the prophecy of Esaias, which saith, By hearing ye shall hear, and shall not understand; and seeing ye shall see, and shall not perceive: For this people's heart is waxed gross, and their ears are dull of hearing, and their eyes they have closed; lest at any time they should see with their eyes, and hear with their ears, and should understand with their heart, and should be converted, and I should heal them."* The Prince of Peace, the Lord Jesus Christ, was in their midst! However, Israel stumbled and the Jews fell deeply into unbelief because they had wanted the kingdom and the king on their own terms!

Israel Isolated Through Judgment

After the children of Israel refused to obey God and keep His commandments, which would have separated them from the heathen nations around them, God used the nations as a tool of judgment to separate the Jews from their land and scatter them across the entire world!

Since the destruction of the Temple by the Roman forces

in A.D. 70, the Jews have been severely persecuted throughout the world.

Volumes have been written about the horrible suffering of the Jewish people during the course of the last 2,000 years.

God ordained them to be distinctly identified, isolated, and separated: not for the purpose of uniqueness in a positive sense, but often for discrimination, oppression and even death.

Israel's Miraculous Birth

This century has witnessed the greatest slaughter in the history of the Jewish people. Through Hitler's Nazi killing machine, more than six million Jews perished, not because of any crime or wrongdoing on their part, but simply because they were Jews. They were different!

It is extremely difficult, if not impossible, to understand why God permitted such horrifying judgment upon His chosen people. Many have asked the question without receiving a definite answer. All we know is that Israel arose immediately after the Holocaust and became a nation. The horrible injustices suffered by the Jewish people contributed to the United Nations' decision to grant them the right to establish a homeland in the territory named by the British–Palestine.

At the beginning of this century, the Jews and Arabs lived together in relative harmony in the Holy Land. However, with the founding of the state of Israel on May 14, 1948, and the wars that followed as a result, Israel became divided from her Arab neighbors. The division of these two groups caused the world to pressure Israel into compromise regarding the coexistence between them and the Arab-Palestinians.

Even today, Israel desires peaceful coexistence with all the Arabs, and undoubtedly, this division will be dealt with in a democratic fashion so that one day Israel will live in peace with all of her Arab neighbors. I must stress, however, that this peace will only be temporary because it is a false peace.

Palestinian Statehood And The Coming Peace

Israel had successfully gained territory through war but lost most of it through negotiation. When looking at a map that shows the territories of the Arab-Palestinians within the territory of Israel, you should quickly realize that two nations cannot exist on this small piece of real estate. You can't have two diverse nations living together in peace and harmony. Although it may seem impossible, a negotiated peace will be created. The prophetic Scripture clearly indicates that Israel will live in peace temporarily, and this will be considered miraculous.

We know that peace will come about because the Bible declares, *"For they have healed the hurt of the daughter of my people slightly, saying, Peace, peace; when there is no peace"* (Jeremiah 8:11). Israel will make peace with the Arabs, and will be led into a federation with the new and final Gentile superpower, the European Union. Then for the first time in Israel's relatively short history, a secure peace will seem like it has finally arrived.

Israel's Desire For "Normalcy"

On the political level, Israel now has diplomatic relations with more nations than ever before. Voices are being heard throughout Israel and the Jewish world proclaiming, in effect, "We are a normal nation."

In 1993, a diplomatic relationship was established between Israel and the Vatican, which has always been a bitter

214

enemy of the Jewish people.

Why has Rome so bitterly opposed the Jews for so many years? Because Rome has fundamentally refused to accept the authority of the Scripture, and has taught that the Roman church has REPLACED Israel in God's plan. The Roman church claimed to be the inheritor of ALL of God's promises of blessing; the Jews were left with the curses. This ideology enabled them to justify their vicious persecution and murder of the Jews throughout history, under the guise of claiming to do God's will. While Martin Luther rejected many of Rome's heresies, he did amplify Rome's attitude toward the Jews. Thus Protestantism was also infected with Rome's fundamental error.

The Danger Of Assimilation

Although the Jews dwelt in the midst of other nations, they have managed to maintain their identity for over two millennia, even when faced with persecution and death. Today, for the first time, they are beginning to integrate themselves as "normal people" with all the other nations of the world. That means that the greatest danger is not necessarily the possibility of being annihilated by the Arab powers, but by being integrated into the Gentile family of nations!

That is the policy of virtually every Israeli politician. They try desperately to position Israel as a nation just like any other. As a result, Israel denies her calling to be a special, chosen people of the Lord.

It is important to point out that the word "chosen" does not necessarily have a positive connotation. The Jews have suffered terribly like no other people because they are "chosen" of God. Humanly speaking, we cannot blame them for refusing to be "chosen."

Today, Israel wishes to be identified as part of the world, not separate from the world.

The People's Democracy

The global arising of a new philosophy is loudly proclaiming: "All people are equal!" With this philosophy, an idea has been proposed and promoted that all countries, including Israel, can obey the same law. Consequently, a world government is a very realistic possibility for the coming days!

In the past, such an idea was rejected, but due to today's global economy, finance, and ecumenically-oriented religion, world unity is becoming a reality. Today's politically correct philosophy of tolerance is bridging the existing problems, making the idea of a global governance much more widely accepted.

Israel's Uniqueness

We deliberately emphasize Israel's position in relation to the Church and the Gentile nations so that we may understand why it is necessary in these endtimes to expect a supernatural intervention. God must fulfill His Word; *"For thou art an holy people unto the LORD thy God, and the LORD hath chosen thee to be a peculiar people unto himself, above all the nations that are upon the earth"* (Deuteronomy 14:2). How can God make Israel a special, chosen people above all the nations of the world if they are expected to become one with the world? Additionally, we can ask: Should Israel go its own way, separating themselves from the nations of the world? I don't think so. Even if the Jews tried, they would be unsuccessful because the choosing of God does not depend on people's actions. It depends exclusively on His calling, *"...the Lord has chosen thee to be a peculiar people unto Himself...."*

Now that we are witnessing the integration of the Jews with the nations of the world, we are forced to ask, "How much longer will it be until God must supernaturally interfere in order to maintain the national identity of His chosen people?" Read on!

Israel: The Origin Of The Church

Many readers might be asking, "Does Israel have a direct relationship with the Church and the Rapture?" The answer is "yes" because Israel has been given to us as an example. Therefore, we must also analyze the Church in regard to her chosen position as a separate identity, using Israel as our pattern!

Pentecost

In order to fully understand the position of the Church, we begin with the birth of the Church. Acts 2 records that approximately 120 devout Jews *"...were all with one accord in one place"* (Acts 2:1). There is no question that there was perfect unity among this group. As we read on, we see that *"...suddenly there came a sound from heaven as of a rushing mighty wind, and it filled all the house where they were sitting. And there appeared unto them cloven tongues like as of fire, and it sat upon each of them"* (verses 2-3). This documents the birth of the Church of Jesus Christ, a one-time event.

The Abiding Spirit

You may be wondering whether the disciples were already believers at that time. The answer is yes; however, they were not born again of the Spirit of God. Read what Jesus said to His disciples about the Holy Spirit, *"Even the Spirit of truth; whom the world cannot receive, because it seeth him not, neither knowth him: but ye know him; for he dwelleth with you, and shall be in you"* (John 14:17). Notice that Jesus says, *"For he (the Spirit) dwelleth **with** you."* Before the outpouring of the Holy Spirit at Pentecost, the Holy Spirit came upon a person to fulfill a certain task. Thus, the Holy Spirit was with the disciples but not *"in"* them.

Verse 17 reveals that He *"shall be in you."* This prophetic word from the Lord Jesus to His disciples was fulfilled on the day of Pentecost!

What Greater Works?

When we understand the significance of the rebirth, the statement that Jesus made in John 14:12 begins to make sense. *"Verily, verily, I say unto you, He that believeth on me, the works that I do shall he do also; and greater works than these shall he do; because I go unto my Father."* How is it possible for us to do *"greater works"* than the Lord did? What are these works that are supposed to be so great? They obviously must surpass opening the eyes of the blind, the ears of the deaf, causing the lame to walk, and raising the dead to life.

The answer is relatively easy when we understand that these people who were healed by the Lord, or raised from the dead, did not continue to live forever. They are no longer among us, just as the Bible declares, *"It is appointed unto man once to die."*

When the Lord said we will be doing "greater works," He was speaking of the outpouring of the Holy Spirit leading to the new birth resulting in the reborn person becoming an eternal person! By our preaching the Gospel, people will be born again. That is indeed greater works! This, dear friend, is our God-given responsibility. Whether by praying, by going to the mission field, or by giving, we are preaching the liberating Gospel of our Lord Jesus Christ to the outermost parts of the earth so that many more will be born again and added to the kingdom of God.

The First Church

The first Church was so rare and so segregated that there was no question regarding her identification. Its uniqueness was based on perfect unity. After reading the first few chapters of the book of Acts, I have concluded that the early Church believed in the establishment of the visible kingdom of God on earth in Israel at that time. Acts 4:34 seems to support this: *"Neither was there any among them that lacked: for as many as were posssessors of lands or houses sold them, and brought the prices of the things that were sold."* Of course, sharing of possessions didn't last, as we will see later.

Is The Church God's Kingdom On Earth?

How would you like to join a church today that expects you to sell everything you have, regardless of how much, and donate it all to the church? Few of us would be willing to do so. I am not convinced God intended to establish the kingdom of God on earth through the Church in Jerusalem at that time. It would seem natural for the early Church to strive towards the establishment of the kingdom of God on earth because they were all Jews residing in the land of Israel and were indeed waiting for the imminent return of Jesus.

We all know that this did not happen. As a matter of fact,

it was against God's will. By establishing this new communal system for the Church, they neglected to obey the commandment of the Lord to go out from Jerusalem into Samaria and to the outermost parts of the world. Thus, persecution was the tool that God used to get the first Church to obey His instruction. This is evident from Acts 8:1, *"...at that time there was a great persecution against the church which was at Jerusalem; and they were all scattered abroad...."*

For this reason, we warn about the various religious groups which require their members to surrender all of their worldly possessions to their leaders or the organization. This is completely contrary to God's intention for the individual. The Church is not composed of the kingdom of God on earth; it does not have a physical, geographical or political promise to do so.

The Original Church

Acts 5 gives an account of the early Church. It is evident that the Church was perfectly united and the Spirit of God's judgment was present. Let's see what transpired.

Ananias and his wife Sapphira, two church members, acted hypocritically and were judged instanteously in the presence of the Church. Here is the report: *"But a certain man named Ananias, with Sapphira his wife, sold a possession, And kept back part of the price, his wife also being privy to it, and brought a certain part, and laid it at the apostles' feet. But Peter said, Ananias, why hath Satan filled thine heart to lie to the Holy Ghost, and to keep back part of the price of the land? Whiles it remained, was it not thine own? and after it was sold, was it not in thine own power? why hast thou conceived this thing in thine heart? thou hast not lied unto men, but unto God. And Ananias hearing these words fell down, and gave up the ghost: and great fear came on all them that heard these things. And the young men arose, wound him up, and carried him out, and buried him. And it was about the space of three hours after, when his wife, not knowing what was done, came in. And Peter answered unto her, Tell me whether ye sold the land for so much? And she said, yea, for so much. Then Peter said unto her, How is it that ye have agreed together to tempt the Spirit of the Lord? behold, the feet of them which have buried thy husband are at the door, and shall carry thee out"* (Acts 5:1-9).

This event illustrates that the apostles had no authority over private property. When believers gave up their possessions, they did so voluntarily. It is vital that we exercise discernment and caution when someone attempts to pressure us regarding how we manage our private property, our giving, or even our tithes. While we are expected to be good stewards, we are at liberty to do with our property as we wish.

The Church Segregated

The result of this act of judgment is described in verse 13, *"And of the rest durst no man join himself to them: but the people magnified them."* These words are very clear. The Church of Jesus Christ consisted exclusively of born again believers; no one dared to be part of this group. At that time, the Church was 100% identifiable.

As I said before, it was not God's intention to establish a geographical identity through the Church, not even in His city of Jerusalem. He had commanded the people to go out of Jerusalem, into Samaria and into the outermost parts of the world to preach the Gospel of Jesus Christ to all people. In the beginning, however, they became an exclusive club so that *"the people magnified them* (the Church).*"*

Segregation And Infiltration

There is a distinct difference between Israel and the Church: Israel was to be united as a special, peculiar people segregated from the rest of the world. On the other hand, the Church was to infiltrate the entire world, preaching loudly and clearly that Jesus saves and that He is coming again!

In the beginning, the Church continued to grow. Acts 6:7 says, *"And the word of God increased; and the number of the disciples multipled in Jerusalem greatly; and a great company of the priests were obedient to the faith."* Jerusalem was the holy city for the Church, yet the rest of the world remained in darkness.

We know from the report given in the Acts of the Apostles that great persecution happened next. From that point on, the early Christians were chased by their enemies to every corner of the earth and they preached the Gospel wherever they went. God fulfilled His intentions through the enemies of the Church!

Having finally reached Rome, the apostle Paul reported, *"To all that be in Rome, beloved of God, called to be saints: Grace to you and peace from God our Father, and the Lord Jesus Christ. First, I thank my God through Jesus Christ for you all, that your faith is spoken of throughout the whole world"* (Romans 1:7-8). The persecution of the Church flamed the fire of the Gospel so it encompassed the world!

A Holy Nation

For almost 2,000 years, the Word of God has been proclaimed and millions have been added to the Church worldwide. Israel is the visible manifestation of God's selection on earth. However, the Church is in the world but not of the world; it is not an organization but a living organism. In biblical terms, it is the body of Christ.

The Church is not a visible entity, yet it is everywhere. First Peter 2:9 states, *"But ye are a chosen generation, a royal priesthood, an holy nation, a peculiar people; that ye should shew forth the praises of him who hath called you out of darkness into his marvellous light."* The Church cannot be identified despite the fact that she is a "holy nation;" on the other hand, Israel can be identified.

Universities, colleges, and seminaries are filled with books about the history of the Church; however, no one can scientifically explain the Church of Jesus Christ. No geographical, political or cultural boundaries identify the extent of the Church.

The Church In Danger Of Annihilation

Because the Church has no earthly parameters, and consists of individual members who walk among people of all races and nationalities, the Church is in danger too, just as Israel is in uniting with the world.

It is no wonder that the Church is continuously admonished not to be part of this world. Romans 12:2 warns, *"...be not conformed to this world; but be ye transformed by the renewing of your mind, that ye may prove what is that good, and acceptable, and perfect, will of God."* James also supports this statement when he says, *"...know ye not that the friendship of the world is enmity with God? whosoever therefore will be a friend of the world is the enemy of God"* (James 4:4). John compassionately cautions us, *"Love not the world, neither the things that are in the world. If any man love the world, the love of the Father is not in him, For all that is in the world, the lust of the flesh, and the lust of the eyes, and the pride of life, is not of the Father, but is of the world"* (1st John 2:15-16). Clearly, we are in the world but not of the world. We walk among the people of this world with no physical or visual distinction between us. We are citizens from every country on the face of the earth; nevertheless, we are different! As Christians, we have no promise of an abiding place on this earth because we are destined for Heaven.

The danger in which the Church finds herself lies in the possibility of being integrated into the world which is contrary to the instructions given in the verses we just read.

These days the spirit of integration is so strong that it will become virtually impossible to keep our identity as Christians. Therefore it becomes important to realize that God must interfere supernaturally by taking the entire Church out of this world. It will happen in the twinkling of an eye. We will be heading toward the clouds of Heaven to meet the Lord in the air which is another reason for the Rapture.

In its January 1996 issue, *The Berean Call* highlighted the threat of integration:

Compromise may be more difficult to resist even than sensual sin-and it is becoming increasingly necessary to compromise to retain the favor of today's evangelical leadership. The very correction which the Bible requires is no longer acceptable. Yet everything else must be accepted. The following fax arrived at this very moment from the former host of a Christian radio talk show: "Our show was cancelled...on Oct. 6, amidst a tremendous protest from listeners...a couple of weeks ago [my replacement] did a show on false teachings...Promise Keepers came up [from a caller], caused the usual flap...management hauled [him] in for a dressing down and pulled him from the show... As a 30-year pro in broadcasting, I can see 'Christian' broadcasting locking into a religiously correct format...and that is tragic for the body as a whole. The effort to smash free speech and thought is worse in religious media than in secular. We have lost the vision of eternity, and heaven has become the place that everyone wants to go to-but not yet.

Persecution Or Integration?

The greatest threat to the Church of Jesus Christ will not be persecution as many think, but rather it will be a friendly, tender, and peaceful invitation to be part of the great global church which will encompass all the religions of the world.

Let us learn from Israel, which, as we have discussed, is to be separate, holy, and not part of this world. Likewise, we, the Church of Jesus Christ, must not be integrated into this world. The entire world, as far as economy, finance, politics, and religion are concerned, is undeniably becoming one. There is absolutely no escape for the Church except by the shout of the archangel and the trump of God which will call us to our heavenly home!

In my book, *How Democracy Will Elect the Antichrist*, I have documented detailed evidence regarding the deception of the world and the preparation for the coming Great Tribulation.

At this point, we are experiencing the greatest time of peace and prosperity in modern history, particularly in the western world. I, for one, enjoy this prosperity, the freedom associated with it, and the increased power to obtain material things. However, this advantage has a hidden danger which paves the way for the rise and rulership of the Antichrist. For example, how can the Antichrist economically control the entire world if various nations and their respective businesses are individually controlled and operated? It's not possible. Today we are seeing many businesses merging with other businesses. I'm always amazed when reading the newspaper of how many large corporations are being swallowed up by even larger global corporations. A few years ago, we saw Chrysler, the American car manufacturer, merge, or to be more precise, get swallowed up by the Mercedes Corporation. This process is advantageous for all of us but it will lead to a united global world which ultimately will be controlled by one man, the beast called Antichrist.

To reinforce our point, here is an excerpt of a letter we received from a reader of *Midnight Call:*

"You seem to support globalization in your writings and I am astonished to realize that you don't oppose it."

If this letter had been written in the 1800's, it would have been totally understandable; however, today, such a statement is completely unrealistic. Am I a globalist? Do I support globalism? Am I in favor of the New World Order? My answer is absolutely and unconditionally "Yes"! Why? Because every person, particularly in the developed world, is automatically–even without his or her full knowledge–a globalist in every sense of the word.

To further explain, let me ask you a few questions: What type of car do you drive? Is it made in the United States, Japan, Germany, or Korea? You don't need to answer that question because ALL cars are manufactured by global car builders!

When you shop at your local grocery store, unless it is a "Mom-and-Pop" store, you are supporting globalism. You shop at the most modern supermarket because you want better quality, at a lower price! I am not trying to be offensive, but you are a globalist!

Is the existence of a modern world outside of globalism possible? Absolutely not!

In the United States, a lot of "right-wing" political philosophies propose total independence of the United States. Whether one agrees or not, the fact remains that the United

States cannot exist outside of the global community.

An article in a recent issue of Midnight Call quoted a news report which stated that four out of five new jobs in the United States are created by foreign firms. The highest wage-earning countries in the world are now exporting their jobs to the U.S. Globalism is not going to take over the world somewhere in the distant future; it has done so already. As a matter of fact, we are already being integrated into the New World Order.

Absolute Global Success

We are already beginning to experience the new global system which is making the nations of the world rich. The ones who are excluded from the system, such as communist Cuba and communist North Korea, are suffering tremendously. The rest of the world is enjoying an increasing prosperity as never experienced. Does that sound like Revelation 18:3, *"...and the merchants of the earth are waxed rich through the abundance of her delicacies"*?

The more I study the Word of God, the more I see that the deception, induced by the spirit of Antichrist, will not be accomplished by weapons of war. Man will deliberately follow in the footsteps of the New World president with his most remarkable, successful, democratic, free-enterprise system.

Self-Declared God

We know from Scripture that the Antichrist will declare himself to be God, sitting in the temple of God commanding worship.

This is not at all unusual. The popular message being proclaimed by todays "teachers" is that man is able to become God. Not only do we hear this from other religions, but its coming out of the mouths of the "professing" Church of Jesus Christ as well! It may be hard to believe, but many preachers are proclaiming such heresy.

This new "theology," that men can "become" God is finding fertile ground in our day. Although man is created in the image of God, deep down in his heart he knows there is a living God. Therefore his conscience will be particularly bothered by the true message of these two prophets who will loudly and clearly proclaim that the peace, prosperity and security the world is experiencing is only temporary. That's the real torture!

Think of the billions of people–who will have invested their lives in this marvelous, successful, prosperous system–being told that all was in vain. I believe that will be the real "torment" of the tribulation. As a result, when their death is witnessed by all the people around the world via satellite television, people will begin to rejoice and exchange "Christmas presents."

In a similar manner, Israel's integration will not stop until the sudden appearance of the Lord Jesus Christ on the Mount of Olives.

The answer for the Church is also the Lord Jesus Christ whose sudden appearance in the clouds of Heaven will prevent total integration of the Church into the world.

A recent article in *The Futurist* proclaims the following under the headline, "The Changing Face Of Protestantism In America":

That "old-time religion" is making something of a comeback in the United States, as the secularization of mainline Protestantism is driving conservative Evangelicals to split away from established churches and start new sects.

"Since World War II, the sprawling and loosely organized conservative Evangelical movement has become the new establishment, the largest single religious faction in the United States," according to Richard N. Ostling, a religion writer for the Associated Press. The newer Evangelical Protestant sects are growing in membership while older denominations have been suffering declines in new membership since the 1960s.

"Without understanding this great two-party split in Protestantism, one cannot understand American religion today," says Ostling. "Conservative Presbyterians have more in common with conservative Lutherans today than either has with more liberal believers carrying the same denominational label."

Like European society before it, American society has secularized as it advanced economically and technologically. But unlike Europeans, Americans are now more "churched" than ever: About 17% of Americans were "churched" in the eighteenth century, rising to 37% in the nineteenth, to about 50% at the beginning of the twentieth century, and to more than 60% currently according to Ostling.

Instead of making America less religious, the secularization that came with development has extended into Protestant churches themselves. The United States now has a "high level of religiosity," with a wider variety of sects to choose from.

Whether the Evangelical movement has staying power is uncertain. As Ostling notes, Evangelicals as a group are more diverse than mainline Protestants, including factions ranging from "Old Fundamentalists" mired in anti-Catholic, anti-Semitic, and racist sentiments to conservative members of mainline churches who are too moderate to be called fundamentalist - and a wide variety of believers in between.

Younger people in the United States are redefining religion as something more inner-directed or "spiritual," detaching themselves from traditional Christian concepts such as the belief in Jesus as the "unique savior of mankind" or the idea of moral absolutes.

- The Futurist, Aug-Sept/1999, P.12

What is the message here? Simply put; the Church is becoming worldly and the world is becoming more church-related.

Ministers of the Gospel often tell audiences that America used to be a "Christian nation." However, historical documents do not support such a claim. During the century this country was founded, 83% of the population was unchurched, today, only 40% is unchurched. Clearly, religion is now the accepted status quo for a modern society and as a result, the boundary that once separated Christians who are born again and those who just "play church" is being erased. That will prove itself to be the greatest tragedy as we approach the Great Tribulation.

To summarize, Israel and the Church are two distinct entities; Israel has an earthly calling and the Church has a heavenly calling. Israel has an unmistakable geographical promise which they will have to claim possession of in due time. On the other hand, the Church has been given no such promise. The Church is a "chosen nation" with no political identity whose task is to be a light to the world and to proclaim that Jesus alone saves and that He is coming again!

CHAPTER 9

THE COMFORT OF THE RAPTURE

The Bible clearly describes the event of the Rapture in 1st Thessalonians 4:13-18, *"But I would not have you to be ignorant, brethren, concerning them which are asleep, that ye sorrow not, even as others which have no hope. For if we believe that Jesus died and rose again, even so them also which sleep in Jesus will God bring with him. For this we say unto you by the word of the Lord, that we which are alive and remain unto the coming of the Lord shall not prevent them which are asleep. For the Lord himself shall descend from heaven with a shout, with the voice of the archangel, and with the trump of God: and the dead in Christ shall rise first: Then we which are alive and remain shall be caught up together with them in the clouds, to meet the Lord in the air: and so shall we ever be with the Lord. Wherefore comfort one another with these words."* The apostle Paul emphasizes that the message is *"...by the word of the Lord."* He concludes with an admonition that we *"comfort one another"* with these words.

The late evangelist John Woodhouse, who emceed our

prophecy conference, would close the sessions with the words, "See you here, there, or in the air." What a wonderful way to be dismissed! They were simple words, and they did in fact *"comfort one another."*

It is very easy to imagine just how necessary and comforting it was for believers, being severely persecuted to hear that the Lord could come at any moment. They needed that type of reassurance because they knew that the result was their being in the presence of the Lord forever!

James E. Robinson wrote the following in his message, "The Rapture Of The Church," under the subtitle "Timing of the Rapture:"

> We must remember that the Bible teaches that the apostle's letters to the New Testament churches were divinely inspired. We will also discuss what Jesus Christ taught concerning His Second Coming. This will be done by answering several questions from the Word of God. Each question will be answered using at least three different Scriptures.
>
> 1) Did the apostles believe and teach that the Rapture would happen in their lifetimes?
> 2) Did the apostle Paul expect that the Rapture would occur before the Great Tribulation?
> 3) Did Jesus and Paul teach that the Church would escape the Great Tribulation?
> 4) What is the "wrath of God" and the "day of the Lord," and for whom is it intended?

The Disciples' Belief About The Return Of Jesus Christ

The apostles thought that Christ's return was imminent. Webster defines the word "imminent" as ready to occur at any moment. The apostles fully expected Jesus to return in their lifetimes. These quotes from the New Testament show this very clearly.

Peter: *"...The end of all things is at hand..."* (1st Peter 4:7)

John: *"...Little children, it is the last time..."* (1st John 2:18)

James: *"...the coming of the Lord draweth nigh..."* (James 5:8)

James: *"...behold the judge standeth before the door..."* (James 5:9)

Paul: *"...Maranatha* (come Lord Jesus)*..."* (1st Corinthians 16:22)

The apostles repeatedly used the word "we" when they wrote about the Rapture. Webster defines the word "we" as a group of people that includes me. Their use of the word "we" indicates that they fully expected to be a part of the body of Christ that would be alive at the Rapture.

> *"...now, little children, abide in him; that, when*
> *he shall appear, we may have confidence, and not*
> *be ashamed before him at his coming."* –1st John 2:28
>
> *"...we know that, when he shall appear, we shall be*
> *like him; for we shall see him as he is."* –1st John 3:2

In his second letter to the church at Thessalonica, the apostle Paul stated that Christians both alive and dead would be "raptured" or "caught up in the clouds" at Christ's return. He called these two groups, *"we which are alive"* and *"them which are asleep."* Paul always included himself in the group which would be alive. This again indicates that he expected to be alive at the Rapture.

> *"...which are alive and remain unto the coming of the*
> *Lord shall not prevent (precede) them which are asleep* (the
> dead in Christ)" (1st Thessalonians 4:15).
>
> *"Then we which are alive and remain shall be caught up*
> *together with them* (the dead in Christ) *in the clouds, to*
> *meet the Lord in the air: and so shall we ever be with the*
> *Lord"* (1st Thessalonians 14:17).
>
> *"...We shall not all sleep, but we shall all be changed.*
> *In a moment, in the twinkling of an eye, at the last*
> *trump: for the trumpet shall sound, and the dead shall*
> *be raised incorruptible, and we shall be changed."*
> (1st Corinthians 15:51-52).

From these verses, I think it is correct to say that the apostle Paul believed in the Pre-tribulation Rapture of the Church. The apostles suffered much persecution and most of them were killed, but they also knew that the Great Tribulation spoken of by Jesus in Matthew 24 & 25 had not occurred.

Old Testament Prophecies About The Rapture

The Old Testament contains several prophecies concerning the Rapture.

> *"For I know that my redeemer liveth, and that he shall stand at the latter day upon the earth: And though after my skin worms destroy this body, yet in my flesh shall I see God"* (Job 19:25-26).
>
> *"Thy dead men shall live, together with my dead body shall they arise. Awake and sing, ye that dwell in dust: for thy dew is as the dew of herbs, and the earth shall cast out the dead"* (Isaiah 26:19).

Both of these Old Testament writers lived hundreds of years before the birth of Jesus. Unlike the apostles, they knew that the Rapture would not occur in their lifetimes." (Taken from *Timing of the Rapture* by James E. Robinson, reader of *Midnight Call* magazine)

Our Comfort

Therefore, we must recognize what our comfort is and where we can find it. Paul is concerned that as believers, we should not be *"ignorant brethren."* We are to know what happened to our loved ones who died believing in Jesus. While those who do not believe in Christ have absolutely no hope, we do have hope. As a result, we do not remain in sorrow and hopelessness, but we have comfort. Those who have gone before us in the Lord are now in His presence!

Paul testifies, *"For I am in a strait betwixt two, having a desire to depart, and to be with Christ; which is far better"* (Philippians 1:23). Notice that he does not say "to depart and sleep in Christ" but rather, *"...to depart and to be with Christ...."* Those who believe in "soul sleep" are probably very uncomfortable with this verse.

Therefore, if we are already in the presence of the Lord at

death, why is it necessary for the Rapture to take place? This is a frequently asked question and needs an explanation.

Trinity Of Man

Man is a triune entity consisting of body, soul and spirit. First Thessalonians 5:23 reads, *"And the very God of peace sanctify you wholly; and I pray God your whole spirit and soul and body be preserved blameless unto the coming of our Lord Jesus Christ."*

Spirit

The spirit of a born again believer is born of the Spirit of God. It is the Spirit of God which guarantees our inheritance of glory, *"Which is the earnest of our inheritance until the redemption of the purchased possession, unto the praise of his glory"* (Ephesians 1:14). Note the words, *"...the earnest of our inheritance."* Martin Luther translated this as *"the deposit of our inheritance."* The Spirit we have received, which remains with us forever, assures us that the best is yet to come!

Our bodies and souls must be subject to the Spirit which is of God.

In Hebrews 4:12 we read, *"For the word of God is quick, and powerful, and sharper than any two-edged sword, piercing even to the dividing asunder of soul and spirit, and of the joints and marrow, and is a discerner of the thoughts and intents of the heart."* Have you noticed that the Word of God divides the soul from the spirit? When we become spiritual people, we divide those things that we have experienced in our soul from those that we have experienced through the spirit which is of God.

Our born again spirit belongs to God; it is *"the earnest of our inheritance."* The spirit is God's and we are His *"…and the spirit shall return unto God who gave it"* (Ecclesiastes 12:7).

The Bible also says, *"…he who is of God sinneth not."* If we apply this verse to ourselves knowing that we do sin, then we may come to the false conclusion that we are still the children of the devil. However, the Bible says *"…now ye are the sons of God."* We can't be children of the devil and sons of God! This seems like a contradiction, but it is not if we "divide the Word of God" correctly. When the Word says, *"He who is of God sinneth not,"* it is not speaking of our flesh and blood, but of our spirit. Therein lies our great comfort. We know that the salvation accomplished by the Lord Jesus Christ on Calvary's cross is eternal and perfect because it is God's work and He is from everlasting to everlasting. We must realize that while our flesh and blood perish, our newly-born spirits are eternal.

I am afraid that many "believers" within Christendom today are being led astray by a false spirit which they perceive through their souls and not through the Spirit of God. The Spirit of God never contradicts Scripture. For that reason we read this strong warning in 1st John 4:1, *"Beloved, believe not every spirit, but try the spirits whether they are of God; because many false prophets are gone out into the world."*

Soul

The soul is part of the triune man which both scientifically and medically cannot be identified. Every man, woman and child has one. We can't go to a physician and ask him to remedy the problems of our souls. A surgeon can't operate and repair our souls. The soul is the avenue by which we connect to the visible world; therefore, the soul is subject to our flesh and blood. The soul controls our emotions. The soul perceives joy and sadness which enables us to weep bitterly at times and exalt in some of the pleasures of life at other times. However, that which pertains to the soul must not be confused with the things of the Spirit.

The Great Conflict

Differences between a person's soul and spirit can cause conflict within the Church of Jesus Christ. Many may have had a conversion in their soul that never led to the rebirth of the spirit. Some have experienced miraculous answers to prayers including physical restoration of the body. These things do not necessarily relate to the spirit and are not to be considered a confirmation of spirituality or regeneration.

Lying Signs And Wonders

Reading the literature of Buddhists, Moslems, Hindus and others, we frequently find testimony of great miracles, supernatural signs, and healing of the body. As a matter of fact, I believe that the very tools that Satan is using to deceive the world today are in the form of lying signs and wonders. In 2nd Thessalonians 2:9-10, we read this description of Antichrist, *"Even him, whose coming is after the working of Satan with all power and signs and lying wonders, And with all deceivableness of unrighteousness in them that perish; because they received not the love of the truth, that they might be saved."*

It is important that you understand that if someone performs a miracle, even done in the name of Jesus, he is not necessarily a Christian. Remember, Satan is transformed into an angel of light for the sole purpose of deceiving the multitudes in order to hide the true way to Christ.

A decisive quality in the life of a Christian is the fruit of the Spirit. The Lord Jesus said, *"...by their fruits ye shall know them"* (Matthew 7:20).

Healing Service In Bible Times

How then should we deal with our own physical infirmities? James instructs us regarding physical ailment, *"Is any sick among you? let him call for the elders of the church; and let them pray over him, anointing him with oil in the name of the Lord"* (James 5:14). Is James saying, "Go to a healing service at church?" Does he give authority to the pastor of the church to call the sick person to him or have him come to an altar to be healed? No he does not; however, the instructions are clear! The person with the physical infirmity should call the elders of the church to pray over him; anointing him with oil. If we follow these simple instructions, we will avoid the sensationalism promoted today by many denominations. This type of sensationalism is contrary to the truth of the Scripture, and leads to deeper deception.

False Christians

As a matter of fact, Jesus identifies a certain group of people who look like Christians, act like Christians, and talk like Christians, but are not Christians. *"Not every one that saith unto me, Lord, Lord, shall enter into the kingdom of heaven; but he that doeth the will of my Father which is in heaven. Many will say to me in that day, Lord, Lord, have we not prophesied in thy name? and in thy name have cast out devils? and in thy name done many wonderful works?"* (Matthew 7:21-22). Jesus is not referring to pagans who worship idols, or are involved in some strange religion. He is speaking of those who, in the name of the Lord, do mighty things such as prophesying, casting out devils, and *"many wonderful works."* But Jesus refuses their testimony, *"...then will I profess unto them, I never knew you: depart from me, ye that work iniquity"* (Matthew 7:23).

These verses are extremely serious. We must take the time and exert the energy to investigate our own personal lives before the countenance of the Lord to see whether we stand in the truth or not.

He Must Know You

Consider the following. Some people have experienced amazing works, can testify of great miracles and eagerly work for the Lord whom they believe they serve in truth and sincerity. Yet, one day when they stand before Him, He will utter the words, *"I never knew you: depart from me, ye that work iniquity."* Can you afford to take that risk? Be absolutely sure that Jesus knows you!

Notice that this passage does not say "you never knew ME," but, *"I never knew YOU."*

Dr. John Ankerberg, a speaker at one of our prophecy conferences, has illustrated this fact in a very impressive way which I will paraphrase: Many American citizens have had the opportunity to participate in an event in which a president was the guest of honor. It is customary that the President shakes hands with a great number of people, and each has a picture taken. Let's say I shook the hand of the President. With a picture of that event in my hand, I can say, "I know him; I shook his hand; I saw him; I talked with him" which would be a truthful statement. However, if you were to ask the President if he knew John Ankerberg, he would say "I never heard of him, I never met the man." There is a distinct difference between me knowing the President and the President knowing me!

If you were to ask former President Bush if he knew Dan Quayle, he would not hesitate with an affirmative answer. He would know Mr. Quayle because he worked with him during the four years of his presidency.

Therefore, you must ask yourself an urgent question: How can you be sure that Jesus knows you? The answer is only found in His Word! *"We shall know them by their fruits…"* (Matthew 7:16).

Body

The third part of man is his body; his flesh and bones. The soul agrees with the body. It pampers the body and seeks advantages for the flesh while here on earth. As we have already seen, the spirit is the dividing factor in relation to the soul and spirit. As far as our bodies are concerned, we read in Galatians 5:16-17, *"This I say then, Walk in the Spirit, and ye shall not fulfil the lust of the flesh. For the flesh lusteth against the Spirit, and the Spirit against the flesh: and these are contrary the one to the other: so that ye cannot do the things that ye would."* Have you noticed that the flesh *"lusteth"* against the Spirit? The flesh loves to pride itself on being "spiritual."

Read further to identify the works of the flesh, *"Now the works of the flesh are manifest, which are these; Adultery, fornication, uncleanness, lasciviousness, Idolatry, witchcraft, hatred, variance, emulations, wrath, strife, seditions, heresies, Envyings, murders, drunkenness, revellings, and such like: of the which I tell you before, as I have also told you in time past, that they which do such things shall not inherit the kingdom of God"* (verses 19-21).

It is of great significance that the apostle Paul, inspired by the Holy Spirit, named eighteen characteristics of the works of the flesh. The late Dr. Wim Malgo often used these verses to illustrate the number 666. The number eighteen is composed of three (the number constituting triune man) sixes. The Antichrist's number, 666, is evident in the works of our flesh!

Addressing his spiritual son Timothy, Paul speaks of an endtime prophecy, *"This know also, that in the last days, perilous times shall come"* (2nd Timothy 3:1). Again he names eighteen characteristics of endtime Christians which I have listed in three groups.

"For men shall be:
1)lovers of their own selves, 2)covetous, 3)boasters,
4)proud, 5)blasphemers, 6)disobedient to parents,

1)unthankful, 2)unholy, 3)Without natural affection, 4)truce-breakers, 5)false accusers, 6)incontinent,

1)fierce, 2)despisers of those that are good, 3)Traitors, 4)heady, 5)highminded, 6)lovers of pleasures more than lovers of God" (verses 2-4).

Paul summarizes these religious people and describes them as, *"Having a form of godliness, but denying the power thereof: from such turn away"* (verse 5). Notice that they have *"...a form of godliness....*" These are the people who believe in God, not in idols, or in strange religions. They seem to be true believers that can speak the language of Christianity, but do not have the Spirit of God.

CHAPTER 10

THE SIGNIFICANCE OF THE NUMBER EIGHTEEN

I believe that 2nd Timothy 3:2-4, which we dealt with in the previous chapter, is very important. Paul listed 18 characteristics of sinful tendencies in the lives of Christians who "deny the power" of God. We need to examine additional details about the number eighteen. Dr. Ed Vallowe, in his remarkable book, *Biblical Mathematics*, writes about this number on page 126:

EIGHTEEN - BONDAGE

Eighteen is the number that stands for bondage. In Luke 13:16, Jesus said, *"Ought not this woman, being a daughter of Abraham, whom Satan hath bound, lo, these eighteen years, be loosed from this bond on the Sabbath day?"* Jesus said, *"Whosoever committeth sin is the servant of sin"* (John 8:34). There were eighteen sinners, or people, who were in bondage to sin in Luke 13:4-5, *"Those eighteen, upon whom the tower in Siloam fell, and slew them, think ye that they were sinners above all men that dwelt in Jerusalem? I tell you, Nay: but, except ye repent, ye shall all likewise perish."*

On two different occasions in the book of Judges, the children of Israel are found in bondage to their enemies for eighteen years. *"So the children of Israel served Eglon the king of Moab eighteen years"* (Judges 3:14). *"And the anger of the LORD was hot against Israel, and he sold them into the hands of the Philistines, and into the hands of the children of Ammon. And that year they vexed and oppressed the children of Israel: eighteen years, all the children of Israel that were on the other side of Jordan in the land of the Amorites, which is in Gilead"* (Judges 10:7-8). Stephen said, *"And God spake on this wise, That His seed* (Abraham's) *should sojourn in a strange land; and that they should bring them into bondage, and entreat them evil four hundred years"* (Acts 7:6). Stephen is quoting from Genesis 15:13.

In the Old Testament, bondage is spoke about in eighteen places.

The fifth time the word "bondage" occurs is in Exodus 6:5. The covenant referred to here was the covenant made with Abraham, Isaac and Jacob (vs. 3). According to Genesis 15:17-18, Abraham offered five sacrifices the day God made the covenant with him. Romans 4:13-16 states that the promise to Abraham and his seed was through the righteousness of faith, and by faith, that it might be by grace. So the fifth occurrence of the word "bondage" is where God says He remembered the covenant made with Abraham, and He announced His purpose of redeeming Israel from bondage.

The reader will also see that the tenth mention of bondage is in Exodus 20:2. Read that verse and the next one, *"I am the LORD thy God, which have brought thee out of the land of Egypt, out of the house of bondage. Thou shalt have no other gods before me."*

Notice the word "bondage" in the first commandment. Also notice that it is the tenth time Israel's Egyptian bondage is mentioned. Paul calls the law the "yoke of bondage," *"Stand fast therefore in the liberty wherewith Christ hath made us free, and be not entangled again with yoke of bondage"* (Galatians 5:1).

Only God could have arranged it so the tenth mention would be followed by the first word in the Ten Commandments (or law), which is called the "yoke of bondage."

The number thirteen stands for a rebellious, sinful, depraved heart and nature. In Mark 7:21-22, Jesus mentioned thirteen evil things that come out of the heart of man. The thirteenth time the word "bondage" is found in the above list is in Deuteronomy 8:14. That verse warns the Israelites that their hearts should not be lifted up, *"Then thine heart be lifted up, and thou forget the Lord thy God, which brought thee forth out of the land of Egypt, from the house of bondage."*

So the thirteenth use of the word "bondage" is when Israel is warned against having a rebellious heart.

Consider the seventeenth time the word "bondage" occurs in the above list, remembering that seventeen stands for victory. In Joshua 24:17, Joshua mentions Israel's victory over all her enemies, *"For the Lord our God, he it is that brought us up and our fathers out of the land of Egypt, from the house of bondage, and which did those great signs in our sight, and preserved us in all the way wherein we went, and among all the people through whom we passed: And the Lord drave out from before us all the people"* (Joshua 24:17-18).

This describes victory for Israel over all her enemies, and occurs in connection with the seventeenth time Israel's bondage is mentioned.

Nothing short of divine wisdom could arrange this. This number is used twenty-two times in the Bible.

The eighteenth time the word "bondage" is found in the above list is in Judges 6:8, *"That the LORD sent a prophet unto the children of Israel, which said unto them, Thus saith the LORD God of Israel, I brought you up from Egypt, and brought you forth out of the house of bondage...And I said unto you, I am the Lord your God; fear not the gods of the Amorites, in whose land ye dwell: but ye have not obeyed my voice"* (verse 10).

At the time the prophet spoke these words, the Israelites were in bondage to the Midianites (Judges 6:1-11). This is evidence that the number eighteen stands for bondage. The eighteenth and last time Israel's Egyptian bondage is referred is when they were in bondage to the Midianites.

The eighteenth time Israel's bondage is referred to, which was in this place, completes the full number of times their Egyptian bondage is mentioned. Now read Judges 6:1, *"The children of Israel did evil in the sight of the LORD: and the LORD delivered them into the hand of Midian seven years."*

Since seven stands for completeness, then the time Israel was in bondage to Midian, seven years, completed the eighteen times their Egyptian bondage is mentioned. This last reference completed the number (eighteen) that stands for bondage.

In addition to the word "bondage" being used eighteen times concerning Israel's experience in Egypt, the word "bondmen" is used four times. Four is the number for the unsaved man. This shows that man in the flesh is in bondage to sin (Galatians 4:3 and John 8:34-36).

CHAPTER 11

WHICH IS THE REAL CHURCH OF JESUS CHRIST?

We have noted that 1st Thessalonians 4 was specifically addressed to the Church. One requirement for the Rapture evident in verse 14, *"...if we believe that Jesus died and rose again...."* Those who do not believe that Jesus died and rose again obviously are not waiting for His coming in the clouds of Heaven because they are not born again. Thus, we must ask two questions: 1) "What is the real Church of Jesus Christ?" and 2) "Who is a real Christian?" I believe these two questions are justified at this point and need to be addressed.

Which Denomination Represents The Real Church?

Today many denominations are found under the umbrella of Protestantism, including: Methodist, Presbyterian, Pentecostal, Baptist, Lutheran, and many others, all of whom consider themselves to be the Church of Jesus Christ. This presents a problem as there are some glaring differences among the doctrine and theology of these Christian denominations. One denomination states that everyone who is baptized as a baby is automatically born again and therefore, is a member of the Church. Others say there is a special second baptism of the Holy Spirit which must be experienced in order to finalize our salvation. If we were to discuss this matter with each denomination, even more contradictory statements would be revealed and as a result additional questions would be raised. Which, then, is the "real" Church?

The word "church" no longer means the same thing it did almost 2,000 years ago. When we hear the word "church," we think of a building where people gather once, twice, three times or more a week for fellowship, worship, singing, and praying. However, that does not qualify any group of people or denomination to be considered the Church of Jesus Christ. Who then comprises the true Church? The answer is rather simple: Jesus stated, *"...where two or three are gathered in my name, there I am among them."* That is the Church of Jesus Christ! Therefore, any local church, denomination, or group of people who claim to be the exclusive representatives of the true Church of Jesus Christ on earth is fundamentally wrong.

Although it's not my intention to target the Catholic Church, it is the most powerful denomination in the world. We need to understand that the organizational structure of the Catholic Church claims absolute jurisdiction over Christianity. The *Catechism of the Catholic Church*, published by Doubleday, says this on page 243,

"...this church, constituted and organized as a society in this present world, subsist in (subsisted in) the Catholic Church,...for it is through Christ's Catholic Church alone, which is the universal help towards salvation that the fullness of the means of salvation can be obtained."

This self-claimed monopoly on salvation can be found as the basic belief of all false religions, whether they are Mormons, Moonies, Jehovah Witnesses, Adventists, or others; all have a similar message. "We are the absolute authority in the Christian religion and we are the way."

On page 239 we read,

"Where there is Christ Jesus, there is the Catholic Church," yet the Bible makes it very evident that, *"Where two or three are gathered in his name, there am I among them."* In addition, the Bible makes it perfectly clear that there are many churches, such as the seven described in the book of Revelation, or a number of different churches organized primarily in believers' homes. For example: *"Likewise greet the church that is in their house. Salute my well-beloved Epaenetus, who is the firstfruits of Achaia unto Christ"* (Romans 16:5); *"The churches of Asia salute you. Aquila and Priscilla salute you much in the Lord, with the church that is in their house"* (1st Corinthians 16:19); *"Salute the brethren which are in Laodicea, and Nymphas, and the church which is in his house"* (Colossians 4:15); and *"And to our beloved Apphia, and Archippus our fellow-soldier, and to the church in thy house"* (Philemon 2). These groups of believers were not accountable to the head church in Jerusalem, and certainly not to Rome, but only to the Head, the Lord Jesus Christ.

The Church Is An Organism

If two or three believers born again of the Spirit of God exist in any local church, then the true Church of Jesus Christ may be found within that particular church building. The moment that there are not any true believers found in a church, the Church of Jesus Christ is not present. They should be considered a supper club, entertainment spot, or cultural center, but not the true Church.

In order to be organized and to obey the laws of our government, we must be registered as a church. We need an infrastructure, programs, staff, equipment, and proper facilities to function. However, we may have all of the above listed essentials, and yet not necessarily represent "the" Church of Jesus Christ.

The Church Is His Body

Ephesians 1:23 refers to the Church of Jesus Christ as, *"His body."* Jesus is the head and we are the members. Chapter 5:30 further explains, *"For we are members of his body, of his flesh, and of his bones."* Notice that it says, *"his flesh, and of his bones."* This cannot be applied to the living members of His Church because our earthly composition is not described as "flesh and bones" but "flesh and blood."

Jesus poured out His blood as full payment for all of our sins. His flesh and bones were transformed at the moment of His resurrection. He testified to His unbelieving disciples, *"Behold my hands and my feet, that it is I myself: handle me, and see; for a spirit hath not flesh and bones, as ye see me have"* (Luke 24:39). Remember that when He was crucified, His bones were not broken. Through His broken flesh, He opened the way to the Holy of Holies, *"By a new and living way, which he hath consecrated for us, through the veil, that is to say, his flesh"* (Hebrews 10:20). At the moment of the Rapture, and not before, we will be instantaneously translated into His likeness!

First Corinthians 12:12-13 reads, *"For as the body is one, and hath many members, and all the members of that one body, being many, are one body: so also is Christ. For by one Spirit are we all baptized into one body, whether we be Jews or Gentiles, whether we be bond or free; and have been all made to drink into one Spirit."* Based on these scriptural facts, we can easily recognize that there is no direct relationship to any organization or denomination.

The true Church of Jesus Christ is a living movement, a channel of blessing from which the Word of God issues forth into the outermost parts of the world. Evidence of a prospering church is where faith is growing, and its primary concern is preaching the Gospel of Jesus Christ.

The Task Of The Church

Believers from around the world, no matter what their nationality, race, or color, have become citizens of Heaven: *"Now therefore ye are no more strangers and foreigners, but fellow-citizens with the saints, and of the household of God"* (Ephesians 2:19). No one can obtain this privileged citizenship by any other means than by trusting Jesus alone as his or her personal Saviour.

In addition, the exclusive responsibility of building the Church is not in the hands of a denomination or a community, but exactly as Jesus prophesied, *"...I will build my church..."* (Matthew 16:18). Not only is Jesus the Creator but He is the very foundation of our faith, *"[We] are built upon the foundation of the apostles and prophets, Jesus Christ himself being the chief corner stone"* (Ephesians 2:20). The Church, consisting of all of its members worldwide, will complete the spiritual temple of God, *"In whom all the building fitly framed together groweth unto an holy temple in the Lord: In whom ye also are builded together for an habitation of God through the Spirit"* (Verses 21-22).

Invisible Church

This great mystery of the Church of Jesus Christ is often misunderstood because there is no visible proof of the existence of the Church. We cannot present a membership list of all who are truly born again. Nor can we show the progress of this spiritual temple to anyone. No wonder so many liberal theologians who have abandoned the faith of the Lord talk about a world-wide church that needs to be organized and visibly manifested through various movements such as the World Council of Churches, the Ecumenical Movement, or the Vatican. These and many other unity-seeking movements and organizations do not represent the Church of Jesus Christ.

The danger of deception does not lie in the obvious but is camouflaged so that it often becomes difficult to analyze who the true Church is.

It would be presumptuous to state that whatever denomination belongs to the Ecumenical Movement is anti-Christian, thus has no members belonging to the body of Christ. Saving faith in Jesus is often not recognized because it is hidden in the confusion of religion.

Not only is the Ecumenical Movement hard at work in uniting various church denominations, but the visible unity-seeking spirit of the endtimes goes much further.

Dave Hunt summarized how religious world unity will

come about:

Although the "whore" is the Catholic Church, all religions will be gathered together under the Vatican. Already we are seeing leading Protestants working together with the Roman Catholic Church and adopting its ecumenism. A new spirit of compromise is sweeping the 'Christian' church and the entire religious world today. The pope's avowed respect for Buddhism is carried the next step by Newark's Episcopalian Bishop John S. Spong, who testifies:

"In the fall of 1988, I worshiped God in a Buddhist temple. As the smell of incense filled the air, I knelt before three images of the Buddha, feeling that the smoke could carry my prayers heavenward. It was for me a holy moment...beyond the words and creeds that each [religion]uses, there is a divine power that unites us...

I will not make any further attempt to convert the Buddhist, the Jew, the Hindu or the Moslem. I am content to learn from them and to walk with them side-by-side toward the God who lives, I believe, beyond the images that bind and blind us."

Such 'unity' will prevail among all religions under the Antichrist. Even many 'Prayer Breakfasts' bringing political and religious leaders together across America and patterned after the one which began in Washington D.C.—originally conceived by evangelicals as opportunities for a clear witness to Jesus Christ—have largely deteriorated into ecumenical platforms for the acceptance of all religions. 'Participating groups' at Los Angeles's annual Interfaith Prayer Breakfast, for example, 'range from the Board of Rabbis and the Buddhist Sangha Council to the Greek Orthodox Church and the Bahai faith.'"

-Dave Hunt, Global Peace, Pages 129-130.

The Spirit of God does not tolerate a mixture of truth and lies. The Spirit corresponds precisely with the written Word. Whenever someone claims to have a special message from God, we must carefully check that message against the Bible. Even well-intended, pro-Gospel statements are not necessarily the works of the Holy Spirit. In our day, many will fall for virtually anything that seems spiritual and is loosely connected to some verse in Scripture. When questioned, supporters of these false teachers say, "It can't be of the devil, they are preaching the Gospel of the Lord Jesus Christ."

Demon At Prayer Time

To emphasize this danger, we turn to Acts 16:16, *"And it came to pass, as we went to prayer, a certain damsel possessed with a spirit of divination met us, which brought her masters much gain by soothsaying."* With this event, it is evident that the infiltration of the spirit from below comes at our most intimate moments—when believers come together and bow before the countenance of the Lord to cast their burdens upon Him during prayer.

Just as this time of prayer was about to take place, we read of *"a certain damsel possessed with a spirit of divination."* After reading the next verse, we find that this lady was "pro-Gospel." She was promoting the apostle Paul and the message of salvation, *"The same followed Paul and us, and cried, saying, These men are the servants of the most high God, which shew unto us the way of salvation"* (verse 17). Under the guise of evangelism, much work being promoted today looks "Christian," but in reality is the work of the great deceiver.

For the average believer, this situation must have been difficult to discern. Apparently this damsel was determined to advertise the works of Paul and his fellow servant. I can easily imagine that today such a person would quickly have a platform on television or radio because she was promoting the Gospel. Evidently, Paul allowed this to transpire for several days, as we see in verse 18, *"...this did she many days."* Finally,

"Paul, being grieved, turned and said to the spirit, I command thee in the name of Jesus Christ to come out of her. And he came out the same hour." How did Paul know that this was a voice from below? Paul was given spiritual insight because his old nature, his flesh, was given over to the death of Jesus Christ. In Philippians 1:21, he testifies, *"For to me to live is Christ, and to die is gain."*

We should learn from this event that not all things that seem good are Christian, but they may be the works of the great deceiver.

It is not our task to eagerly search for mistakes that fellow Christians may make and identify them as *"works of deception"* or even as the "devil's work." Few servants of the Lord today have the authority and ability to identify certain "Christians" who teach, preach and practice that which is contrary to the Bible. In the case of the damsel, we have already noted that Paul did not act instantaneously, but he obviously tolerated her works, *"many days."* Therefore we see that jumping the gun is not necessarily the work of the Spirit of God either.

Dispensation Of The Church

Let me emphasize the fact that the Church, contrary to Israel, has a limited amount of time. To be more precise, our time lies between the rejection and the re-acceptance of Israel. Today, we are witnessing Israel coming back to her land where they have established a powerful, prosperous nation.

But until this day, Israel is still blind to her Messiah for our sake, *"As concerning the gospel, they are enemies for your sakes: but as touching the election, they are beloved for the fathers' sakes"* (Romans 11:28).

For the first time in 2,000 years Israel has become a sovereign nation. As believers, we should recognize this as a great endtime sign for the Church to be ready for the Rapture.

It is impossible for anyone to deny the reality of the Israeli nation any longer, not even her Arab enemies. This is an unprecedented sign in history, and a special sign of the times for the Church. Jesus told us, *"...when these things begin to come to pass, then look up, and lift up your heads; for your redemption draweth nigh"* (Luke 21:28). He is not necessarily encouraging us to be alert and to watch for signs of the Great Tribulation or the coming of the Antichrist, but rather to *"Look up"* for our redemption and our Redeemer!

The Church continues to grow and the Gospel of our Lord Jesus Christ is being proclaimed in the outermost parts of the world. Those who believe in Him are born again, and they become lively stones in this spiritual temple. The moment the last one is added, the spiritual house is complete and will be raptured into the presence of the Lord!

Light Of The World

Another vital task for the Church is to be a light in a dark world. Philippians 2:15 reads, *"That ye may be blameless and harmless, the sons of God, without rebuke, in the midst of a crooked and perverse nation, among whom ye shine as lights in the world."*

Jesus says, *"Ye are the light of the world"* (Matthew 5:14). We must not misunderstand this important statement because Jesus said of Himself, *"I am the light of the world."* He is the ultimate Light. Notice that He did not say *"ye have the light of the world"* but *"ye are the light of the world."* This *"light"* is not physically visible in any way. In other words, we cannot see this light with our physical eyes. The news media cannot come to our churches and report about the light they have seen. The light to which the Lord is referring is a spiritual matter and can only be understood spiritually. Only when a person is born again can he see the light, and subsequently the future kingdom of God.

John 3:3 makes this very clear, *"...Verily, verily, I say unto thee, Except a man be born again, he cannot see the kingdom of God."*

When Jesus walked on the earth, both friends and enemies recognized who He was without any publicity campaign. He did not have promoters, booking agents, press secretaries, or a media staff. His being radiated the glory of God and touched those who were in darkness because they saw the light. His light exposed the sins of those with whom He came in contact. Even the devils cried out, *"...What have we to do with thee, Jesus, thou Son of God?"* (Matthew 8:29).

Fruit Of The Spirit

My dear friend, if you are born again, you are light. Don't hide the light behind your own flesh and blood. In other words, don't place yourself in front of the light in that you show off what a great person you are. The works of the flesh, which we have already identified, are the hindering element in letting your light shine. Examine yourself before the countenance of God as to whether or not your light is shining!

How can you know that your light is shining? Through the exhibition of the fruit of the Spirit, *"But the fruit of the Spirit is love, joy, peace, longsuffering, gentleness, goodness, faith,*

Meekness, temperance: against such there is no law" (Galatians 5:22-23).

Our Works

Often, our problem is that we reverse Matthew 5:16, *"Let your light so shine before men, that they may see your good works, and glorify your Father which is in heaven."* We are not to promote our works for the Lord for our glory. Naturally we like to do that. Jesus plainly tells us in the correct order that first we should *"let your light so shine."* We have mentioned that the light is the "fruit of the spirit." When people recognize this light, they *"see your good works."* Therefore, don't show off your good works because you will hinder the light: rather, let the "fruit of the spirit" be on permanent display in your life so a direct vision of the Word will fall by those who are in darkness and, as a result, they *"will glorify your Father which is in heaven."*

Light Shines Best When Dark

Believers frequently complain about the terrible times in which we live and the darkness coming upon this world. That may be true, but remember, light shines brightest in the darkest places. To illustrate this point, look up. You will not see a star in the sky during the day, but in the darkness of the night, stars shine brightly!

The prophet Isaiah spoke of the contrast between darkness and light, *"Arise, shine; for thy light is come, and the glory of the Lord is risen upon thee. For, behold, the darkness shall cover the earth, and gross darkness the people: but the LORD shall arise upon thee, and his glory shall be seen upon thee"* (Isaiah 60:1-2).

While this is specifically addressed to the children of Israel, we know that spiritually it addresses the Church as well. These verses have not been fulfilled for Israel nationally because the Lord's glory is not seen upon Israel in this day.

A *"gross darkness"* is indeed covering the entire earth, a darkness to the truth of the precious liberating Gospel of our Lord Jesus Christ. Thankfully, this darkness has been removed from the eyes of millions who believe in the Lord Jesus Christ. Each of us who believes has experienced the fulfillment of Isaiah 60:3, *"...the Gentiles shall come to thy light, and kings to the brightness of thy rising."*

Isaiah's prophecy continues in the next verse and has yet to be fulfilled to its fullest extent. *"Lift up thine eyes round about, and see: all they gather themselves together, they come to thee: thy sons shall come from far, and thy daughters shall be nursed at thy side"* (Isaiah 60:4- 5).

Summarizing, the Church of Jesus Christ cannot be identified with a denomination, a local church, or a group of people, but it consists exclusively of individual born again believers in the Lord Jesus Christ. The Church does not have an address, a nationality or a political identity. No one can determine the number of Her members. Yet the Church is a powerful, living reality surpassing everything that is of this world.

In recent years, we have experienced the revelation of the Church behind the former Iron Curtain. While virtually nothing of the Church has been visible in communist countries, we have suddenly seen great activity in the most unexpected places. Believers are gathering in fellowship, praising God, teaching the Word, and waiting for the coming of Jesus. China, where extreme strict measures have been taken against any religion, has particularly surprised us when we read that some estimates place the Church has over 100 million souls. No one can confirm that number, but we do know the Church is alive and well, even during the greatest oppression man has ever seen. As the true Church continues to prosper and grow daily, the Lord is adding those who believe to His body and when the fullness of the Gentiles comes in, the moment of the Rapture will arrive.

CHAPTER 12

THE COMING OF THE LORD

Now that we have determined who comprises the Church and we understand that we are speaking about the entire Church, we will now explore the "coming of the Lord," which occurs in a threefold manner:

The outline below shows the distinction between each coming:

- •<u>First Coming</u>
  His birth in Bethlehem.
- •<u>Second Coming</u>
  His arrival in the clouds of Heaven for the Rapture.
- •<u>Third Coming</u>
  His coming to Israel to rescue His people and end the rule of Antichrist.

The return of Christ, generally known as His Second Coming, will occur in a two-fold phase. This is not very obvious in the Old Testament because the prophets saw the coming of Jesus as one. Only when we combine their visions do we get a detailed picture.

We will use Isaiah 61:1-2 as our example, *"The spirit of the Lord God is upon me; because the Lord hath anointed me to preach good tidings unto the meek; he hath sent me to bind up the brokenhearted, to proclaim liberty to the captives, and the opening of the prison to them that are bound. To proclaim the acceptable year of the LORD, and the day of vengeance of our God; to comfort all that mourn."* This statement was made approximately 700 years before Jesus was born. During those seven centuries, nobody claimed to be the anointed one of the Lord because no one could fulfill the requirements of being able to *"...bind up the broken hearted"* or *"proclaim liberty to the captives."* This prophecy could only be fulfilled by Jesus.

In the fourth chapter of Luke we read, *"The Spirit of the Lord is upon me, because he hath anointed me to preach the gospel to the poor; he hath sent me to heal the brokenhearted, to preach deliverance to the captives, and recovering of sight to the blind, to set at liberty them that are bruised, To preach the acceptable year of the Lord"* (verses 18-19). Notice that Jesus closes this passage with, *"...the acceptable year of the Lord."* Then the next verse says, *"And he closed the book, and he gave it again to the minister and sat down...."* Yet Isaiah continues in the same breath, *"...To proclaim the acceptable year of the Lord, and the day of vengeance of our God...."* Thus, we see that the Old Testament prophets viewed the coming of the Messiah as one event. However, Jesus clearly revealed that this one event would be interrupted by grace, *"...the acceptable year of the Lord."*

Day Of Vengeance

The prophets proclaimed the coming of the Messiah and

gave many details as to how He was to be recognized. Isaiah spoke of the Great Tribulation as *"the day of vengeance,"* without mentioning the time of the Church.

The Spirit of God revealed to the writer that Jesus would come and fulfill those prophecies in detail. He would indeed preach salvation to Israel and the nations, but then Isaiah concludes with the words, *"...the day of vengeance of our God..."* That did not occur at the time of Jesus. Therefore, it stands to reason that a distinct time period would occur between the time of the *"acceptable year of the Lord"* and *"the day of vengeance of our God."*

Today, we are still living in *"...the acceptable year of the Lord...."* Jesus deliberately stopped at that point. He closed the book and then said something remarkable, *"...This day is this scripture fulfilled in your ears"* (Luke 4:21). This information should be sufficient in showing that Jesus' coming almost 2,000 years ago is not His only one. He will come again!

We have already read the words of the prophet Isaiah, but there is no harm done in reading them again, *"Arise, shine; for thy light is come, and the glory of the Lord is risen upon thee. For, behold, the darkness shall cover the earth, and gross darkness the people: but the Lord shall arise upon thee, and his glory shall be seen upon thee. And the Gentiles shall come to thy light, and kings to the brightness of thy rising"* (Isaiah 60:1-3).

These three verses make a powerful but simple statement: Israel saw the light. However, the ultimate fulfillment of that prophecy did not take place, *"...the Lord shall arise upon thee, and his glory shall be seen upon thee."* This most certainly is in the future.

We know from history that the Jews were the most persecuted, despised, and rejected people and no evidence is found that His glory was visible upon them nationally. Israel rejected the Messiah. They cried, *"...Away with him...crucify him!"* They said, *"We have no king but Caesar."* This short statement has profound significance. They are not empty words, but they are the result of the continuous rebellion against the Living God which can be seen in Israel's determined desire to be integrated into the nations of the world even today. Let's look at history.

Israel Requests Equality

In Samuel's time, Israel had collectively requested that a king rule over them instead of God. They desired to be equal with the surrounding nations. We read in 1st Samuel 8:4-5, *"Then all the elders of Israel gathered themselves together, and came to Samuel unto Ramah, And said unto him, Behold, thou art old, and thy sons walk not in thy ways: now make us a king to judge us like all the nations."* This intense decision did not reflect on Samuel and his disobedient sons, but on Israel's democratic rejection of the leadership of God, who told Samuel, *"...they have rejected me, that I should not reign over them"* (verse 7).

After Samuel had listed the disadvantages of having a king rule over them we read, *"Nevertheless the people refused to obey the voice of Samuel; and they said, Nay; but we will have a king over us; That we also may be like all the nations; and that our king may judge us, and go out before us, and fight our battles"* (verses 19-20).

Before Samuel died, again he testified to the people and reminded them of their mistake, *"...ye said unto me, Nay; but a king shall reign over us: when the LORD your God was your king"* (1st Samuel 12:12). We must emphasize this event because it marks the first time Israel expressed her desire to be equal with the nations of the world.

This has so much to do with the Rapture because the Rapture finalizes the election of God's spiritual people on earth and therefore relates to the election of God's heavenly people, the Church.

We have already dealt with the subject of separation and integration and learned that the Church, consisting of born-again believers, must be separated from the world.

Through the separation of the children of Israel, God brought forth His only begotten Son, the Lord Jesus Christ. Ironically, this separation was recognized by the heathen prophet Balaam. He answered Balak, *"...lo, the people shall dwell alone, and shall not be reckoned among the nations"* (Numbers 23:9). Today, this remains a sore point for Israel and the world. Our modern society does not tolerate segregation, and insists that no one is special. Equality is the gospel of the endtimes and it is "politically correct" to treat all nations, races, and religions equally.

However, one nation is different: Israel. She, in fact, will not be counted equally with all nations of the world. At this point, that is exactly what modern Israel wants; she seeks equality and will obtain it. This will lead to the most successful integration the world has ever seen. But it's only temporary.

Jesus Condemned By The World

When the first church was persecuted, a significant statement exposing Israel's union with the nations was uttered in prayer , *"For of a truth against thy holy child Jesus, whom thou hast anointed, both Herod, and Pontius Pilate, with the Gentiles, and the people of Israel, were gathered together"* (Acts 4:27). The enemies of Christ are listed as: Herod, a half-Jew; Pontius Pilate, a Roman; the Gentiles; and Israel. In a united front they opposed the Lord Jesus Christ at His first coming!

We can easily imagine that at the Second Coming of Christ, the nations will reject Him as prophesied. The Gentile nations, *"…and the people of Israel were gathered together."* It is impossible for Israel to accept the Antichrist unless someone comes forward looking like the real Messiah of Israel.

Unbelief In Prophecy

So much was prophesied in the Old Testament about the coming Messiah. Yet when the time came for Jesus' birth in the prophesied town of Bethlehem in Judea, no preparations were being made in Jerusalem for the birth of the King. It is only mentioned that some Gentiles from the east came to Jerusalem to announce His birth. *"Now when Jesus was born in Bethlehem of Judaea in the days of Herod the king, behold, there came wise men from the east to Jerusalem"* (Matthew 2:1). They asked the right question to the right people in the right place, *"Where is he that is born King of the Jews? for we have seen his star in the east, and are come to worship him"* (verse 2). The fact that Jerusalem was unprepared and Jesus came to the world unexpectedly is evident from the next verse, *"When Herod the king had heard these things, he was troubled, and all Jerusalem with him"* (Verse 3). What was King Herod to do? From historic writings, we know that he was paranoid, extremely fearful and took excessive precaution for his security. Then he heard of these foreigners who were coming from far away to announce the birth of a new King of the Jews. Naturally, Herod found this intimidating because He was the King of the Jews. If another was born, Herod would no longer be king.

Prophecy Fulfilled, But Not Believed

The king called his advisers, *"And when he had gathered all the chief priests and scribes of the people together, he demanded of them where Christ should be born"* (Verse 4). Herod asked the right people, for they knew the Scripture, read the prophets, and studied the Word of God.

He received an immediate answer, *"...they said unto him, In Bethlehem of Judaea: for thus it is written by the prophet, And thou Bethlehem, in the land of Juda, art not the least among the princes of Juda: for out of thee shall come a Governor, that shall rule my people Israel"* (Verses 5-6). This is as plain as day, the King born in Bethlehem was to rule Israel.

When we continue to read about this event, we notice something very strange. There is no report of the chief priests or scribes going to Bethelehem to witness the fulfillment of Bible prophecy. This proves that these "Bible believers" grasped the prophetic Scripture intellectually but had no living faith to produce action.

Again, we highlight the fact that the tangible fulfillment of Bible prophecy, the miraculous announcement of the birth of Jesus Christ, and the signs in the heavenly constellation did not produce living faith, but rather, unbelief.

Believing Prophecy Is Required

I take this opportunity once again to emphasize that no matter how great your experience is with the Lord, how many of your prayers have been answered, how often you have been healed, how many prophetic utterances you proclaim in the church, or how frequently you have the gift of healing the sick and even raising the dead, it is all insignificant compared with the simple faith that Jesus is who He says He is.

He poured out His blood on Calvary's cross for our sins, was buried, arose the third day, and ascended to Heaven with the clear message that He will come again. This knowledge does not come from any experience we may have had or from seminary training, nor can we obtain it through any other educational process. This knowledge comes from the living Word of God, the Bible!

The Suffering Servant

The New Testament describes the fulfillment of Isaiah 53 in detail. To reinforce this fact, let's read just a few verses of this beautiful Messianic chapter, *"He is despised and rejected of men; a man of sorrows, and acquainted with grief: and we hid as it were our faces from him; he was despised, and we esteemed him not. Surely he hath borne our griefs, and carried our sorrows: yet we did esteem him stricken, smitten of God, and afflicted. But he was wounded for our transgressions, he was bruised for our iniquities: the chastisement of our peace was upon him; and with his stripes we are healed"* (Isaiah 53:3-5).

He did not protest, *"He was oppressed, and he was afflicted, yet he opened not his mouth: he is brought as a lamb to the slaughter, and as a sheep before her shearers is dumb, so he openeth not his mouth"* (verse 7).

He was crucified between two criminals and buried in the tomb of a rich man, *"And he made his grave with the wicked, and with the rich in his death; because he had done no violence, neither was any deceit in his mouth"* (verse 9).

Faith In The Word

It insults our Lord when we desire special confirmation or supernatural manifestation in order to validate the truths of the written Word. As believers, we can completely trust every detail in the Bible.

When we come across places in Scripture which we do not understand, or which may seem contradictory, we can be assured that God does not lie. Scripture supports Scripture and it is only because of our limited intellect that we fail to grasp the deeper truths presented in the Bible.

Jesus was despised and rejected at His first coming. Pouring out His blood, He died on Calvary's cross and became *"...the Lamb of God which taketh away the sin of the world"* (John 1:29).

While Jesus was on earth, He promised that He would come again, *"...I will come again, and receive you unto myself..."* (John 14:3), *"...I go away, and come again unto you..."* (John 14:28). Jesus desires to be with us; He purchased us with His own blood! Just think, if you make a purchase, don't you want the product? How much more does our Lord Jesus Christ, who loved us so much that He gave His life so He might receive us unto Himself? Read His prayer in John 17:24, *"Father, I will that they also, whom thou hast given me, be with me where I am; that they may behold my glory, which thou hast given me: for thou lovedst me before the foundation of the world."* The announcement of His return is indisputably clear in the Scriptures.

Rapture Is Not The Last Resurrection

The Church of Jesus Christ, consisting of those who have died in Him and those who are still alive at the moment of the Rapture, *"...shall be caught up together with them in the clouds to meet the Lord in the air..."* (1st Thessalonians 4:17). This can't be made any clearer, and should not be misunderstood.

Yet some say that this verse speaks about the last resurrection when all people will stand before the white throne of judgment. The Bible does not teach that we will see Jesus at the Great White Throne. Revelation 20:11 says, *"...I saw a great white throne, and him that sat on it, from whose face the earth and the heaven fled away; and there was found no place for them."* This is the ultimate judgment of all those who have rejected salvation in Jesus Christ.

Even the dead will be resurrected, as the next verse indicates, *"And I saw the dead, small and great, stand before God...."* Again, there is no Lamb of God, no grace, no more salvation, only judgment. That will be the most horrible time for those who must stand before the throne of God. Undoubtedly they will know they could have been saved, but will now realize that it is too late; there is no escape. Verse 13 categorically states, *"And the sea gave up the dead which were in it; and death and hell delivered up the dead which were in them: and they were judged every man according to their works."* This judgment leads to condemnation. The result is described with the words, *"And death and hell were cast into the lake of fire. This is the second death. And whosoever was not found written in the book of life was cast into the lake of fire"* (verses 14-15).

The resurrection that we read of in 1st Thessalonians 4 has no relation to the one mentioned in Revelation 20. The Church *"...shall be caught up together with them in the clouds to meet the Lord in the air: and so shall we ever be with the Lord"* (verse 17).

Who Are The Two Witnesses?

It is my understanding that Moses and Elijah, two great men of Israel, will fulfill the office of the "two olive trees" and "two candlesticks" spoken of in Revelation 11.

Elijah was a servant of God who shut the heavens so that it would not rain. Moses raised his rod and turned the waters into blood. Revelation 11:5-6 reads, *"...if any man will hurt them, fire proceedeth out of their mouth, and devoureth their enemies: and if any man will hurt them, he must in this manner be killed. These have power to shut heaven, that it rain not in the days of their prophecy: and have power over waters to turn them to blood, and to smite the earth with all plagues, as often as they will."* By supernatural power, these two witnesses will be in Jerusalem testifying the truth of God to the world.

During that time, the Church of Jesus Christ, the light of this world, will be in the presence of the Lord. Israel will remain blind, having accepted the Antichrist as her redeemer. As a result, God will supernaturally interfere, to leave a testimony on earth by sending Moses and Elijah as His witnesses.

Prophets Must Be Killed In Jerusalem

However, we read that these two prophets will be killed by the beast who rises up out of the sea. Their bodies will openly lay in the streets of Jerusalem as a testimony against the world. Revelation 11:8 confirms this by reporting, *"...their dead bodies shall lie in the street of the great city, which spiritually is called Sodom and Egypt, where also our Lord was crucified."*

Jerusalem, the most glorified city, will have experienced a negative transformation. No longer will she be considered the city of the peace and joy of the Lord, but she will be called *"Sodom and Egypt."* Sodom was the epitome of sin against the Lord because of the Sodomites—or in today's vernacular, homosexuals—who ruled that city with their publically exhibited practice, which is an abomination to the Lord.

Romans 1:24 testifies, *"Wherefore God also gave them up to uncleanness through the lusts of their own hearts, to dishonour their own bodies between themselves."*

To be called "Egypt" would remind Jerusalem of the land of bondage, which prophetically shows that Israel will come into the bondage of the Gentile nations. This time, however, it will not be by force, but voluntarily, for Jesus prophesied that when another shall come in His name, they will receive him.

The fact that these two great prophets will die in Jerusalem reminds us of the words of the Lord *"...for it cannot be that a prophet perish out of Jerusalem"* (Luke 13:33). Elijah did not see death, but was raptured into Heaven therefore he did not die in Jerusalem. He crossed the Jordan River and then ascended into Heaven outside the borders of the Promised Land. Neither Moses nor Elijah have fulfilled Luke 13:33 in that they did not die in Jerusalem or in the Promised Land.

These two great prophets will return to Jerusalem, the center of the world, where they die, but will resurrect after 3 1/2 days and ascend into Heaven. Again, we see the Rapture demonstrated right in the city of Jerusalem.

When these two prophets are resurrected after 3 1/2 days, they will be raptured into the clouds of Heaven in view of all the people. As a result, a great earthquake will occur and, *"...the remnant were affrighted, and gave glory to the God of heaven"* (Revelation 11:13). Subsequently, the Rapture of the true prophets will result in a revival among "the remnant" which undoubtedly refers to Israel, and they will give God the glory.

On the other hand, when the Rapture of the Church takes

place, we find no indication in the Bible that it will result in repentance or the glorification of God. However, I believe that the "remnant" of Gentiles left behind, whose family members have been raptured, will indeed be very afraid and many will give God the glory and be converted.

The effect of the testimony of these two witnesses in Jerusalem points to Israel's preparation for the outpouring of the Spirit of grace and supplication at the coming of Jesus.

Non Believers-Non Repentance

Let's look at the different reactions to God's supernatural interference as outlined for us in the book of Revelation. At the opening of the sixth seal we see that man is totally unrepentant. Beginning in Revelation 6:15-16 we read, *"...the kings of the earth, and the great men, and the rich men, and the chief captains, and the mighty men, and every bondman, and every free man, hid themselves in the dens and in the rocks of the mountains; And said to the mountains and rocks, Fall on us, and hide us from the face of him that sitteth on the throne, and from the wrath of the Lamb."* Instead of repenting they try to hide from the wrath of the Lamb!

After one-third of the world's population is killed, we read in Revelation 9:20-21, *"...the rest of the men which were not killed by these plagues yet repented not of the works of their hands, that they should not worship devils, and idols of gold, and silver, and brass, and stone, and of wood: which neither can see, nor hear, nor walk: Neither repented they of their murders, nor of their sorceries, nor of their fornication, nor of their thefts."*

When the fourth and fifth angel pour out their vials we hear this shocking testimony, *"...the fourth angel poured out his vial upon the sun; and power was given unto him to scorch men with fire. And men were scorched with great heat, and blasphemed the name of God, which hath power over these plagues: and they repented not to give him glory. And the fifth angel poured out his vial upon the seat of the beast; and his kingdom was full of darkness; and they gnawed their tongues for pain, And blasphemed the God of heaven because of their pains and their sores, and repented not of their deeds"* (Revelation 16:8-11). Instead of repentance there is blasphemy! This should have been enough to bring everyone to their knees. Verses such as this leave no room for the mocking attitude of those who say, "Well, I only believe what I see." The people referred to in Revelation 16 see the indisputable evidence of the God of Creation with their own eyes, yet they still find no room for repentance, or space to believe.

Michael The Archangel

The book of Daniel specifically identifies Michael the archangel as being on Israel's side, *"And at that time shall Michael stand up, the great prince which standeth for the children of thy people: and there shall be a time of trouble, such as never was since there was a nation even to that same time: and at that time thy people shall be delivered, every one that shall be found written in the book"* (Daniel 12:1). This verse is referring to the Great Tribulation. Michael the archangel is standing for the defense of Israel. We can well imagine that when the Rapture takes place, the "shout" that is heard will be the voice of Michael, for he will come in defense of Israel.

With the Church gone, there will be no more prayers for Israel, resulting in total darkness for her. For the first time in history, the Jews will be in danger of losing their identity. Therefore, it is absolutely necessary that Michael come into action for this people because the Church is gone.

It is significant to note that Michael's action on behalf of Israel will not be evident from the beginning. When the Church is raptured, the Jews' trouble will have only just begun. After Israel has accepted the Antichrist as her Messiah, they must go through to the end of the seven-year tribulation...only then will Israel experience salvation.

The Meeting Place

Jesus is not coming to earth at the time of the Rapture. That will only happen when Jesus' feet literally stand upon the Mount of Olives. This event will be fulfilled only after the Rapture takes place. In the very same manner He left Israel, He must return for Israel.

According to the Acts of the Apostles, when Jesus ascended into Heaven, the disciples looked up toward Heaven. Two unidentified men dressed in white gave this message, *"...Ye men of Galilee, why stand ye gazing up into heaven? this same Jesus, which is taken up from you into heaven, shall so come in like manner as ye have seen him go into heaven"* (Acts 1:11). Jesus will physically come back to the Mount of Olives for Israel just as the prophets declared, *"And his feet shall stand in that day upon the mount of Olives, which is before Jerusalem on the east, and the mount of Olives shall cleave in the midst thereof toward the east and toward the west, and there shall be a very great valley; and half of the mountain shall remove toward the north, and half of it toward the south"* (Zechariah 14:4).

The meeting place for the Church with her Lord is

described very clearly, *"...in the clouds to meet the Lord in the air...."* This first phase of the Second Coming, which we call the Rapture, is not for Israel or the world; it is only for His blood-bought believers, Jews and Gentiles!

Two Rapture Categories

The Rapture involves two categories of believers: those who have already died in the Lord and those who are still alive at that moment. It is this great hope that the Church of Jesus Christ has had for many centuries: the sudden removal and translation of our bodies which leads us into the presence of the Lord.

The apostle Paul's prayer and deep yearning gave him the comfort, *"For we that are in this tabernacle do groan, being burdened: not for that we would be unclothed, but clothed upon, that mortality might be swallowed up of life"* (2nd Corinthians 5:4). He had a living hope of the reality of the Rapture!

The apostle Paul also accepted the possibility that he would have to die and be separated from his physical body which he reveals in 2nd Corinthians 5:6, *"Therefore we are always confident, knowing that, whilst we are at home in the body, we are absent from the Lord."* In verse 8 he confesses, *"We are confident, I say, and willing rather to be absent from the body, and to be present with the Lord."* This is a demonstration of genuine faith, *"...for we walk by faith, not by sight."* From the beginning, his hope, and by association, the hope of the Church, was the coming of the Lord in the clouds of Heaven. The early Christians were waiting for the Rapture to take place at any moment, just as we are today. Nevertheless, they fully accepted the possibility that they might have to die first.

The Glorified Body

What is the difference between dying now and being in the presence of the Lord, or not dying and being raptured into the presence of the Lord? We have already seen the desire expressed by Paul in 2nd Corinthians 5:4 to be *"...clothed upon, that mortality might be swallowed up of life."* In other words, to have their body instantaneously translated into the likeness of His glorious body, which believers are to receive the moment of the Rapture. Read Paul's words: *"For in this we groan, earnestly desiring to be clothed upon with our house which is from heaven: If so be that being clothed, we shall not be found naked"* (2nd Corinthians 5:2-3).

To understand this better, let us take a look at one of the mysteries that the Bible reveals in relation to the Rapture, *"Behold, I shew you a mystery; We shall not all sleep, but we shall all be changed, In a moment, in the twinkling of an eye, at the last trump: for the trumpet shall sound, and the dead shall be raised incorruptible, and we shall be changed. For this corruptible must put on incorruption, and this mortal must put on immortality"* (1st Corinthians 15:51-53). This will take place instanteously. A Dutch translation says *"...in an inseparable moment of time...."* In simple words, this means that the bodies in which we now dwell have no promise or future on earth.

Knowledge Of Death Brings Wisdom

May I urge you, dear reader, to recognize that day by day, we are getting older. You may have more aches and pains and some parts of your body may not function like they used to. If you are physically fit, you can rest assure that it won't last. As impossible as it may sound, do not despair-but rejoice, for the end of this very short earthly life is the beginning of eternity. We do well to heed the admonition found in Psalm 90:12, *"...teach us to number our days, that we may apply our hearts unto wisdom."* When our hope and faith is anchored securely in Jesus and not in our own works, we can rejoice with the full assurance that the best is yet to come!

Glory Without The Body

For this reason we should not spend too much time or energy promoting the healing of the body. The Bible says *"...it is appointed unto men once to die, but after this the judgment."* While the body is important, as we have seen in Moses' case, we must understand that our flesh and blood are only part of the outer shell which contains the new person. All who have died in the Lord Jesus are already in His presence without their glorified bodies. This means they are not *"made perfect."* They are saved for all eternity, are secure forever and are already experiencing the glory of the Lord. Yet they must wait until they receive their glorified body which will take place at the Rapture.

Receiving our glorified bodies also includes the Old Testament saints. Hebrews 11 is the chapter of faith that begins with its definition: *"Now faith is the substance of things hoped for, the evidence of things not seen"* (Hebrews 11:1). Followed by the definition is the testimony of a great host of saints who claimed the victory because they believed.

Verse 35 reveals the difference between physical resurrection unto life and the better resurrection unto eternal life, *"Women received their dead raised to life again: and others were tortured, not accepting deliverance; that they might obtain a better resurrection."* The last two verses summarize their reason for waiting, *"And these all, having obtained a good report through faith, recieved not the promise: God having provided some better thing for us, that they without us should not be made perfect"* (Hebrews 11:39- 40). In simple terms, the saints cannot be translated until the Bridegroom receives His Bride: the Church.

The Best Is Yet To Come

To further clarify this matter, we read again from 1st Thessalonians 4:15, *"For we say unto you by the word of the Lord, that we which are alive and remain unto the coming of the Lord shall not prevent them which are asleep."* What does it mean to *"not prevent them which are asleep"*? Luther translated it this way, *"We shall not advance* (or be ahead) *of those who sleep."* Verse 16 concludes with the following statement, *"...the dead in Christ shall rise first."* They have been waiting longer than us and will be the first to receive their glorified bodies.

A Warning

At this point I must express to you a strong warning. When the Rapture does take place, it will be too late for you to belong to the Church. If you are not born again at that time you will definitely be left behind! The Rapture is the perfecting of the Bride of Christ. If you are left behind it will be too late to belong to the Church.

Dr. Wim Malgo used this example: "This change, the sudden renewal, will take place as quickly as the response of an electric lightbulb to the operation of a switch that is turned on. Suddenly, it is light! Only a moment before, the bulb looked grey and dismal but because it is connected to the power supply and the switch is operated, it is instantly transformed. This can be seen every evening in towns and cities everywhere, as thousands upon thousands of little glass bulbs are transformed in an instant when the switch is operated. This is a wonderful illustration of the transformation of God's children when Jesus comes."

Everything you have done for Jesus up until that point will count for eternity. In the same way, everything you have neglected to do or postponed will be a loss for all eternity!

No Endtime Signs For The Rapture

No signs will precede the coming Rapture. How vain is the attempt of man to think that he can pick the mind of the Almighty God by using mathematical theories to calculate the day of the Lord's return? Many have been put to shame in the past and great damage has been done to the Church of Jesus Christ because some have tried to "figure out" the exact date of the Rapture.

Waiting For Him Alone

Virtually all Bible-believing Christians agree that the Word of God warns us to be ready at any time. That being the case, any statement regarding the timing of the Rapture is contrary to Scripture. If someone tells us that the Rapture will take place at the beginning, middle, or even after the Great Tribulation, then we logically wouldn't have to wait for the Lord today. If we are told to wait for something else to happen, such as the tribulation or the appearance of the Antichrist, our priority will shift: we do not need to wait for Jesus because something else is to take place first.

When we transfer this to the event of the Rapture, it becomes extremely dangerous because now we would have to change Titus 2:13 from, *"Looking for that blessed hope, and the glorious appearing of the great God and our Saviour Jesus Christ,"* to, "Looking for the coming of the Great Tribulation and the appearance of the Antichrist." If that were true, we would have to wait for the beginning of the tribulation, or as recently popularized, the beginning of the Pre-wrath period.

Such an idea is extremely dangerous and diametrically opposes the teaching of the Holy Scripture.

Someone may object to this and say, "Hasn't the Lord given us many signs that we should take notice of preceding His coming?" Yes, that is true. However, these signs were given for His physical coming to earth, or to be more precise, for Israel when He comes to the Mount of Olives. He was specifically addressing the people of Israel and gave them signs to notice. When He sent out His disciples, Jesus told them not to go to the Gentiles but only to the house of Israel because a promise was given to them that the kingdom of God would come on earth. In general, the signs of the Bible are given to the Jewish people, but the Jews themselves are a sign to us!

The fact that Israel became a nation in 1948, and is being established today as one of the power centers of the Middle East, indicates that the time is drawing near. We must heed the Lord's words more than ever, *"...when these things begin to come to pass, then look up, and lift up your heads; for your redemption draweth nigh"* (Luke 21:28).

CHAPTER 13

ISRAEL AND PEACE

W e have already dealt with the nation of Israel in relation to the Church, but it is equally important to briefly summarize Israel's modern history.

When the first Jewish pioneers returned to the land of Israel at the turn of the century, they were faced with insurmountable obstacles. The land was deserted and agriculturally unproductive. In spite of these severe odds, Israel was reborn as a nation in 1948. The Jews defended themselves successfully against the overwhelming Arab majority during military conflicts. Today, it is almost unthinkable for any Arab country to pick up arms and attempt to annihilate Israel. They have learned the hard way that Israel is a reality that is here to stay.

In the meantime, a new generation born in the land of Israel has grown up. This generation no longer has the determined pioneer spirit of the first immigrants who thought their calling was to reestablish the original biblical borders as identified by God to their forefathers. The new generation, which has also suffered, and is still paying a price for its freedom, sees the possibility of a peaceful coexistence with the Arabs as a priority.

Gentile Against Israel

One can easily sense how the devil so desperately tries to hinder the implementation of God's prophetic Word. From the beginning, in Egypt, he moved Pharaoh to kill all male babies. Why? To eliminate God's chosen people! But Pharaoh's demise occurred in the same way he had planned to destroy Israel; he drowned.

Later in history, Haman, another evil man, tried to wipe out the entire Jewish race. He was hung on the gallows that he had prepared for Mordechai, the Jew.

In recent history, Adolf Hitler, a diabolical man, came to rule the central European country of Germany and slaughtered over 6 million Jews. Why? Because without the Jews, there would be no Israel. If there was no Israel, the Messiah could not come back and, as a result, Satan could establish his own thousand-year kingdom of peace.

Hitler also died in fire, just as the Jews he murdered in Auschwitz, Dachau, Treblinka and the many other concentration camps he established. He, too, failed to annihilate the Jewish people.

Yasser Arafat and his cohorts have, for a long time bitterly fought the Jewish nation of Israel. However, for the first time, there seems to be a faint indication that negotiated peace may be realized after all. Yet this progress toward "peace" brings the Jews into the most dangerous period of their entire history. Their real enemies are no longer "Pharaohs," "Hamans," or "Hitlers," ...now their enemies are the nations of the world!

Presently, Israel's best political ally is the United States of

America, despite the fact that they are also pressuring Israel by using political and economic force to coerce her into surrendering areas of the Promised Land to Arab-Palestinian settlers.

The U.S.'s official policy is that Israel should maintain security control only over parts of Judea and Samaria. The U.S. says that Jerusalem should not be under Jewish sovereignty, but should be internationalized; part of it should become the capital of a Palestinian state based on the dictates of the Vatican.

If Israel's best friend begins to oppress her to such a degree, what will her enemies do?

In the end, there is good news; the Jews are coming back to the land of their fathers and are establishing an energetic, vibrant nation in the Middle East. Therefore, promises such as Zechariah 12:10 will be fulfilled, *"And I will pour upon the house of David, and upon the inhabitants of Jerusalem, the spirit of grace and of supplications: and they shall look upon me whom they have pierced, and they shall mourn for him, as one mourneth for his only son, and shall be in bitterness for him, as one that is in bitterness for his firstborn."* For the Jews to look upon Him whom they have pierced, it is absolutely necessary that the Jews are back in Israel, particularly Jerusalem.

Israel Or Palestine?

As this book was being written, a number of towns and cities in Judea and Samaria were handed over to Israel's former Arab enemies: the PLO. Negotiations with Syria over the surrender of the Golan Heights continues. The legitimization of the proposed Palestinian state was demonstrated through the PLO election in January 1996. It is important to understand that this is only the beginning. The Arabs won't be happy with a small area of land within the so- called former West Bank. In order to fulfill their dreams of a Palestinian state, Israel will have to surrender much more of the Promised Land territory. The previous argument that Israel must have the land for security is no longer seen as an absolute. With today's modern weapons, distance no longer plays a major role, which makes such arguments relatively insignificant. No one desires peace more than the Israelis and the negotiation process that is going on right now promises peace.

Jerusalem: The Stumbling Stone

The next great step is the city of Jerusalem, which Israel has sworn never to divide. However, the Arabs equally lay claim to Jerusalem. This monumental problem will not go away. Nevertheless, Israel continues to prosper and any peace will contribute more towards their prosperity. The process of negotiations will continue, and according to our understanding of the prophetic Word, Jerusalem will be included in the negotiations.

The European Union To The Rescue

A great entity arising today is the European Union, in which Israel desperately seeks membership. This political, economic, military, and religious union, an outgrowth of the Treaty of Rome signed in 1957 by Italy, France, Germany, Belgium, Luxembourg, and the Netherlands, promises unity and prosperity with peace. Only in Europe do we see the borders being erased and people living in peace and prosperity.

Land Without Borders

During my recent travel through Europe, I was astonished at the virtual non-existence of borders. Once in a while, travelers are questioned at a border crossing, but in general, traffic flows unhindered through previously secured national boundaries. It's rather amazing when we compare this with the border between the United States and Canada where vehicles are stopped and their drivers interrogated. The U.S. border to the south is also fortified in spite of NAFTA and other treaties in the works today.

On the other hand, Europe's borders have been dismantled because of prevailing peace. That is exactly what Israel needs. Therefore, any guarantee from the European Union that would lead to an eventual full membership for Israel in the E.U. would include a guarantee of peace. When this occurs, Israel will finally feel secure. Through the negotiation process, as we have already mentioned, Israel is being integrated into the nations of the world.

At this moment, the only remaining obstacle is the Church of Jesus Christ, which the Lord says is *"...the light of the world."* As long as the Church is present on earth, this sinister dark power that is working with lying signs and wonders, success, prosperity, and peace cannot fully take over.

The Day Of Christ

Although we have already dealt with 2nd Thessalonians 2, relating to the events of the *"day of Christ"* and our *"gathering unto Him,"* I sense an urgency in taking another look at these important passages, due to the fact that we are seeing the beginning of *"lying signs and wonders"* in our day.

The Church, evidence of God's truth, is still on earth; darkness cannot prevail because light is stronger than darkness. When the apostle Paul spoke about the revelation of the Antichrist in relation to the coming of the Lord at the Rapture, he said, *"Now we beseech you, brethren, by the coming of our Lord Jesus Christ, and by our gathering together unto him, That ye be not soon shaken in mind, or be troubled, neither by spirit, nor by word, nor by letter as from us, as that the day of Christ is at hand"* (2nd Thessalonians 2:1-2). Paul is making a distinction between two events: our gathering to Him via the Rapture and the return of the Lord, when His feet stand on the Mount of Olives.

Apparently during Paul's time, someone was teaching the Church that the *"day of Christ,"* or His coming to the Mount of Olives in Israel, was at hand. The apostle countered this rumor by telling the Church that the Rapture hadn't taken place yet, therefore, the *"day of Christ"* was even further away. He then revealed the conditions for the revelation of the man of sin, the son of perdition: the Antichrist.

The Bible does not leave us in the dark, but gives the reason why the *"day of Christ"* cannot take place. In 2nd Thessalonians 2:6-7 we read, *"And now ye know what withholdeth that he might be revealed in his time. For the mystery of iniquity doth already work: only he who now letteth will let, until he be taken out of the way."* Only after the light (the Church of Jesus Christ) is taken out of the way will iniquity have a free hand. Satan, is the god of this world and is also known as the prince of darkness. Only in darkness will he have free reign to do as he pleases. The light which remains in the form of the Church will have departed. That is the reason for the *"day of Christ;"* His coming to the Mount of Olives to rescue Israel and end the deceptive One-World government and the Antichrist. In order for Him to come for the *"day of Christ,"* His saints must be with Him, as the Bible says, *"...the Lord cometh with ten thousands of his saints"* (Jude 1:14).

The Great Deception

Paul describes the Antichrist's activity in very precise terms. He is the one who *"...opposeth and exalteth himself above all that is called God, or that is worshipped; so that he as God sitteth in the temple of God, shewing himself that he is God"* (2nd Thessalonians 2:4). This is the same person about which the Lord prophesied, *"...if another shall come in his own name, him ye will receive"* (John 5:43).

Today, we are witnessing a systematic integration of the nations of the world. Europe, as I have already mentioned, is becoming one. The United States and Canada, the North American powerhouse, is becoming less significant and will have to become more and more united with Europe. "Let's unite" is the desperate cry of those in South America. Looking to the Far East, we see that Asia is becoming a mighty economic bloc and Africa envisions its only future in unity.

More and more, Israel is being accepted, even by their most bitter of enemies, the Arabs. Peace is more probable than ever before.

Animal Sacrifice

After supporting the Jews in their effort to rebuild their temple, and allowing them to reinstitute animal sacrifice, presenting himself as the coming Messiah, Israel will be deceived by Antichrist. However, he will come under pressure from the world, specifically animal rights groups, to call for an end to animal sacrifices. As a result *"...he shall cause the sacrifice and the oblation to cease..."* (Daniel 9:27).

There is much justification for the protection of animals, so this animal rights movement will intensify as the days go by. On a daily basis, we hear news about animal rights groups and their aim. Just recently, a group was fighting for equal rights for animals. It was said that just as parents are duty-bound not to neglect their children, so animal owners are duty-bound to protect, nourish and look after the well-being of animals.

Often when we hear the word "Antichrist," we make the mistake of thinking that everything he does and stands for is against Christ. However, in actuality, the name "Antichrist" means that he is in place of Christ, an imitator of the real Christ. By his success, he will deceive the entire world into believing that he is the Christ.

In view of the ecumenical development in our days, we can well understand that Israel will stick out like a sore thumb when reinstituting animal sacrifices. Some may object that "the Antichrist is not going to listen to animal rights groups because he is the ultimate dictator." I beg to differ. The Antichrist will be elected democratically and will be a devout leader, greatly beloved and respected by the world's population. The Bible says, *"...all the world wondered after the beast"* (Revelation 13:3). The Amplified translation reads, *"...the whole earth went after the beast in amazement and admiration."* This does not indicate an expression of fear, but rejoicing, which is confirmed in verse 4, *"they* [the world] *worshipped the beast, saying, Who is like unto the beast? who is able to make war with him?"*

The notion that the Antichrist establishes his domain through brutal dictatorship is a great error. He will listen carefully to various groups of people just as politicians do today.

Of course, the Antichrist will be faced with opposition as well. However, based on the Holy Scriptures, he is the ultimate Gentile world ruler, *"...he shall confirm the covenant with many for one week: and in the midst of the week he shall cause the sac-*

rifice and the oblation to cease..." (Daniel 9:27).

Israel's Tribulation

Israel will be pressured in a manner she has never experienced before. Everything her people have worked for, hoped for, and prayed for is going to come to naught because of the overwhelming power of the Antichrist and his world government. For this reason, Jesus must come to put an end to the wicked one, *"...then shall that Wicked be revealed, whom the Lord shall consume with the spirit of his mouth, and shall destroy with the brightness of his coming"* (2nd Thessalonians 2:8).

Experience Placed Above Faith

We now come to a very important point in our study: the identification of the avenues Satan uses to deceive mankind. This deception is going on right now and is running rampant even in the professing Church of Jesus Christ. I have spoken to believers who have had such wonderful testimonies, but also believed that certain experiences they've had superceded their testimony. I have talked with these people about the Bible and showed them that their miraculous experiences were insignificant, maybe even questionable. Nevertheless, with sheer determination, they have stuck to their stories even if Scripture clearly did not confirm them. One person once said, "I cannot deny my experience." While he may not have denied his experience, he surely denied his faith.

The Bible teaches, *"While we look not at the things which are seen, but at the things which are not seen: for the things which are seen are temporal; but the things which are not seen are eternal"* (2nd Corinthians 4:18). Reliance on miracles and experiences is exactly what Satan wants. He is the great miracle worker, but the Bible exposes him and reveals, *"…the working of Satan with all power and signs and lying wonders"* (2nd Thessalonians 2:9). Having said this, examine yourself; where is your faith grounded? Is it grounded in miracles, healings, tongues, and physical experiences, or is it grounded in the invisible Lord who reveals Himself through His Word? Please do not take this lightly; it makes an eternal difference.

There will be a temple, a sacrifice, and an authority who will cause the sacrifices to cease. Not only does the world at large honor, praise, adore, and even worship the Antichrist, but he will become the epitome of pride, *"Yea, he magnified himself even to the prince of the host, and by him the daily sacrifice was taken away, and the place of his sanctuary was cast down"* (Daniel 8:11). During his self- exaltation, Israel will realize that this man is not the promised Messiah, but an imposter.

Church Differs From Israel

The great error that has crept into the Church is its failure to distinguish between Israel and the Church. Israel is God's people on earth, while the Church is God's heavenly people. At the moment of this writing, the Church is not complete, therefore it is unable to be in its final place; Heaven. We are not home yet, our job is not done, the Gospel still needs to go out into the outermost parts of the world. *"Go ye"* is still a valid command. At any moment the last of the Gentiles may be added and the Church of Jesus Christ will be complete. The fullness of the Gentiles will have come in and the Rapture will take place!

Satan's deception is camouflaging the differences between the Church and Israel. The entire Bible, including the New Testament, is a Jewish book. However, the whole Bible is profitable at all times for the Church, *"All scripture is given by inspiration of God, and is profitable for doctrine, for reproof, for correction, for instruction in righteousness"* (2nd Timothy 3:16).

We understand that the Old Testament was given specifically to the people of Israel so that they would learn to be obedient to the commandment of God and recognize the eternal One, the Creator of Heaven and earth. In the New Testament, we see the fulfillment of the Old Testament in detail, all taking place in the land of Israel among the Jews. Subsequently, the Lord plainly and emphatically stated, *"...salvation is of the Jews"* (John 4:22). The Gentiles were later added to the Church. Virtually all cults and false religions emphasize that Israel has lost their original calling and the Church has arisen to replace it.

The Church Has Not Replaced Israel

I have an old Bible in which each chapter is preceded by a couple of lines explaining the content. For example, Joel 3 begins with these words, "God's judgment against the enemies of his people and his blessing on the church." Yet this chapter describes a geographical area such as Judah and Jerusalem. Verse 2 speaks of *"all nations"* and mentions a geographical area again, *"the valley of Jehosaphat."* In addition, it specifically emphasizes that all the nations will be punished *"for my people and my heritage Israel."* At the end, we find the reason for such terrible judgment upon the nations when it says that the nations have *"parted my land."* It is extremely difficult for anyone to explain that *"parted my land"* refers to the land of the Christians. Christians may be owners of parcels of land but no provision is made in the Bible for a Christian nation to exist.

Any attempt to create such an identity is destined to fail because in reality it would be anti-Christian.

The conclusion of Joel 3 says, *"But Judah shall dwell for ever, and Jerusalem from generation to generation. For I will cleanse their blood that I have not cleansed: for the Lord dwelleth in Zion"* (Joel 3:20-21). Again, we see that Judah, Jerusalem and Zion are mentioned, not Christians. In spite of this, "Churchianity" claims that such promises are "his blessing on the Church."

When it comes to judgment, the caption of my old Bible proclaims "punishment of sinful Jewish people." The great deceiver has been successful in infiltrating the Church by twisting inerrant Scripture to the point of direct falsehood.

Israel; The Root Of The Church

We know from Romans 11:28 that the Jews are enemies of Christ, *"As concerning the gospel, they are enemies for your sakes: but as touching the election, they are beloved for the fathers' sakes."* That does not change the fact that they are God's chosen people for eternity. Everything we have comes from Israel. The apostle Paul emphasizes in Romans 11:13, *"For I speak to you Gentiles..."* and warns us, *"Boast not against the branches. But if thou boast, thou bearest not the root, but the root thee. Thou wilt say then, The branches were broken off, that I might be grafted in. Well; because of unbelief they were broken off, and thou standest by faith. Be not highminded, but fear: For if God spared not the natural branches, take heed lest he also spare not thee. For if thou wert cut out of the olive tree which is wild by nature, and wert grafted contrary to nature into a good olive tree: how much more shall these, which be the natural branches, be grafted into their own olive tree?"* (Romans 11:18-21,24).

Gentiles Accepted Into The Church

Despite the fact that in the beginning the Church was made up of Jews, James emphasized that the Gentiles have now become first in relation to the building of the Church. He confirmed this by quoting the prophetic Word.

We understand that the Church does not constitute the end of Israel, but represents an intermission in God's eternal plan of salvation to establish the kingdom of God on earth through His people.

What was the result of the apostle's analysis of the Gentiles? They received the instruction, *"Wherefore my sentence is, that we trouble not them, which from among the Gentiles are turned to God: But that we write unto them, that they abstain from pollutions of idols, and from fornication, and from things strangled, and from blood"* (Acts 15:19-20).

Therefore, it is futile to begin instructing the Church to observe certain days or abstain from certain food and drink because the Church has no such law.

Paul wrote to the Romans, *"One man esteemeth one day above another: another esteemeth every day alike. Let every man be fully persuaded in his own mind"* (Romans 14:5). He also stressed this point to the Colossians, *"Let no man therefore judge you in meat, or in drink, or in respect of an holyday, or of the new moon, or of the sabbath days"* (Colossians 2:16).

CHAPTER 14

PROPHETIC SHADOWS OF THE RAPTURE

The apostle Peter makes a profound statement in 1st Peter 2:5, *"Ye also, as lively stones, are built up a spiritual house, an holy priesthood, to offer up spiritual sacrifices, acceptable to God by Jesus Christ."* Peter is describing the believers as "lively stones:" stones used to build a spiritual house.

To build a house you need stones, bricks, blocks, lumber, steel, and concrete. The ultimate destiny of all these materials is to be used in putting the house together so that it can be occupied.

As the work progresses, the day comes when the last stone is placed into the walls of the house and it is finished. What happens then? The owner comes and occupies the house!

Solomon's Temple Made By Gentiles

We already have used Solomon's temple as the spiritual temple, but it seems necessary to take a second look at the building of the temple. Unlike the tabernacle in the wilderness that was built by the Israelites, the glorious temple that stood on Mt. Moriah in Jerusalem was prefabricated by Gentiles. We find the record of this project in 2nd Chronicles 2:17-18, *"...Solomon numbered all the strangers that were in the land of Israel, after the numbering wherewith David his father had numbered them; and they were found an hundred and fifty thousand and three thousand and six hundred. And he set threescore and ten thousand of them to be bearers of burdens, and fourscore thousand to be hewers in the mountain, and three thousand and six hundred overseers to set the people awork."* The miracle of this prefabricated temple never ceases to amaze me because it was a perfect masterpiece.

Today's modern machinery manufactures all kinds of goods for average people to put together. Most of us have bought furniture such as a shelf or a cabinet that needed to be assembled. Excitedly we brought it home, took it out of the box, unwrapped it, and looked at all the parts. After carefully reading the instructions, we assembled it. Yet, often we were disappointed because the parts did not fit together perfectly. We might have had to drill an extra hole or enlarge an existing one. If that has been your experience, you are not alone. This kind of thing happens every day.

During my time in the construction business, I saw many building components that had to be realigned. Sometimes concrete had to be broken up in order to allow certain pipes or cables to pass through; walls had to be removed because they were not in the right place, or prefabricated door frames did not fit.

Yet, when we read about the assembling of the temple in Jerusalem, we notice it was absolutely perfect, *"...the house, when it was in building, was built of stone made ready before it was brought thither: so that there was neither hammer nor axe nor any tool of iron heard in the house, while it was in building"* (1st Kings 6:7). For all practical purposes, we can say that the temple built of stone in Jerusalem was a technological miracle.

The Spiritual Temple Will Be Finished

After the temple was finished, it was dedicated. We read of this in the fifth and sixth chapters of 2nd Chronicles. Solomon prayed extensively and in very precise detail, then followed God's answer in chapter 7, *"Now when Solomon had made an end of praying, the fire came down from heaven, and consumed the burnt offering and the sacrifices; and the glory of the Lord filled the house. And the priests could not enter into the house of the LORD, because the glory of the LORD had filled the LORD's house. And when all the children of Israel saw how the fire came down, and the glory of the Lord upon the house, they bowed themselves with their faces to the ground upon the pavement, and worshipped, and praised the Lord, saying, For he is good; for his mercy endureth for ever"* (verses 1-3). God took possession of His house. Even the service of the priests became insignificant; the holiness of the Lord had filled the temple.

Church And World Look Alike

This is a wonderful picture of the Church of Jesus Christ. Right now, we are insignificant "stones" in our earthly tabernacle, yet nothing is apparent of the glory of God which already dwells within us.

In an airport, a shopping center, or a large city, thousands of people walk by, none of whom have any visible characteristics that would identify them as Christians. That is because we are still in our "old tabernacles" which have no promise. However, within these old tabernacles are the perfect "stones" that will fit perfectly into this new glorious spiritual temple, but will remain hidden from all natural eyes.

Silently, without any spectacles, and neither depending on nor disregarding the organizational structure of the local church, Christian ministries and denominations, the Lord is building His Church, adding to it daily such as should be saved. The moment the last "stone" is added to the temple, *"fire will come down from heaven,"* that is, Jesus will appear in the clouds of Heaven and our old, natural body will be consumed and translated in a split-second. In the twinkling of an eye, we will suddenly be transformed into the likeness of His glorious body. In that instant, we will recognize the perfect, glorious, spiritual habitation of God!

Prophetic Necessities Of The Rapture

While no signs are directly connected to the Rapture, we do know that the regathering of the nation of Israel is a visible sign that the time is close at hand. At this moment, Israel is still blind and remains an enemy of the Gospel for our sake. But we know that God will fulfill every promise He has given His people. In the near future, they will recognize Him whom they have pierced.

The fact that this time grows closer every day, and that at least seven years must lie between the Rapture of the Church and Israel's salvation, we realize that time is indeed running out. Are you ready?

Another Gospel=Another Church

The apostle Paul's great concern was the building of the body of Christ. Read his words, *"For I am jealous over you with godly jealousy: for I have espoused you to one husband, that I may present you as a chaste virgin to Christ"* (2nd Corinthians 11:2). Paul's concern was justified because many were preaching another Jesus. *"For if he that cometh preacheth another Jesus, whom we have not preached, or if ye receive another spirit, which ye have not received, or another gospel, which ye have not accepted"* (2nd Corinthians 11:4). False doctrine produces a false gospel, a false Jesus, false apostles, a false angel of light, and false ministers of unrighteousness. Let's read this important statement, *"For such are false apostles, deceitful workers, transforming themselves into the apostles of Christ. And no marvel; for Satan himself is transformed into an angel of light. Therefore it is no great thing if his ministers also be transformed as the ministers of righteousness; whose end shall be according to their works"* (verses 13-15).

This warning exposes the fact that Satan, with his cunning devices, is imitating the Church of Jesus Christ. What is his reason? So that people will not be able to distinguish between the counterfeit and the genuine! Jesus is building His Church based on election and segregation; only those who believe can become genuine members. The devil builds his global church through integration; all become one in his religion.

When Will The Church Be Complete?

The fact that the Lord used a building as an example of the Church helps us to understand that the work of laying the foundation was completed almost 2,000 years ago. The building has been under construction ever since, and it is my personal conviction that it is almost finished. I believe the roof is on the house, the painters are inside and the furniture is being delivered. Therefore, the attempt to raise a Church in the likeness of the original one in Jerusalem is not only destined to fail, but the great imitator is the major driving force behind such ideas. Satan is building another church, but it is a false one!

We have already seen how the Old Testament temple of Solomon was built; it was perfect. The Church of Jesus Christ is perfect. We must not permit ourselves to become ensnared by the imitation being offered today. In the same way that the presence of the glory of God filled the house, God intends His presence to fill His Church. That, however, cannot take place while we remain in our old nature of flesh and blood. Therefore, it is absolutely necessary that the Rapture take place, and at that time we shall receive our glorified bodies. The Church simultaneously constitutes the Bride of Christ and the perfect habitation of God in the Spirit.

Replacement Theology

It is significant that we repeat our admonition to make a distinction between the Church and Israel. In the April 1995 edition of *Pre-Trib Perspectives,* Thomas Ice quoted the following from Arnold Fruchtenbaum's, *Issues in Dispensationalism:*

Six reasons supporting the notion that the Church is a distinct work in God's household from His people Israel.

1) The first evidence is the fact that the Church was born at Pentecost, whereas Israel had existed for many centuries. This is supported by "the use of the future tense in Matthew 16:18 which shows

that it did not exist in gospel history." Since the Church born at Pentecost is called the "Body of Christ" (Colossians 1:18), and entrance into the body is through "Spirit baptism" (1st Corinthians 12:13), Jew and Gentile are united through the Church. It is evident that the Church began on the Day of Pentecost since Acts 1:5 views Spirit baptism as future, while Acts 10 links it to the past, specifically to Pentecost.

2) The second evidence is that certain events in the ministry of the Messiah were essential to the establishment of the Church—the Church does not come into being until certain events have taken place. These events include the resurrection and ascension of Jesus to become head of the Church (Ephesians 1:20-23). "The Church, with believers as the body and Christ as the head, did not exist until after Christ ascended to become its head. And it could not become a functioning entity until after the Holy Spirit provided the necessary spiritual gifts" (Ephesians 4:7-11).

3) The third evidence is the mystery character of the Church. A mystery in the Bible is a hidden truth not revealed until the New Testament (Ephesians 3:3-5, 9; Colossians 1:26-27). Fruchtenbaum lists "four defining characteristics of the Church [that] are described as a mystery.

(a) The body concept of Jewish and Gentile believers united into one body is designated as a mystery in Ephesians 3:1-12.

(b) The doctrine of Christ indwelling every believer, the Christ-in-you concept, is called a mystery in Colossians 1:24-27.

(c) The Church as the Bride of Christ is called a mystery in Ephesians 5:22-32.

(d) The Rapture is called a mystery in 1st Corinthians 15:50-58. These four mysteries describe qualities that distinguish the Church from Israel.

4) The fourth evidence that the Church is distinct from Israel is the unique relationship between Jews and the Gentiles, called one new man in Ephesians 2:15." During the current church age, God is saving a remnant from the two previous entities (Israel and Gentiles) and combining them into a third new object-the Church. This unity of Jews and Gentiles into one new man covers only the church age, from Pentecost until the Rapture, after which time God will restore Israel and complete

her destiny (Acts 15:14-18). 1st Corinthians 10:32 reflects just such a division when it says, "Give no offense either to Jews or to Greeks or to the Church of God."

5) The fifth evidence for the distinction between Israel and the Church is found in Galatians 6:16. It appears logical to view `the house of God' (Galatians 6:16) as believing Jews in contrast to unbelieving Jews called 'Israel after the flesh' (1st Corinthians 10:18). This passage does not support the false claim of replacement theologians who claim that Israel is supplanted by the Church. Instead, the Bible teaches that a remnant of Israel is combined with elect Gentiles during this age to make up a whole new entity the New Testament calls the Church (Ephesians 2).

Replacement theology tries to teach that because Gentile believers are described as the "seed of Abraham" (Galatians 3:29) that this is equivalent to saying that they are Israel. This is clearly not the case. Paul's description of Gentile believers in Galatians 3:29 simply means that they participate in the spiritual (salvation) blessings, i.e., that come through Israel (Romans 15:27; 1st Corinthians 9:11, 14). "Those who are the spiritual seed are partakers of Jewish spiritual blessings but are never said to become partakers of the physical, material, or national promises." Therefore, Israel's national promises are left intact awaiting a yet future fulfillment.

6) In the book of Acts, both Israel and the Church exist simultaneously. The term Israel is used twenty times and ekklesia (church) nineteen times, yet the two groups are always kept distinct."

Thus, the replacement theologian has no actual biblical basis for his claim that Israel and the Church have become one, or that the Church has replaced Israel as the fountain of God's blessing and the Jews are cursed forever for rejecting Christ.

The Significance Of The Distinction

If Israel and the Church are not distinguished between, then there is no basis for seeing a future for Israel or for the Church as a new and unique people of God. If Israel and the Church are merged into a single entity, the Old Testament promises for Israel will never be fulfilled. These promises are usually seen by replacement theologians as spiritually fulfilled by the Church. The merging of Israel's destiny into the Church's not only molds into one what the Scriptures understand as two, but it also removes the need for the future restoration of God's original elect in order to literally fulfill His promise that they will one day be the head and not the tail, *"...the Lord shall make thee the head, and not the tail; and thou shalt be above only, and thou shalt not be beneath; if that thou hearken unto the commandments of the Lord thy God, which I command thee this day, to observe and to do them"* (Deuteronomy 28:13).

The more the believer sees the distinct plan for Israel and the Church, the more he realizes the two separate callings.

A distinction between Israel and the Church, as taught in the Bible, provides a basis of support for the Pre-Trib Rapture. Those who merge these two entities, or replace Israel with the Church, cannot logically support the biblical arguments for the Pre-Trib position.

Before The Foundation Of The World

We do well to understand that the act expressed by our Lord Jesus Christ on Calvary's cross with the words, *"...It is finished"* was an accomplished fact from eternity and for all eternity. But it had to be fulfilled in *"...the fulness of time."* Jesus was before the foundation of the world because He is from eternity. In John 17:24, we read, *"...for thou lovedst me before the foundation of the world."* And Ephesians 1:4 makes this statement, *"...he hath chosen us in him before the foundation of the world...."* Peter confirms, *"Who verily was foreor-*

dained before the foundation of the world, but was manifest in these last times for you" (1st Peter 1:20).

Jesus came in the fullness of time and demonstrated His status as Messiah with great power, accompanied by signs and wonders. He defeated the devil on Calvary's cross, died, was buried, arose on the third day and ascended into Heaven. He was Raptured! With His Rapture, He became the firstfruit from among the dead.

Victory Over Death

While victory over death has already been accomplished, it is not a visible reality as far as the body is concerned.

Every day, countless believers in the Lord Jesus Christ die and are buried, fulfilling the Scripture, *"...absent from the body, and...present with the Lord"* (2nd Corinthians 5:8). However, the visible final victory over the last enemy, which is death, has not been fulfilled so the Rapture is absolutely necessary.

First Corinthians 15:25-26 reads, *"For he must reign, till he hath put all enemies under his feet. The last enemy that shall be destroyed is death."*

In order to solve this problem, the apostle Paul begins verse 51 with these words, *"Behold, I shew you a mystery; We shall not all sleep, but we shall all be changed, In a moment, in the twinkling of an eye, at the last trump: for the trumpet shall sound, and the dead shall be raised incorruptible, and we shall be changed. For this corruptible must put on incorruption, and this mortal must put on immortality"* (1st Corinthians 15:51-53). The mystery is beginning to be revealed to us; we shall be changed. Our mortal body will be translated into a glorious body of immortality.

Verse 54 explains why this is necessary, *"So when this corruptible shall have put on incorruption, and this mortal shall have put on immortality, then shall be brought to pass the saying that is written, Death is swallowed up in victory."* Only at the Rapture will death finally be defeated for the Church! Triumphantly, the next verse exclaims, *"O death, where is thy sting? O grave, where is thy victory?"* (verse 55).

In view of this wonderful prophetic fulfillment that is yet to come, the apostle Paul cautions believers, *"Therefore, my beloved brethren, be ye stedfast, unmoveable, always abounding in the work of the Lord, forasmuch as ye know that your labour is not in vain in the Lord"* (verse 58).

CHAPTER 15

THE BELIEVERS' LAST BATTLE

"The night is far spent, the day is at hand: let us therefore cast off the works of darkness, and let us put on the armour of light" (Romans 13:12).

"...It is appointed unto men once to die, but after this the judgment" (Hebrews 9:27).

These two verses summarize the last battle for the believer. You may be wondering why a battle would be necessary if the Lord has already won. I believe that the answer to that question is because light and darkness are mutually exclusive. Keep in mind that light is always stronger than darkness. It makes no difference how dark the darkness may be because when light appears darkness is instanteously defeated and all that the darkness attempted to hide is exposed. Only in the absence of light is darkness powerful. Since the Lord said, *"Ye are the light of the world,"* complete darkness cannot set in. Works of darkness are continuously exposed by our presence.

It is significant to remember that the light that exposes darkness is not accomplished by "flesh and blood." Don't ever be deceived by well-meaning Christians who play politics to expose the darkness that exists in our land and heal our society as a result. It will never happen. It is not promised in the Bible and those attempts are actually the work of the great enemy.

Some of you may be shocked to read such a statement but based on what the Bible teaches, I am convinced that it is true. The Lord Jesus told us that His kingdom was not of this world; otherwise, His disciples would fight. The Lord Jesus Himself was born and lived His entire life under foreign occupation but He never lifted a finger against the political and military authority of Rome. As a matter of fact, He even endorsed the payment of taxes to the foreign government with His statement, *"Render unto Caesar the things that are Caesars."*

When we follow the life of Paul and the lives of the other apostles we also see that they were not politically active in any way, but were consumed with the desire to preach the Gospel and follow Jesus even unto death.

Your motives may be noble in fighting against the various ills of our society. But if you do, please remember that the Bible holds no promises that you will succeed. How then do we fight against the powers of darkness? Simply by being and acting like Christians, letting the fruit of the Spirit show through our lives. That light is much stronger than any political power in the world. Fighting against such practices as abortion, homosexuality, atheism and drug abuse will not produce fruit for His glory but will entangle us in the affairs of the world. As a result, our strength will be wasted upon the things of this world.

For the work of darkness—including the deception of the world—to reach fruition, the light must be removed from planet Earth. Until that happens, we are light-bearers although we remain in our sinful flesh and blood.

The fact that the apostle cautioned us to *"cast off the works of darkness"* clearly indicates that by nature, Christians are in danger of participating in the work of darkness.

It also reveals that when we are born again of the Spirit of God, we are not automatically separated from darkness while we are in our flesh.

Paul also spoke of the sin which so easily besets us. In other words, Christians are capable of committing the same sins as the children of the world.

We are redeemed from the power and guilt of sin; however, we are not redeemed from the presence of sin. Subsequently, our last battle is based on our continuous stand in direct opposition to temptation and sin.

Our stand in faith will determine our position regarding the rewards that will be given to those who have faithfully held on to their Lord. We are strongly warned and reminded of this in 2nd John 1:8, *"Look to yourselves, that we lose not those things which we have wrought, but that we receive a full reward."*

We can outline this chapter in five points:

1) When light became darkness
2) The battle between light and darkness
3) The battle between spirit, soul and body

4) The battle against deception

5) The battle of silence

1) When Light Became Darkness

Isaiah supplies us with a view of prophecy that looked back in time. He showed us the history of darkness in chapter 14:12-14, *"How art thou fallen from heaven, O Lucifer, son of the morning! how art thou cut down to the ground, which didst weaken the nations! For thou hast said in thine heart, I will ascend into heaven, I will exalt my throne above the stars of God: I will sit also upon the mount of the congregation, in the sides of the north: I will ascend above the heights of the clouds; I will be like the most High."* These verses describe the birth of darkness.

Lucifer, the "son of the morning," was indeed an excellent personality in the presence of God. Only the King James translation adds the word *"Lucifer"* so as not to confuse him with the only bright and morning star. The Hebrew-English translation reads, *"How art thou fallen from heaven, O shining one, son of dawn!..."* Luther translates this verse, *"How has thou fallen from heaven, thou beautiful star of the morning...."* This is a vivid description of the birth of sin. Of course it is incomprehensible to us because our limited human intellect cannot grasp the terrible catastrophe that took place at that time.

This "morning star," so full of light, so boundlessly beautiful and glorious, conceived in his heart the desire to be equal with the Most High. His self-exaltation and pride is clearly expressed in the five-fold "I will" of the fallen star cited in the Isaiah passage. Deception was born in his heart and caused his downfall. As a result, light became darkness.

Fall Of Angels

The calamity of his sin was not limited to the "star of the morning" because the Bible reports that one-third of the angelic host fell into the deception of Satan as well. Jude wrote about these angels in verse 6, *"...the angels which kept not their first estate, but left their own habitation, he hath reserved in everlasting chains under darkness unto the judgment of the great day."*

Revelation 12:4 confirms that one-third of the angelic inhabitants of Heaven were cast to the earth: *"...his tail drew the third part of the stars of heaven, and did cast them to the earth: and the dragon stood before the woman which was ready to be delivered, for to devour her child as soon as it was born."* The fallen angels became the devil's helpers.

Lucifer, the leader of this rebellious host, is described in Revelation 12:9 with the following titles:

1) the great dragon
2) that old serpent
3) the devil
4) Satan

"...the great dragon was cast out, that old serpent, called the Devil, and Satan, which deceiveth the whole world: he was cast out into the earth, and his angels were cast out with him."

Demon Possession

Matthew 8:28-29 reports a whole legion of demons possessing two men, *"...when he was come to the other side into the country of the Gergesenes, there met him two possessed with devils, coming out of the tombs, exceeding fierce, so that no man might pass by that way. And, behold, they cried out, saying, What have we to do with thee, Jesus, thou Son of God? art thou come hither to torment us before the time?"*

The translation of "devils" is incorrect because there is only one devil according to Revelation 12. The correct word would be "demons."

In Luke's account of a demon-possessed man, we read *"...art thou come hither to torment us before the time?"* Thus the demons knew that Jesus' coming would cause them to be cast *"into the deep."* However, they also knew that it should not happen during Jesus' first coming on earth, thus, their protesting question, *"art thou come...before the time?"* When Jesus asked the demon, *"What is thy name?"* he replied, *"'Legion' because many devils were entered into him."*

The word "legion" in the Roman army meant a force numbering anywhere between three and six thousand men. This one man was possessed by between three and six thousand demons. Can you imagine the number of demons which are now at work in the children of darkness? How encouraging for those who know the Bible and the Lord to know that He has defeated all the powers of darkness for all eternity!

Fall Of Animals

The fall of the "morning star" also led to the fall of the serpent; an animal. In the first pages of our Bible we read of the prince of darkness hard at work. He had already deceived one-third of the angelic host; the next step was the newly-created animal world, *"Now the serpent was more subtil than any beast of the field which the Lord God had made. And he said unto the woman, Yea, hath God said, Ye shall not eat of every tree of the garden?"* (Genesis 3:1).

We may think that this serpent was the devil himself, which seems to be reinforced by Revelation 12:9 where it says "that old serpent." However, in that chapter we receive additional information which clearly identifies that it is the devil who is spoken of. He has a four-fold title: the great dragon; the old serpent; the devil and Satan. The serpent introduced in Genesis 3 cannot be the devil because he is clearly identified as one of the *"beast of the field which the Lord hath made."* This "serpent" is part of God's created animal world and has no direct relation to the fallen "morning star." No evidence in Scripture indicates that Satan was in the Garden of Eden in the form of a serpent because in Genesis 1:31 God called His creation *"very good."* This "Genesis serpent" became partner with the "old serpent" called the devil.

Therefore, I am forced to believe that this serpent was one of the many animals God had created. Notice that *"the serpent was more subtile."* Another translation says, *"smarter than the others"* and the new JPS Hebrew-English translation says *"the shrewdest of all thy beast."* Based on the interpretation of these verses, the serpent must have been deceived by the devil.

Furthermore, when Adam fell into sin, the Lord pronounced judgment against the serpent, *"...the LORD God said unto the serpent, Because thou hast done this, thou art cursed above all cattle, and above every beast of the field; upon thy belly shalt thou go, and dust shalt thou eat all the days of thy life"* (Genesis 3:14). This verse makes it unmistakably clear that the serpent was not the devil because this serpent was condemned to slither on its belly and eat dust all the days of its life. This reveals that prior to the Lord's judgment, the serpent must have had legs to walk on. God said, *"...thou art cursed above all cattle, and above every beast of the field....*" So the serpent is part of God's animal kingdom; not Satan himself.

Curse Not Completely Fulfilled

It is significant to point out that the latter part of the curse, "*...dust shalt thou eat...*" has not been fulfilled yet.

In our part of the world, we have a number of serpents, including rattlesnakes, cottonmouths, copperheads, and water mocassins. They eat all kinds of animals such as rabbits, mice, rats, even fish and frogs; they don't eat dust.

However, when Jesus comes back and establishes the thousand-year kingdom of peace on earth, the animal world will be redeemed from bondage, as we read in Isaiah 65:25, "*The wolf and the lamb shall feed together, and the lion shall eat straw like the bullock: and dust shall be the serpent's meat. They shall not hurt nor destroy in all my holy mountain, saith the Lord.*" Interestingly, the serpent will eat dust at that time.

The Fall Of Man

The process of deception continued when the serpent asked Eve a simple but cunning question, "*...hath God said, Ye shall not eat of every tree of the garden?*" You can almost sense this to be a trick question. The serpent was obviously aware of the commandment that God had given, so he began with a question that he knew would lead into a religious discussion.

Eve immediately corrected him and said, "*... We may eat of the fruit of the trees of the garden: But of the fruit of the tree which is in the midst of the garden, God hath said, Ye shall not eat of it, neither shall ye touch it, lest ye die*" (Verses 2-3). The ecumenical discussion was now in full swing!

Based on the previous verse, notice that the woman, already trapped in the first step of temptation, added something to God's commandment, *"...neither shall ye touch it."* Seeing his golden opportunity, the serpent, inspired by Satan, realized that Eve was ready for a full-fledged deception.

The First Lie

How did Satan answer? *"...your eyes shall be opened, and ye shall be as gods, knowing good and evil"* (verse 5). Satan offered Eve an elevated position: to be *"as god."* This is exactly what the devil had originally intended for himself; he wanted to be like the Most High.

The serpent, the devil's co-worker, very cunningly wrapped the truth in lies when he said, *"... Ye shall not surely die: For God doth know that in the day ye eat thereof, then your eyes shall be opened, and ye shall be as gods, knowing good and evil"* (Genesis 3:4-5). Quite obviously the first part of the statement was a lie, *"ye shall not surely die."* However, the second part is true, as confirmed in verse 22, *"...the Lord God said, Behold, the man is become as one of us, to know good and evil."* The serpent did not explain what he meant by *"ye shall not surely die"* but continued describing the benefits, completely failing to mention that the consequences would indeed be death.

It is not surprising to see that the gospel of Satan camouflaged with the Gospel of salvation is being mightily proclaimed in these end stages of the endtimes. Sinners are no longer called sinners. We are encouraged to love ourselves and continuously build our self-esteem, otherwise we will not be living up to "who we really are in Christ." This false gospel is

318

very destructive and has found its way into many Bible-believing churches in our day.

The Fallen Anointed Cherub

Ezekiel also gave us a look back into the fall of the anointed cherub in chapter 28:11-15, *"Moreover the word of the Lord came unto me, saying, Son of man, take up a lamentation upon the king of Tyrus, and say unto him, Thus saith the Lord God; Thou sealest up the sum, full of wisdom, and perfect in beauty. Thou hast been in Eden the garden of God; every precious stone was thy covering, the sardius, topaz, and the diamond, the beryl, the onyx, and the jasper, the sapphire, the emerald, and the carbuncle, and gold: the workmanship of thy tabrets and of thy pipes was prepared in thee in the day that thou wast created. Thou art the anointed cherub that covereth; and I have set thee so: thou wast upon the holy mountain of God; thou hast walked up and down in the midst of the stones of fire. Thou wast perfect in thy ways from the day that thou wast created, till iniquity was found in thee."*

While this prophecy directly addresses the king of Tyrus, it speaks of the fall of the "morning star." How do we know? Because the king of Tyrus was never *"perfect in beauty,"* nor was he *"in Eden the garden of God."* He was never *"the anointed cherub,"* nor did his feet ever touch *"the holy mountain of God;"* and surely the king of Tyrus was never *"perfect in* [his] *thy ways."* This speaks of the fall of Lucifer - when light became darkness!

Through the evil of King Tyrus, the prophet saw the originator of sin and described the fall of the anointed cherub, the one that lifted himself up in pride against the Living God,

"Thine heart was lifted up because of thy beauty, thou hast corrupted thy wisdom by reason of thy brightness: I will cast thee to the ground, I will lay thee before kings, that they may behold thee" (Ezekiel 28:17).

2) The Battle Between Light And Darkness

As we previously mentioned, light is stronger than darkness. As a child of God, you have received the Light of the world, the Lord Jesus Christ. The powers of darkness are nullified when you stay in the territory of the light. Then, you can exclaim with the Lord, *"The evil cometh and findeth nothing on me."*

To illustrate how light is stronger than darkness, do the following: go into the basement of your house or some other dark place at night when there is no light. When you find yourself in such a place, you literally cannot see your hand in front of your eyes. Everything is pitch black and you do not know what is waiting for you in the darkness.

If you don't move carefully, you may hurt yourself, falling over an object or bumping into a dangerous instrument. For all practical purposes, you are completely paralyzed by the darkness. Any move you make can be dangerous, even fatal.

But then at the very second you turn on the flashlight, darkness is defeated and you can clearly recognize the objects which could have done you harm in the darkness.

The Counterfeit Light

The same can be said about the unsaved who remain in darkness, not knowing where they are going. They live on a day-to-day basis, approaching eternal darkness where no salvation is possible.

Anyone with a little common sense knows that you don't walk around in a dark place where you cannot see. We may wonder why people walk in darkness.

The answer is simple, yet sad; they are following in the footsteps of a counterfeit light. Second Corinthians 11:14 warns, *"...no marvel; for Satan himself is transformed into an angel of light."*

How can a person see the light? Jesus answers that question in John 3:3 when He speaks to Nicodemus the Pharisee, *"...Verily, verily, I say unto thee, Except a man be born again, he cannot see the kingdom of God."* Therefore, the moment a person is born again of the Spirit of God, not only does he see his surroundings, but he sees eternity, *"the kingdom of God."* By faith he sees those wonderful things which are hidden from the eyes of the children of the world.

The believer does not aimlessly wander in this world, but has the light and walks with determination toward eternity.

This can be compared to a ship on the sea, looking for the beacon of the lighthouse. Picture the Lord, the Light of the world who beckons all who are lost in the darkness of sin to come to Him. The lighthouse operator rejoices when on the horizon he sees a little flicker of light from a ship in the far distance being tossed to and fro by the waves. The moment this contact is established, the lighthouse is able to safely guide the ship back to the harbor. The captain of the ship understands the signs aimed at him from the lighthouse, he follows the instructions and ultimately reaches safety. Our lives can be compared to this illustration. We are in the ocean of darkness with no hope, lost for all eternity. Suddenly, in the far distance we see the blinking Light from our heavenly Lighthouse. The moment we cry out for help, Jesus gives us His Light. From that point on, we can communicate with Him directly because our light is now turned toward our heavenly Lighthouse, the Lord Jesus.

Dear reader, if you have not yet received the Lord Jesus, do not delay any longer because it may be your last chance to be saved for all eternity. The alternative is eternal darkness, separation from God, being lost forever.

The wonderful truth is that the Christian walks toward eternity with full assurance that the way has been prepared, the price has been paid, and the guarantee, *"I will never leave you nor forsake you,"* is always valid.

The Sure Word Of Prophecy

A born again Christian does not walk in darkness but uses the sure word of prophecy as his guideline. *"We have also a more sure word of prophecy; whereunto ye do well that ye take heed, as unto a light that shineth in a dark place, until the day dawn, and the day star arise in your hearts"* (2nd Peter 1:19).

The great apostle Peter penned these words under the inspiration of the Holy Spirit at a time when he was aware that his life was soon to come to an end. He testified in verse 14, *"Knowing that shortly I must put off this my tabernacle, even as our Lord Jesus Christ hath shewed me."* It is significant that this apostle emphasized the fact that he had diligently proclaimed the imminency of the Rapture, *"...the power and coming of our Lord Jesus Christ..."* (verse 16). As a result, Peter boldly proclaimed the prophetic Word, the coming of Jesus.

Many Christians fail to realize that the Word of prophecy

climaxes in the return of Jesus and is part of the liberating Gospel we are to preach to all people everywhere.

You can sense the urgency with which Peter entrusted the prophetic Word to the Church. Not only do we have a *"more sure word of prophecy,"* but we are also cautioned to *"take heed"* of it. We are to watch out, to be alert, and to be fully conscious of the events that are taking place in our time which point to the coming of the Lord.

It struck me when I realized that Peter wrote, *"...as unto a light that shineth in a dark place."* Surely it doesn't take much energy to recognize a light in a dark place, because the light, no matter how faint, is easily detected. The light itself does not need to exclaim, "Here, look, this is light!" Light is so powerful that it actually cancels out darkness.

Light Exposes Darkness

This light that the apostle speaks of is the light that gives us perfect and secure guidance amidst the commotion and darkness in this world. When we read the news, listen to the radio or watch television, we are plagued with so many negative things; terrible catastrophes, wars and rumors of wars, misery and tragedy. We are being offered all types of remedies - of which none usually work - except for the Light of the world! But in the midst of the surrounding darkness in our society, we have the sure word of prophecy - the Light that guides us through the darkness.

We must remember that darkness is not going to be obliterated and will be even more powerful as the endtime progresses until there is so much darkness that even children of God are in danger of losing sight of the light.

It is quite obvious that Peter was not only speaking about the coming of the Lord, but was particularly interested in showing us that the day must also dawn in our hearts. How are our hearts enlightened? When "the day star" has taken full possession of our earthly tabernacle and we have totally surrendered to His will and do His bidding!

The Prophetic Light

The light of the prophetic Word is not to be compared to any other light such as daylight. There is no difference between the saved and the lost, the good and the evil, because our daylight is an all-penetrating force that gives light to all men. The light we are speaking of is the Light in the person of the Lord Jesus Christ.

John spoke about this when he began his Gospel account and said, *"In him was life; and the life was the light of men. And the light shineth in darkness; and the darkness comprehended it not"* (John 1:4-5).

This Light shines in the darkness, but as we have just read, the general population does not recognize it. Why is that the case? Isn't this Light available everywhere? The answer is yes, even more than our daylight, which is only poured out on half of the globe at one time.

In verse 9 John makes this very clear that the Light is there for all men, *"That was the true Light, which lighteth every man that cometh into the world."* Every single human being will be confronted with the Light of the world, for it *"lighteth every man that cometh into the world."* But the great tragedy is that *"...the darkness comprehended it not"* (John 1:5).

The Coming Light

Isaiah saw the coming of this Light approximately 750 years before the birth of Christ. He wrote, *"The people that walked in darkness have seen a great light: they that dwell in the land of the shadow of death, upon them hath the light shined"* (Isaiah 9:2).

The New Testament speaks of the fulfillment of this prophecy, *"That it might be fulfilled which was spoken by Esaias the prophet, saying, The land of Zabulon, and the land of Nephthalim, by the way of the sea, beyond Jordan, Galilee of the Gentiles; The people which sat in darkness saw great light; and to them which sat in the region and shadow of death light is sprung up"* (Matthew 4:14-16).

It is important at this point to emphasize the Gentiles' integration and participation in the promised Light. Paul reports the following to us in Romans 15:9-13, *"...that the Gentiles might glorify God for his mercy; as it is written, For this cause I will confess to thee among the Gentiles, and sing unto thy name. And again he saith, Rejoice, ye Gentiles, with his people. And again, Praise the Lord, all ye Gentiles; and laud him, all ye people. And again, Esaias saith, There shall be a root of Jesse, and he that shall rise to reign over the Gentiles; in him shall the Gentiles trust. Now the God of hope fill you with all joy and peace in believing, that ye may abound in hope, through the power of the Holy Ghost."*

You Need Light

Is it dark in your life? Are you bothered by your surroundings? Is your day-to-day life dictated by circumstances which apparently are beyond your control? Then you are not permitting the Word of prophecy to be the light of your life. In other words, you are not really waiting for the coming of our Lord Jesus.

The apostle Paul recognized the danger of not waiting for Jesus and wrote to the Corinthians, *"So that ye come behind in no gift; waiting for the coming of our Lord Jesus Christ"* (1st Corinthians 1:7).

This gift of waiting for His return is something so precious I have no adequate words to describe it. When we wait for Him, everything else that oppresses and burdens us seems to fade away. Therefore, today, begin to seek the better way, the prophetic Word, the Word Himself, the Lord Jesus Christ, so that He can fill your life with the unspeakable and joyful desire of waiting for Him.

3) The Battle Between Body, Soul, And Spirit

We all know of the endtime events which are taking place today such as wars and rumors of wars, pestilence, earthquakes, famine, even signs in the sun, moon and stars, causing great commotion and perplexity on the earth. All we need to do is read the newspaper, listen to the radio or watch the news on TV.

We are continuously overwhelmed by the many catastrophes that are taking place today, whether they are natural, such as tornadoes, floods, and droughts, or caused by the negligence of men such as traffic fatalities, airplane crashes, or fires.

We may consider them as commonplace throughout the ages. Such are not directly related to the personal battles we are involved in daily. Let me make it clear, we are not speaking about everybody else, just you and me.

Flesh Must Be Defeated

The apostle Paul confessed in Romans 7:15, *"For that which I do I allow not: for what I would, that do I not; but what I hate, that do I."* This clearly reveals the battle between body, soul and spirit. In verse 18 he said, *"For I know that in me (that is, in my flesh,) dwelleth no good thing: for to will is present with me; but how to perform that which is good I find not."* This statement exposes the truth about Paul, who did not think much about himself, but nevertheless was confronted with his own sinful nature.

He was fully conscious of the fact that the regenerated person within him was what really mattered. Paul continued, *"For the good that I would I do not: but the evil which I would not, that I do. Now if I do that I would not, it is no more I that do it, but sin that dwelleth in me"* (verses 19-20). He realized that the flesh can never fully submit to the Spirit, and as a result, he exclaimed, *"O wretched man that I am! who shall deliver me from the body of this death?"* (verse 24).

This verse makes it perfectly clear that we cannot serve God with our flesh. In other words, no matter how hard we try to please God, we will ultimately fail. Naturally the question should arise, "How can we serve God if it is impossible for us to please Him in our physical being?" We please God by serving Him in Spirit and in truth!

Worship In Spirit and Truth

When Jesus spoke to the Samaritan woman at the well, He told her, *"But the hour cometh, and now is, when the true worshippers shall worship the Father in spirit and in truth: for the Father seeketh such to worship him"* (John 4:23). This was in response to the woman's attempt to lead Jesus into an ecumenical discussion. But the Lord responded to her with the truth of the prophetic Word, and as a result, she had to confess, *"...I perceive that thou art a prophet"* (verse 19).

In an attempt to justify her comments, she said, *"Our fathers worshipped in this mountain; and ye say, that in Jerusalem is the place where men ought to worship"* (verse 20). Jesus made it very clear that worship of God the Father outside of the truth was impossible.

He made it obvious that the Gentiles were in total darkness when He said, *"Ye worship ye know not what..."* (verse 22) and then emphasized that true worship can only come forth from the truth, *"...we know what we worship: for salvation is of the Jews"* (verse 22).

The Two-Edged Sword

Furthermore, Hebrews 4:12 reveals the way to liberty in Christ through the Word, *"For the word of God is quick, and powerful, and sharper than any two-edged sword, piercing even to the dividing asunder of soul and spirit, and of the joints and marrow, and is a discerner of the thoughts and intents of the heart."* Do you want to serve God? Then the Word of God, the most powerful and sharpest of all two-edged swords, must divide your soul and spirit.

We cannot worship God in the soul; the Word of God forbids it. Not only does the two-edged sword clearly divide the soul from the spirit but it is also the *"discerner of the thoughts and intents of the heart."* Only the Word of God will disclose to us what our thinking process is and will even expose the true intention of our hearts.

For that reason, it is urgent that we unconditionally agree with the Word of God. The moment we deviate from the written Word, we fall among the *"robbers."* The end result is that no fruit will be created for the glory of the Lord Jesus.

Soulish Believers

The statement in Hebrews 4:12 also reveals the tragedy of the endtimes that millions of believers serve the Lord in their souls, not in their spirits.

A person who bases his faith on the soul always depends on tangible circumstances. He is unsure and unstable in all of his ways and continuously needs supernatural guidance, which of course, is supplied by the powers of darkness. In addition, it nullifies the fundamental principle of the gospel of grace; we are to walk by faith, not by sight!

An even greater tragedy is the fact that many consider themselves Christians because they have had emotional experiences in their souls. In reality, their spirits are still dead in sins and trespasses. What a disaster it will be for those when Jesus comes and all who are not born again of the Spirit of God are left behind, despite the fact that they thought they had become new creatures in Christ.

Seven Signs

Certain visible signs take place in the believer's life which confirm and make obvious whether a person has in fact been born again of the Spirit of God. In his book, *Seven Signs of a Born Again Person,* Dr. Wim Malgo points out the following:

• A born again person knows that he is born again.

- The new life becomes visible.
- He has a spirit of prayer.
- He has a hunger for the Word of God.
- He will suffer much adversity.
- He has victory over temptations and sin.
- The truly born again person waits with joy and expectancy for the return of the Lord Jesus.

If any of these signs are not a reality in your own life, then you must ask yourself a very serious question, "Am I really born again?"

The Lust Of The Flesh

The believer's last battle consists of the continuous conflict between the Spirit and the flesh. To the Galatians, the apostle Paul wrote, *"For the flesh lusteth against the Spirit, and the Spirit against the flesh: and these are contrary the one to the other: so that ye cannot do the things that ye would"* (Galatians 5:17). In other words, we must have continuous victory over the works of the flesh through the Spirit. We are guaranteed of this in verse 16, *"... Walk in the Spirit, and ye shall not fulfil the lust of the flesh."*

What is the lust of the flesh? We already learned in chapter nine that Paul lists 18 characteristics which signify the result of the works of the flesh. Remember that the number eighteen is made up of three sets of sixes, which reveal the work of the spirit of Antichrist.

Fruit Of The Spirit

Contrasting the works of the flesh, we read about the fruit

of the Spirit in the next verses, *"But the fruit of the Spirit is love, joy, peace, longsuffering, gentleness, goodness, faith, Meekness, temperance: against such there is no law"* (verses 22-23).

Isn't it significant that in the list of the fruits of the Spirit, there is no indication of the presence of pride, self-love, self-esteem, and other fallacious ideas that are being promoted in today's false gospel movements?

Remember that only by the fruit of the Spirit will the Lord recognize us. It doesn't matter how good we are, or what we have accomplished in our lives, or how much we have given to our churches, missions, or other benevolent organizations. Those things are good, but they will not count when we stand before the Lord. He said, *"...by their fruits ye shall know them"* (Matthew 7:20).

To successfully win the victory over our last battle, we must continue to keep the victory over our flesh at all times. When we walk in the Spirit, we are standing on the Word of God doing His will. As a result, we will not fulfill the lust of the flesh.

Let us conform ourselves to 1st Thessalonians 5:23, *"And the very God of peace sanctify you wholly; and I pray God your whole spirit and soul and body be preserved blameless unto the coming of our Lord Jesus Christ."*

4) The Battle Against Deception

We know from the Bible that sin entered into the world due to pride. Satan, the originator of sin, successfully deceived one-third of the angelic host, the animal world, and man, God's crown created in His image.

The devil is the god of this world and rules supreme. He

has a legitimate right to all the unsaved people on the earth.

The Bible says that all have sinned and fall short of the glory of God. Isaiah 64:6 confirms this indisputable fact with the words, *"But we are all as an unclean thing, and all our right-eousnesses are as filthy rags; and we all do fade as a leaf; and our iniquities, like the wind, have taken us away."*

To further prove this point and show that there are no exceptions to the rule, we read Romans 3:10, *"...There is none righteous, no, not one."* Verse 12 confirms, *"They are all gone out of the way, they are together become unprofitable; there is none that doeth good, no, not one."*

One Escape

Praise God that He has made a way of escape. Only one Man has ever lived who was without sin; Jesus Christ, fully God and fully man who voluntarily sacrificed Himself on Calvary's cross. He poured out His blood for the sin of all men so that anyone who comes to Him will receive forgiveness.

The only way of escape is through Him who said, *"...I am the way, the truth, and the life: no man cometh unto the Father, but by me"* (John 14:6). There is no middle ground, for there is no other name given under Heaven by which man can be saved, and that name is Jesus.

5) The Battle Of Silence

We have explored four important battles thus far and have now come to the final, most difficult one: the battle of silence. This battle is contrary to all that we are and diametrically opposes our sense of righteousness, our desire to justify ourselves, and our inexhaustible need to prove that we are "somebody. "

We begin this subject by reading from the prophet Isaiah in chapter 53:7, *"He was oppressed, and he was afflicted, yet he opened not his mouth: he is brought as a lamb to the slaughter, and as a sheep before her shearers is dumb, so he openeth not his mouth."* This is one of the most shocking verses in the entire Bible. Twice we read that, *"he opened not his mouth"* Jesus suffered in silence!

Incidentally, Isaiah 53 is also the most difficult chapter in the Old Testament for a Jewish person who does not believe that Jesus is the Messiah. Isaiah 53 is a clear documentation inspired by the Holy Spirit over 700 years before the birth of Christ. Jewish rabbis often refuse to read this chapter in the synagogue because it reads like a script straight out of the New Testament trial, condemnation and crucifixion of Jesus.

The Silent Lamb

Who was this Lamb led to the slaughter who did not open His mouth? Why was He seemingly powerless before His executioners? Verse 8 answers this question beautifully, *"...for the transgression of my people was he stricken."* It makes no difference if you are the most learned Bible scholar, or whether you are a Christian or Jew; no one can come up with any identity other than Jesus Christ.

Some people have said that this chapter is talking about the suffering of the Jewish people throughout the centuries; however, verse 5 contradicts this theory when it says, *"...the chastisement of our peace was upon him; and with his stripes we are healed."* What about verse 6? *"...the Lord hath laid on him the iniquity of us all."* Or verse 8? *"...for the transgression of my people was he stricken."* We are clearly reading about a person, not a group of people. Verse 9 unmistakably identifies this person as the Lord Jesus Christ, *"…neither was any deceit in his mouth."*

The apostle Peter later testified, *"Who did no sin, neither was guile found in his mouth"* (1st Peter 2:22). In a very precise manner, Isaiah 53 describes the work, the life, and the death of the Lamb of God who was sacrificed for the sins of the world.

His Grave Was Not His Own

We read of the proclamation in verse 9 that, *"…he made his grave with the wicked."* The New Testament confirms that He was crucified between two criminals. His body was laid in the borrowed tomb of a rich man, Joseph from Arimathea, which corresponds with Isaiah's account, *"…with the rich in his death."*

Without Sin

The verse concludes, *"…neither was any deceit in his mouth."* While confronting His enemies, Jesus challenged them to find any sin in His life. He never spoke too much, or too little. He said what had to be said, and did what had to be done. He was the perfect Man, who became the perfect sacrifice for an imperfect, corrupt, and lost humanity.

Silence Before His Accusers

Christ stood wrongly accused by wicked men and false witnesses. However the Bible says, *"…Jesus held his peace"* (Matthew 26:63). He stood before Pilate, the Roman authority who challenged him, "*...Answerest thou nothing?*" and "*...Jesus yet answered nothing...*" (Mark 15:2,5).

In Luke 23, we read that King Herod "*questioned with him in many words.*" How did Jesus react? "*...He answered him nothing*" (verse 9).

Indeed, He was led silently like a lamb to the slaughter.

Intercession For Sinners

When they crucified Him, Jesus cried, "*...Father, forgive them; for they know not what they do...*" (Luke 23:34).

Seven centuries before that prayer, Isaiah gave the following details, "*...he was numbered with the transgressors; and he bare the sin of many, and made intercession for the transgressors*" (Isaiah 53:12).

Greatest Of All Works

We are all familiar with the wonderful works that Jesus did among His people and the miracles He openly demonstrated confirming Himself to be the Messiah of Israel and Savior of the world. The greatest of all works was when the Son of God remained silent, when through the hands of wicked man, He was nailed Him to the cross where He died.

Matthew described His death in this manner, "*Jesus, when he had cried again with a loud voice, yielded up the ghost. And, behold, the veil of the temple was rent in twain from the top to the bottom; and the earth did quake, and the rocks rent*" (Matthew 27:50-51).

The work Jesus accomplished as the silent suffering Lamb touched the universe. The Bible reports that darkness covered the earth from the sixth to the ninth hour. The moment He died, the veil in the Holy of Holies in the temple was torn from top to bottom, opening up the way to God through the death of Jesus.

The rocks of the earth could not hold their peace, for *"the earth did quake and the rocks rent."* These world-shaking events affected those who stood by, *"Now when the centurion, and they that were with him, watching Jesus, saw the earthquake, and those things that were done, they feared greatly, saying, Truly this was the Son of God"* (Matthew 27:54).

Following Jesus

The fact that Jesus did not defend Himself and permitted sinful men to lead Him to His death is something that the world does not understand, and unfortunately, many Christians don't either.

For the average Christian, it is much easier to fight, stand up for your rights, oppose the wicked, stand for the truth, and let others know what you think. But that, dear friends, is the battle of the flesh, which has no promise whatsoever, and will lead only to defeat.

I am reminded of the words Wim Malgo used to say, "The greatest fight for a Christian is not to fight." How true these words really are.

Jesus went before us; He showed the way; He walked the way; and He finished the way in total obedience to His Heavenly Father. We are admonished to follow Jesus.

The Real Task Of The Church

Of course, it is a noble gesture to fight for civil rights or support moral causes. We are justifiably insulted when we see, for example, how Sodomites not only demand recognition for their practices, but openly demand special assistance from the tax-paying public. To fight against such immorality is as natural as a flower that needs water to survive.

To join picket lines and protest marches against the abominable murder of the unborn is most certainly a good and noble thing to do.

To oppose the propagation of pornography needs courage and is expected of every moral person.

What about fighting for a righteous government? Surely no one can deny that one of the most important items in a functioning civilized society is an honest government.

Investing time and energy in Christianizing the laws, the courts, governments, and institutions is most certainly commendable.

But in light of these good works, we must ask ourselves, "Is this the task of the Church of Jesus Christ?" Based on the verses we have just read, there is absolutely no evidence that Jesus planned for His followers to change the world morally, politically, or economically. Why not? Because He specifically stated *"My Kingdom is not of this world."* His focus was to fish for men, calling those who voluntarily wanted to follow Him, because He is the Way, the Truth and the Life.

Only His Kingdom Counts

He accepted the occupational Roman government of His country, and in regards to morals, He clearly told us that things would get worse.

We have quoted part of John 18:36, but let's read it again,

"Jesus answered, My kingdom is not of this world: if my kingdom were of this world, then would my servants fight, that I should not be delivered to the Jews: but now is my kingdom not from hence."

Jesus came to bring salvation to man; whosoever believes in Him will not perish, but have everlasting life. He does not reject sinful men and women; for His original intention to establish *"on earth, peace, good will towards men"* is yet to take place.

In this verse, Jesus specifically emphasized, *"But now is my kingdom not from hence."* At that time, He did not come to establish His kingdom. Therefore, any attempt by the Church to do a task which the Lord has not entrusted us with will only lead in the opposite direction; to the establishment of the kingdom of Antichrist!

The Battle For The King

In order to gain a better understanding of our non-flesh and blood battle, we turn to the examples given us in 2nd Kings chapter 2 and 2nd Chronicles chapter 23 which describe an event in Israel's history in which chaos reigned. The kingdom was split between the ten tribes of Israel and two tribes of Judah. Both the house of Israel and the house of Judah had fallen into idolatry which resulted in severe judgment.

In 2nd Chronicles 22:3 we read of the turning point in the story of King Ahaziah's mother. We read, *"...for his mother was his counsellor to do wickedly"* (2nd Chronicles 22:3). This wicked counsel ended in tragedy, and ultimately in the death of the king.

The real wickedness of the king's mother Athaliah, was then revealed, *"But when Athaliah the mother of Ahaziah saw that her son was dead, she arose and destroyed all the seed royal of the house of Judah"* (2nd Chronicles 22:10). It is difficult to imagine such brutality taking place today in that a mother would murder all the descendants of her family in order to become queen.

Secure In The House Of God

According to the report given in 2nd Chronicles 22:11-12, only one person was saved from the royal house, *"But Jehoshabeath, the daughter of the king, took Joash the son of Ahaziah, and stole him from among the king's sons that were slain, and put him and his nurse in a bedchamber. So Jehoshabeath, the daughter of king Jehoram, the wife of Jehoiada the priest, (for she was the sister of Ahaziah,) hid him from Athaliah, so that she slew him not. And he was with them hid in the house of God six years: and Athaliah reigned over the land."*

Queen Athaliah had solidified her rulership over Judah and it seemed as though there was absolutely no chance that Joash would ever become king. However, the key to his salvation was that he was *"hid in the house of God."*

That is a lesson we should learn in our daily walk with the Lord. As long as we are hidden in *"the house of God,"* we are spiritually untouchable by the enemy. What does it mean to be in "the house of God"? Simply put, whenever and whatever you do, if you do it in the name and for the glory of Jesus, you are in "the house of God." If your thoughts are influenced by dishonesty, lusts of the flesh, and the like, then you are not in "the house of God" and you are in extreme danger. The apostle Peter warned, *"Be sober, be vigilant; because your adversary the devil, as a roaring lion, walketh about, seeking whom he may devour"* (1st Peter 5:8).

Where can we find a safe place to hide from the devil? Jesus revealed that safe haven to us when He said, *"I in them, and thou in me, that they may be made perfect in one; and that the world may know that thou hast sent me, and hast loved them, as thou hast loved me"* (John 17:23). Ask yourself, "Do I really love Jesus?" If your answer is yes, then you are in holy territory, "the house of God," and the evil one cannot successfully accuse you.

The closer you are to Him, the safer you are. However, the further you distance yourself from Jesus, the more you place yourself in danger of being devoured by the wicked one, the adversary, the devil.

Jehoida: The Priest

When reading the event that took place in 2nd Chronicles chapter 23, we notice that Jehoida busied himself with a strategy to install the king of Judah and virtually ignored Queen Athaliah.

His plan was presented to the Levites, (those in charge of the temple service), *"And they went about in Judah, and gathered the Levites out of all the cities of Judah, and the chief of the fathers of Israel, and they came to Jerusalem. And all the congregation made a covenant with the king in the house of God. And he said unto them, Behold, the king's son shall reign, as the Lord hath said of the sons of David. This is the thing that ye shall do; A third part of you entering on the sabbath, of the priests and of the Levites, shall be porters of the doors; And a third part shall be at the king's house; and a third part at the gate of the foundation: and all the people shall be in the courts of the house of the Lord"*

(2nd Chronicles 23:2-5).

Not Conspiracy But Determination

This plan does not include a conspiracy or outright attack against the wicked queen but rather a strengthening of all that belongs to the Lord.

They did not advertise their intentions nor their plans to anyone, *"But let none come into the house of the Lord, save the priests, and they that minister of the Levites; they shall go in, for they are holy: but all the people shall keep the watch of the Lord"* (verse 6). The object was to protect the king based on the Word of God, *"...the king's son shall reign as the Lord has said of the sons of David."*

We must take careful notice that Jehoida, the priest gave no command to attack the enemy or to include the properties outside the house of God in his defense strategy. He clearly separated church and state, doing what Jesus later commanded, *"Render unto Caesar the things that are Caesar's, and to God, the things that are God's."*

In addition, he took the defense of the king very seriously, *"Moreover Jehoiada the priest delivered to the captains of hundreds spears, and bucklers, and shields, that had been king David's, which were in the house of God. And he set all the people, every man having his weapon in his hand, from the right side of the temple to the left side of the temple, along by the altar and the temple, by the king round about"* (verses 9-10).

Our Battle Is To Stand

This preparation should remind us of the New Testament's admonition to, *"Put on the whole armour of God, that ye may be able to stand against the wiles of the devil. For we wrestle not against flesh and blood, but against principalities, against powers, against the rulers of the darkness of this world, against spiritual wickedness in high places. Wherefore take unto you the whole armour of God, that ye may be able to withstand in the evil day, and having done all, to stand. Stand therefore, having your loins girt about with truth, and having on the breastplate of righteousness; And your feet shod with the preparation of the gospel of peace; Above all, taking the shield of faith, wherewith ye shall be able to quench all the fiery darts of the wicked. And take the helmet of salvation, and the sword of the Spirit, which is the word of God"* (Ephesians 6:11-17).

This New Testament instruction is identical to the one found in the Old Testament revealed with the word, "stand." We are not to attack the powers of darkness, we are to stand in faith grounded on Calvary.

We are warned however, to be fully aware of the intention of the principalities of darkness. As long as we remain in the Light, we are able to clearly identify the works and intentions of the adversary. Second Corinthians 2:11 cautions us, *"Lest Satan should get an advantage of us: for we are not ignorant of his devices."*

As long as we continue to stand in the Light darkness cannot overcome us. We are to stand based on the already accomplished victory of the Lord Jesus. In order to properly stand, we must be prepared as we are so clearly instructed in the above verses.

Moving back to our text in Ephesians we find the content of the real battle, *"Praying always with all prayer and supplication in the Spirit, and watching thereunto with all perseverance and supplication for all saints"* (Ephesians 6:18).

Whenever the powers of darkness attempt to discourage or oppress you, stand in faith on the already accomplished work at Calvary. You may oppose any and all attacks from the world of darkness when you consistently believe with all of your heart that Jesus fully accomplished victory over the devil when He exclaimed *"It is finished!"*

Only with the proper spiritual attire are you able to withstand the fiery darts of the wicked one. When you clothe yourself in the armor of God you will be able to continue to proclaim the Gospel of peace to people everywhere; whether it be done through testimonies, the preaching of the Word, sending forth of missionaries, or distribution of tracts. All things work together for the building of His Church. We are admonished to continue in prayer so that the Gospel of the Lord Jesus Christ will not be hindered.

The King Installed

In all of his preparation to install the king, we never see Jehoida attack anyone or plan an invasion. He simply ignored the political reality that Athaliah was the queen and that she had power over life and death in the kingdom. All this faithful priest had was the promise of God that a descendant of David should be king.

After having made all the necessary preparations for the security of the king, *"...they brought out the king's son, and put upon him the crown, and gave him the testimony, and made him king. And Jehoiada and his sons anointed him, and said, God save the king"* (2nd Chronicles 23:11).

These people put their lives on the line for the truth proclaiming *"God save the king"* or as the Hebrew reads "Let the king live."

Jesus Lives!

What a tremendous message we have to announce, "Jesus lives!" We don't need to fear the enemies; nor should we be afraid of the government or those who wish to eliminate the testimony of the Gospel of Jesus Christ.

Our task is the same as it was almost 2,000 years ago; to proclaim the Gospel, telling people everywhere that salvation is available through faith in the Lord Jesus Christ. He died for our sins, arose victoriously on the third day, and is coming again.

This message of salvation has been declared for almost two millenia, and an uncounted number of souls have responded to the call and now herald the reality of the resurrection of the Lord Jesus Christ!

The Enemy Exposed

What is so remarkable about this story is that the priests who were minding their own business and ignoring political realities were the key to the exposure of the enemy, *"Now when Athaliah heard the noise of the people running and praising the king, she came to the people into the house of the Lord; And she looked, and, behold, the king stood at his pillar at the entering in, and the princes and the trumpets by the king: and all the people of the land rejoiced, and sounded with trumpets, also the singers with instruments of music, and such as taught to sing praise. Then Athaliah rent her clothes, and said, Treason, Treason"* (2nd Chronicles 23:12-13). It is demonstrated here that light was stronger than darkness and evil could hide.

In the end, we see that the victory of truth was a total victory over the forces of the enemy and it is reported that, *"...all the people of the land rejoiced: and the city was quiet, after that they had slain Athaliah with the sword."*

May I take this opportunity, dear child of God, to remind you that your battle does not consist of opposing the evils you may be faced with, whether they be in your own home, at work, at school, in your government, or even in church.

When you have put on the whole armour of God you become untouchable to the powers of darkness and you can fulfill the office the Lord has called you to, *"Praying always with all prayer and supplication in the Spirit, and watching thereunto with all perseverance and supplication for all saints"* (Ephesians 6:18).

CONCLUSION

"Thou hast put all things in subjection under his feet. For in that he put all in subjection under him, he left nothing that is not put under him. But now we see not yet all things put under him. But we see Jesus, who was made a little lower than the angels for the suffering of death, crowned with glory and honour; that he by the grace of God should taste death for every man. For it became him, for whom are all things, and by whom are all things, in bringing many sons unto glory, to make the captain of their salvation perfect through sufferings. For both he that sanctifieth and they who are sanctified are all of one: for which cause he is not ashamed to call them brethren" (Hebrews 2:8-11).

These marvelous words reveal to us that not only is Jesus the Author and Finisher of our faith, but all things will be put under His subjection. Jesus, the Living Word of God, has created all things and *"for whom are all things, and by whom are all things"* including our perfect salvation! It is both literally and physically impossible for me to fully comprehend the last line of this verse, *"he is not ashamed to call them brethren."* However, my admission does not change the fact that we have indeed become His brethren, sons of God. We are so much a part of God's family that no earthly family can ever compare. The final answer to the Lord's high priestly prayer is yet to be fulfilled, *"I in them, and thou in me, that they may be made perfect in one"* (John 17:23).

If we as believers would realize just a fraction of the glorious things God has wrought for us, we would not take ourselves too seriously. We would worry much less about things we can't change and while we remain on earth, our lives would be filled and overflowing with the peace that passes all understanding.

I wanted to convey these few words of encouragement to you in my conclusion of *The Great Mystery of the Rapture.*

Throughout this study, we laid down some indisputable facts regarding the reality of the Rapture–facts which cannot be moved or removed by any interpretation. Jesus said that He will come again to take us to Himself. In order for that to happen, certain events in history had to first take place.

We must never be so naive as to think that such events as the uproar of the nations, wars and rumors of wars, earthquakes, floods, fires, pestilences, and others take place coincidentally. That is far from the truth because these phenomena serve only one purpose: to call out a people for His name. God does not make mistakes, nor does He need to apologize. His resolutions are eternal because He is from everlasting to everlasting.

When we understand God's plan for mankind we shouldn't have much difficulty comprehending the words of Amos 3:6, *"...shall there be evil in a city, and the LORD hath not done it?"* (Amos 3:6). When we grasp these things spiritually, we see that we do not need to worry about the frightening events taking place in the world today. In holy reverence, we can sing with the hymn writer, "He's got the whole world in His hands...."

Calling Out Of His People

We have thoroughly discussed the relationship between Israel and the Church. God chose Abraham, from whom He brought forth a nation, Israel. She in turn brought forth the man-child Jesus, *"...who was to rule all nations with a rod of iron"* (Revelation 10:5). Jesus: Son of God, and Son of man. On Calvary's cross, He accomplished the greatest redemptive work in history when He cried out, *"It is finished."* Since then, the final selection process has been progressing. From Israel and all the nations of the world, God is gathering a new people, born again of His Spirit, for His heavenly kingdom. This selection is no longer limited to Israel, who received a distinct promise of territory. Today, anyone who has an ear to hear may respond to the message, believe it, and as a result, be added to the innumerable host of heavenly citizens comprising the Church of Jesus Christ.

The selection process has been taking place since 33 A.D. and will be completed when the fullness of the Gentiles comes in, at which time the Rapture will take place.

In the Bible, God has given us many examples of His intention to save mankind. One example was the salvation of Noah and his family. Only those who entered the ark by faith were saved from the flood. The same principle is valid today;

those who enter the heavenly ark through the door (Jesus Christ) are saved for eternity.

Light And Darkness

During these many centuries, God in His grace has not sent destructive judgment upon the powers of darkness, but He has permitted darkness to exist parallel to the light. Every person born on planet Earth must either decide to continue in the way of darkness or to come to the Light. John testifies of Jesus when he says, *"That was the true Light, which lighteth every man that cometh into the world"* (John 1:9). It is the job of the children of light to exemplify the way to the Light to those in darkness, which is why Jesus said to His Church, *"ye are the light of the world."* Darkness includes all things on earth. Everything we see, hear, or touch outside of the Gospel is subject to darkness. Every nation and every government on our planet is subject to darkness. The god of this world, the prince of darkness, rules the earth, as evident in 2nd Corinthians 4:3-4, *"But if our gospel be hid, it is hid to them that are lost: In whom the god of this world hath blinded the minds of them which believe not, lest the light of the glorious gospel of Christ, who is the image of God, should shine unto them."* This dark force cannot destroy the children of light because, as we illustrated earlier in the book, light is stronger than darkness. However, God in His counsel has determined that darkness will eventually cover the entire world. We concluded that this cannot take place while the Church is still present.

The Great Tribulation

The prophets of both the Old and New Testaments, as well as Jesus Himself, prophesied that the Great Tribulation would come on planet Earth and that it would be a time such as has never been experienced before, nor will it be repeated. In those days of darkness mankind will voluntarily believe the great lie, the lie that is believed by virtually everyone in the entire world. The lie is that salvation may be obtained through good behavior and does not depend on any particular form of religion. This philosophy is accepted today as "politically correct." The continuous success of the world in relation to peace and prosperity will reinforce humanity's belief that they should be centered on themselves instead of the Savior. Second Thessalonians 2:9-10 says, *"Even him, whose coming is after the working of Satan with all power and signs and lying wonders, And with all deceivableness of unrighteousness in them that perish; because they received not the love of the truth, that they might be saved."* The truth is that man cannot save himself; he is lost. He's not lost because of the bad deeds he may have committed, but because he is a sinner by birth. To the question, "What must you do to end up in Hell?" the answer is nothing! Everyone from birth is destined to Hell. For that reason, God the Father sent Jesus so that whoever believes in Him will not perish but have everlasting life. Just as a person does not have to do anything particularly bad to remain Hellbound, the same applies to a person who wants to go to Heaven but does not have to do anything to get there other than believe. Virtually all religions, including much of Christianity, are proclaiming that man must either work for his salvation or at least contribute his part so that he may qualify. That is the great deception of Satan. Those who embrace that belief do not love the truth. Continuing in verse 11, we read, *"...for this cause God shall send them strong delusion, that they should believe a lie."*

The great contradiction of the present day is the existence of the Church. Within the Church, there is a light which stands in opposition to darkness. As long as this light remains on Earth, the Great Tribulation, the epitome of darkness, cannot take place. The moment the Church is removed, darkness will prevail and the lie will be accepted as truth, which has been clearly and thoroughly addressed in this book.

The Spirit Must Depart For Jesus To Return

Israel's salvation cannot take place as long as the Church is present on earth. We find support of this in Jesus' response to the disciples, *"...It is expedient for you that I go away: for if I go not away, the Comforter will not come unto you; but if I depart, I will send him unto you"* (John 16:7).

Plainly, Jesus was saying that if He did not depart, the Comforter would not come; but when He did depart, the Comforter would indeed come.

Now this will take place in reverse. Jesus cannot literally and physically come back to earth as long as the Comforter [the Holy Spirit] remains on earth.

The Comforter dwells in the heart of the believer! Therefore, it is impossible for Jesus to come back with His saints unless they are first taken out of the way so that He can come back to earth with them!

What Are You Waiting For?

Please allow me again to ask, "What are you waiting for?" If you are waiting for the Great Tribulation, then you cannot be waiting for Jesus. If you are waiting for the appearing of the Antichrist, then you cannot be waiting for Jesus. If you are waiting for better times, for peace and prosperity, then you cannot be waiting for Jesus. If you are not waiting for Jesus, you are not a child of God.

If you are not a child of God, at this point you should be asking yourself, "How can I become a child of God?" It is almost too easy to be true, yet it is true! Believe on the Lord Jesus and you will be saved! Right after you have read the last lines of this book, get down on your knees and confess to God that you are a sinner. Admit that you cannot save yourself. Realize that you are in need of redemption. Someone else must pay for your sins; you can't do it yourself. If that is the case, you are on the right track toward salvation. You may pray a simple prayer: "Dear God: I realize that I am a sinner and I believe that Jesus Christ paid for my sins when He died on Calvary's cross, pouring out His blood as full payment for my sins. I now consciously and deliberately ask Jesus to save me from my sins, come into my heart and make me a child of God." When you sincerely pray this, then the prophetic Scripture will be fulfilled, *"Him that cometh unto me, I will in no wise cast out."* And the wonderful promise of John 3:36 will be instantly fulfilled in your life: *"He that believeth on the Son hath everlasting life!"*

SUBJECT INDEX

▋▋▶ *Tap into the Bible analysis of top prophecy authorities...*

12 issues/1 yr. $28.95
24 issues/2 yr. $45

Midnight Call is a hard-hitting Bible-based magazine loaded with news, commentary, special features, and teaching, illustrated with explosive color pictures and graphics. Join hundreds of thousands of readers in 140 countries who enjoy this magazine regularly!

▋▋▶ *The world's leading prophetic Bible magazine*

▋▋▶ *Covering international topics with detailed commentary*

▋▋▶ *Bold, uncompromising Biblical stands on issues*

▋▋▶ *Pro-family, Pro-life, Pro-Bible*